JOSEPH

'HIS ARMS WERE MADE STRONG'

JOSEPH

'His Arms Were Made Strong'

David C. Searle

THE BANNER OF TRUTH TRUST

THE BANNER OF TRUTH TRUST
3 Murrayfield Road, Edinburgh EH12 6EL, UK
P.O. Box 621, Carlisle, PA 17013, USA

*

© David C. Searle 2012

ISBN: 978 1 84871 165 5

*

Typeset in 11/15 Adobe Caslon Pro at
the Banner of Truth Trust, Edinburgh

Printed in the USA by
Versa Press, Inc.,
East Peoria, IL

This book is for

Maddy and Katya

two dearly loved granddaughters

Contents

Foreword

Writing this Foreword for *Joseph: 'His Arms Were Made Strong'* has coincided with two things I am currently reading. First, in my daily Bible Reading I have reached in Genesis the record of Joseph's life. It has prompted me to see afresh what an illustration he is of New Testament teaching: for example, that Christian slaves (for us, employees) should show how attractive the teaching about God our Saviour is by our conduct (*Titus* 2:9, 10). Whether, as I read this morning in Genesis 41, Joseph was in a position of prominence in Potiphar's household or in prison having been falsely accused, his behaviour shows what it means to have the Lord with us in all we say and do in life.

Alongside my daily Bible reading I have been rereading *The History of Redemption* by Jonathan Edwards, written in the early eighteenth century. He underlines how it was by the instrumentality of Joseph that the family from whom our Lord Jesus Christ was to come was saved from perishing. Edwards carefully draws attention to ways in which Joseph's story resembles the salvation our Lord brings to us.

There can be no doubt that Joseph's story is a vital part of salvation history. On the road to Emmaus the risen Jesus explained to Cleopas and his companion from Moses and all the Prophets what was said in all the Scriptures concerning himself. It would be fascinating to know what place he gave to Joseph—what comparisons might he have drawn from this man's life?

I know that resemblances between the life of Joseph and our Saviour can be forced and fanciful. The Venerable Bede suggested that the coat of many colours made by Jacob for his son signified the variety of people from all the nations of the world to be gathered into the body of Christ. But fear of such allegorizing must not lead us to neglect how the gospel can be clearly taught from Old Testament narratives. *Joseph: 'His Arms Were Made Strong'* helpfully demonstrates this.

The author is aware of how Joseph's life and example were especially prominent in the sermons and writings of the early church fathers. In several footnotes he refers to the writings of John Chrysostom (c. A.D. 347-407) who gave Joseph prominence in his preaching. Similarly he calls on the writings of Ambrose (c. A.D. 339-97) who devoted an entire volume to Joseph. And these early Christians were right to do so. They were following the Apostle Paul who, writing in the context of our vulnerability to temptation and referring to God's people in the Old Testament, tells us, 'These things happened to them as examples and were written down as warnings to us' (*1 Cor.* 10:11). 'Everything that was written in the past was written to teach us, so that through the endurance taught in the Scriptures and the encouragement they provide we might have hope' (*Rom.* 15:4). David Searle stands firmly in this biblical tradition.

The book also emphasises two important biblical truths concerning the priority of the fear of God and our need of the wisdom only he can give, and how the two concepts are closely entwined. It shows how Joseph exemplified both. Further, it clearly integrates the teaching of the New Testament with the Old, and interprets the Old in the light of the New. The wise and gracious providence of God is plainly brought out and applied through Joseph's whole life, encapsulated in his words to his brothers: 'You intended to harm me, but God intended it for good to accomplish what is now being done, the saving of many lives' (*Gen.* 50:20).

Joseph: 'His Arms Were Made Strong' also provides illustrations of many other essential truths. It is not only a good read but will be spiritually beneficial to both young and old. It is relevant to contemporary trends and opinions both in society and the church. It draws upon long pastoral experience and is replete with down-to-earth examples. What is unusual but refreshing is David Searle's directness in addressing the reader personally as if you were sitting in front of him and on occasions asking some personal questions. This underlines the spiritual helpfulness of the lessons drawn from Joseph's life and makes the reading a stimulus and guide to spiritual growth and personal holiness.

I recommend reading a chapter a day so as to allow time for the truths expressed in each chapter to be thought about, understood and allowed to do their work.

DEREK PRIME
Edinburgh
January 2012

Preface

As far back as I can remember I have always been fascinated by the book of Genesis. It began with a children's story book which my mother read to us every evening. My imagination was captivated as I listened to the account of the three patriarchs and on to the 'novella' of Joseph.

It was hardly surprising, therefore, that in my first pastorate in the village of Ewhurst, Surrey, in the three years there I preached through these same stories. I did the same in the other churches where I ministered—Newhills (Aberdeenshire), Larbert (Stirlingshire) and Hamilton Road Church (Bangor, Northern Ireland). Each of those four series of expositions deepened both my love for and appreciation of this first book of the Old Testament Scriptures. Most recently (2008) I was invited to give the mid-week Bible Study at the Town Mission, Arbroath and it has been that final, fifth revision of the earlier work that has formed the basis of this book.

About twenty years ago a friend whose parents had worked long years in China with the former China Inland Mission, asked me which two books of the Bible I thought would have been most effective in bringing Chinese people to the Christian faith. The answer was Genesis and Romans, the reason being that they give a biblical world-view. The Chinese found these two books a compelling and comprehensive introduction to the Christian faith.

The works listed in the Select Bibliography have combined to put me in debt to their authors. In varying degrees these are the writers whose works have nurtured me, expanded my understanding and pointed me in the direction of how to teach the Scriptures. Chief among these have been W. H. Griffith Thomas, whose devotional readings greatly helped me in my early twenties; William Still, whose Daily Bible Reading Notes enabled me to feed my own soul that I might provide spiritual sustenance for others (I later edited them for publication); and John Calvin, who trained me to use the reformed framework of theology both as a pastoral tool to build up the people of God in their faith, and as a firm evangelical foundation from which to sound forth the gospel of God's mercy and grace in Christ Jesus.

I am grateful to the following friends who have checked my scripts and made helpful suggestions, most of which I have adopted: Ian Barter, Donald Fraser, Frances MacLeod and Alistair Simpson. My thanks also to the staff at the Banner of Truth Trust, for their help, courtesy and good counsel. Finally, I acknowledge my immense debt to my wife whose 'crits' of my sermons I always dreaded, but from which I learned so very much.

DAVID C. SEARLE
Arbroath, 2012

CHAPTER ONE

Joseph the Dreamer—Genesis 37

I F we were able to take a kind of time-machine which enabled us to pass momentarily out of our present four dimensional world of space and time into some other dimension from which we could look down and briefly survey human history, a little bit like some cosmic astronaut thousands of miles above the earth being able to view our planet, what do you think we would see as we surveyed human history from its beginning to its fulfilment? I believe that we would see that the centre and heart of history, the focal point around which everything else circulates, is the cross and resurrection of Jesus Christ. From our momentary vantage point, quite outside of earthly time, we would discover that from its very beginning human history moved inexorably forward *towards* the cross; and then we would also discover that human history has continued to move forwards *from* the cross.

But something that would, I suspect, take us rather by surprise and fill us with awe and wonder would be that we would realize that the shadow of the cross falls both backwards in time as well as forwards to its consummation in eternity. You and I can easily understand that the shadow of the cross falls forwards, because we live under the protective, redemptive shade of the events of Good Friday and Easter Morning. However, it would be the backward shadow of Calvary that I think would amaze us. We would see, for example, our first parents after the Fall clothed with animal skins whose blood had been shed so that their nakedness and shame might be covered; that would be the very first shadow of the cross. We would see Abraham climbing Mount Moriah along with Isaac carrying the wood on his shoulders, and we would hear the father's beloved son asking, 'My father . . . Behold the fire and the wood, but where is the lamb for a burnt offering?' And we would hear Abraham's reply, 'God will provide for himself the lamb for a burnt offering, my son.' Again, that long backward shadow of the cross.[1]

However, perhaps nowhere in the whole of the Old Testament (apart from in the elaborate ritual of the Day of Atonement) would we see the shadow of the cross more clearly than in the life of Joseph. For Joseph stands so vividly as a type of Christ that one might be tempted to ask if, when this mini-biography was recorded, the writer actually knew what would happen to Jesus and deliberately paralleled in Joseph's story the Lord's life, his betrayal, his suffering, his descent into the grave, and his final exaltation. Let us look then at the opening episode in Joseph's life—his unimpeachable integrity, his strange dreams and his betrayal by his brothers into slavery.

A Family's Sin

In a moment we shall notice how the Apostle Paul in his didactic letters such as Romans and Ephesians spells out doctrinally the nature of human sin and fallenness. But what we have in Genesis, covering several generations, is a large tapestry, woven in an intricate pattern, portraying in human lives the same doctrines as Paul outlines in theological language. The narrative of Genesis is like a physician's comprehensive file containing the medical case history of a whole family. When you or I move from one town to another, the doctor with whom we register receives our medical files with a full account of our records of any past illnesses, treatment or surgery. And when you pay your first visit to your

[1] Genesis 22:7, 8.

new medical practitioner, he will glance through your records to familiarize himself with your story, problems you may have, your earlier visits to a surgery and the medication prescribed. Before he commits himself to deciding on any new course of treatment, your GP[2] will want to have before him as full a picture of you as he can gather from your records.

I am not going to deal here with Genesis 34 and 38, but they form a vital part of the case history of the family of Jacob. Later on in this book we will read about Reuben's act of incest—all part of the notes in the family file. Tucked away in the record are other details too, sordid, sad and shameful. But let us try and summarize briefly what we learn.

Jacob had met with God at Peniel and there God changed his name from 'Supplanter' to Israel, 'Prince of God'. From that day on he was disabled and limped as he walked, leaning heavily on his staff. But sadly, even after that event, he was still up to his old trickery, promising his brother Esau he would meet up with him in due course at Seir. Yet we are explicitly told that he deliberately took another route to Shechem to avoid that promised reunion. In spite of his vision of angels and his wrestling with God, he still had much of the old, fallen nature in him. Arriving at Shechem, he bought land and settled down. But there ten of his sons become involved with the local people and chapters 34 and 38 tell us of that involvement—and how degrading and wicked it was!

Nevertheless, we need both of these two awful chapters to give us the full picture because we are learning certain important lessons which are absolutely essential to the great onward movement of salvation-history and the work of God in the souls of men and women. I mention just two of those lessons. The first is that Jacob's unhappy, divided home life on account of his polygamy produced

[2] General Practitioner, a doctor who treats patients for most illnesses or complaints, referring other cases to specialists.

sons who were evil men. All the quarrelling between Rachel and Leah, the tension, bitterness and favouritism, has reaped a tragic harvest in a family of which Jacob is deeply ashamed. Immorality, incest, idolatry, murder, cruelty, deception—the spiritual records in that family file are quite horrifying. And Jacob openly acknowledges it. He says to his ten sons, 'You have brought trouble on me by making me stink to the inhabitants of the land, the Canaanites and the Perizzites.'[3] That says it all, does it not?

The second lesson we draw from the case notes of Jacob's family is that God appears to have chosen the worst possible raw material on which to found his chosen people and the Old Testament church. One of the key symbolic numbers in the New Testament book of Revelation is the number twelve, and this number is used to describe the redeemed, the new Jerusalem, the heavenly city inhabited by very God. Twelve thousand multiplied by twelve is the one hundred and forty-four thousand redeemed souls; twelve foundations, twelve gates, twelve pearls, twelve names, twelve angels, twelve kinds of fruit. And where does that number come from? In the Old Testament from Jacob's twelve sons, of course. Yet reading the story of the twelve sons we find all this wickedness, lust and hatred. Surely it is nothing short of astonishing that God chose such miserable material on which to build his church. These men and their descendants were actually the foundation stones of the church!

But is this not also the message the New Testament? "'Go to the main roads and invite . . . as many as you can find . . ." and those servants went out into the roads and gathered all whom they found, both bad and good.'[4] The material God begins with is always sinful, sordid material. For that material is you and me: at one time 'dead in trespasses and sins . . . following the prince of

[3] Genesis 34:30.
[4] Matthew 22:9, 10.

the power of the air, the spirit that is now at work in the sons of disobedience—among whom we all once lived in the passions of our flesh ... children of wrath'. Again, we were 'futile in our minds ... darkened in our understanding, alienated from the life of God because of the ignorance that is in us, due to the hardening of our hearts ... callous, given up to sensuality and impurity'.[5] These are the apostle's words describing human nature, the raw material God has to work with to build his church and produce a spotless bride for his beloved Son.

So come with me for just a moment into this family circle. What strikes us straightaway? Surely that although this family is a complete scandal, the eleventh son is different. He is quite different for various reasons. As we pore over the family's case history, we find he was born when his father had entered a new stage of spirituality, for immediately after this boy's birth Jacob knew he must return to the land of promise; the record is very clear—after announcing Joseph's arrival into the world, the very next sentence states Jacob's resolve to return to the land of promise.[6] Therefore the environment of his upbringing had been different on the human level. But on the higher, symbolic level, he was different because he was going to be a type of Christ, foreshadowing the Lord in a remarkable way. And so while he was bound to have had faults, for he was a sinner like us all, the record passes over them because the writer's intention was that we should understand that Joseph was set apart from his birth.

Probably when his age is given to us as being seventeen years the intention is to tell us that he was old enough to join his brothers and learn the herdsman's trade, for he is now working with his ten older siblings. I remember reading how when just a boy Luis Palau, the South American evangelist, fell in with a truck driver

---

[5] Ephesians 2:1-3; also alluded to is 4:17-19.
[6] Genesis 30:24, 25.

who thrust pornography into his hands, saying it was time for him to learn the facts of life, thereby polluting his young mind. Palau wrote how he was tormented for weeks, unable to sleep, by the sudden shock of the filth that had engulfed his very soul. It would appear that Joseph's brothers similarly decided it was time to initiate him into their ways and show him a thing or two.

They may have tried to involve him in dishonest trading. They grazed their sheep and goats in a region through which passed one of the great trade routes from east to west and merchants were constantly travelling past, easy prey for unscrupulous nomadic herdsmen. But Joseph was different. He was troubled and grieved by what he saw. He realized his father's name was being scandalized by the deceit and trickery of his older brothers. More, we will find in the next chapter that he feared God and knew very well right from wrong. So he told his father what was going on.

Our concern under the first heading of 'A Family's Sin' is not to ask whether he was justified in informing his father of the evil reputation spreading throughout the land regarding his name and family. Our concern is rather to note that the kind of upbringing children receive and the environment in which they are reared will ultimately shape their lives in later years. Having said that, it is also true that when these men were in their formative years, Jacob was serving Laban; Jacob had been scrupulously honest, though ten times Laban had changed his wages.[7]

But the four women in Jacob's life, his two wives and their maid-servants, could not have made for an harmonious family environment, especially when we find the eldest son sleeping with one of the maid-servants who was mother of his step-brothers. We reap what we sow. Yes, our sins are forgiven, but as King David also discovered generations later, though God accepts the sacrifice of a broken and contrite heart, we have to live with the consequences

[7] Genesis 31:41.

of what we have done. Jacob, chosen of God that he was, had lived according to his sinful nature and now he was reaping a bitter harvest of scandal and depravity. A family's sin indeed!

A Favourite's Suffering

Joseph's father had sent him from Hebron to Shechem, a full day's walk. But when he reached Shechem, the brothers had moved on and enquiries established they were now a further fifteen miles away at Dothan, an area with naturally irrigated pasture lands. Rather than giving up and returning home, Joseph pressed on the search for his ten brothers.

When I was in my early teens and was given a difficult job to do by one of my parents, I often thought of Joseph sent by his father to find his brothers and his perseverance until at last he located them. I used to think that his persistence had been an excellent trait on his part and I tried to follow his example of sticking in until he fulfilled the task. However, I knew perfectly well that I fell very far short of his example.

His ten brothers hated him for at least three reasons. First, they hated him because they were spiritually filthy and he had resolved to keep himself pure. Second, they hated him because Jacob foolishly made it obvious that Joseph was his favourite, his beloved Rachel's son; of course, these two reasons were inseparably intertwined. But third, they hated him for his dreams; those two dreams intensified their jealousy.

Scholars are divided in their opinions about Joseph's motives in relating his dreams to his family. Some regard him as having been an impudent young pup, arrogant and conceited. I disagree. I am sure there must have been more to it than that.[8] Even if there was

---

[8] 'The prophetic substance [of the dreams] is unmistakable, and yet Joseph is at the same time chided on their account. One cannot lessen the paradox by the explanation that Joseph was censured only because he told the dreams. A vision was

pride in him, he had to tell them his dreams so that years later, when they were reunited with him in Egypt, he could point to those dreams as evidence that his life's sufferings and successes had all been planned by God.[9] Further, his family had to know that 'that word of the Lord proved him true'.[10] Therefore we cannot pin their jealousy of Joseph entirely on their father's blatant favouritism. His unpopularity was inevitable. There was no way round it. It was part of the cross he had to carry.[11]

We do not hear much these days about the cross Christ asks us to carry. When Peter wrote his first letter, believers were about to face severe persecution, similar to that of Christian believers in Orissa and the neighbouring provinces in North East India and in many other parts of the world in these early years of the 21st century. The word 'suffering' occurs no less than fifteen times in Peter's short epistle.[12] Paul had earlier written that 'all who desire to live a godly life in Christ Jesus will be persecuted'.[13]

Few living in the West expect to suffer in this generation. I wonder if we have not cut the cloth of the New Testament in such a way that fits exactly the comfortable kind of lives we want to live. Is the truth not that too often there is only a measured, partial obedience in our Christian living, while there is a certain hidden disobedience that we think we are clever enough to get away with? When a man

---

for the ancients so important and obligatory that a demand to keep it tactfully to oneself would not have occurred to them.' Von Rad, pp. 346-47. Contrast the view of Joseph's disclosure of his dreams: '… boastfulness and [an] error of judgment … his unwisdom in the way in which he spoke … the immature manner in which he apparently acted.' Still, p. 166.

[9] Genesis 50:20.

[10] Psalm 105:19.

[11] A comment on verse 11, 'his father kept the saying in mind': 'This phrase is the origin of the words in Luke 2:51, "kept all these sayings in her heart." Jacob rebuked Joseph but evidently was so deeply impressed with the remarkable and seemingly improbable character of the twice repeated dream, that he secretly cherished a presentiment of its fulfilment (42:6).' Ryle, p. 352.

[12] Fifteen times as Gk *pascho*, and 3 times as Gk *pathema*.

[13] 2 Timothy 3:12.

or woman is one hundred percent faithful to the Lord, that person will be the favourite of some, but resented by others. For 'through many tribulations we must enter the kingdom of God'.[14]

Later on in Genesis, there is a flash-back and we learn that Joseph was distressed and begged for his life when his brothers seized him and threw him into the pit. We are also told that the Ishmaelite traders put iron fetters on his wrists and his ankles. He was sold for twenty pieces of silver and it seemed his dreams were mockery and had turned to ashes.[15] Those mysterious night visions and his beautiful ornamental coat were all in ribbons.

John Newton was only eighteen years old when a press-gang seized him and he was carried off, kicking and screaming, to become a sailor in His Majesty's navy. A terrible life for a teenage boy! It must have been like that for Joseph. How would you have felt if you were kidnapped, drugged, sold to some evil person who ran a sweat-shop factory; then you found yourself in some eastern land where you did not know a word of the language and had to toil sixteen hours every day? How would you cope? Give a thought, too, to Joseph being dragged along the hot desert sands of the Sinai desert, chained to the saddle of some Midianite merchant's camel. Think of his burning thirst, his exhaustion, the pitiless sun. I have done that journey by air-conditioned coach with plenty of chilled soft drinks available from the coach's refrigerator; even so, it was quite exhausting. I cannot begin to think of what it must have been like in chains, and having to run to keep up with a camel's steady stride. 'Why? O God, why? Why is this happening to me? Why did you not preserve me from my brothers' hatred, Lord God? Why?'

Joseph's only recorded personal cause for offence was his honesty, purity and integrity. 'Surely', we say, 'God should have looked after him. Surely God should never have allowed such foul and

---

[14] Acts 14:22.
[15] Genesis 42:21; Psalm 105:18; Genesis 37:28.

horrible things to happen to him.' But often our thinking and opinions are wrong. We assume all suffering is evil.

For starters, Joseph was being given the awesome privilege of being a type of Jesus Christ.[16] His suffering, cries, pain and the lash of the whip across his innocent back were all foreshadowing the cross and the sufferings of our Lord. Someone says, 'But Christ has suffered for us, so that we should no longer suffer.' In one way that is right: by our Lord's sufferings we are preserved from the wrath of the righteous God.

But there are other dimensions to Christ's suffering. Peter explicitly tells us in his First Letter, spelling it out in language that cannot be interpreted any other way, that Christ also suffered to leave us an example, and that we should follow in his steps. There are times when believers are called upon to walk in his shoes. He suffered silently, without threats or retaliation, as an example to us in our suffering when it is for righteousness' sake.[17]

Yet is it not true that as soon as any pain, frailty or suffering crosses our paths, we throw up our hands in horror and demand that God must get rid of our pain instantly! We arrange for people to be busy praying that our suffering will end quickly. We assume that God should intervene to stop it. Sometimes that might be right. But sometimes it might not be his will at all. Think of Joseph: a lamb to the slaughter, hated by his brothers for his dreams, which were nothing less than God's word to him; hated for his

---

[16] One of the early church Fathers, Caesarius of Arles (470–543), comments: 'Upon seeing Joseph, his brothers discussed his death; just as when the Jews saw the true Joseph, Christ the Lord, they all resolved with one plan to crucify him. His brothers robbed Joseph of his outside coat; the [soldiers] stripped Christ of his bodily tunic at his death on the cross. When Joseph was deprived of his tunic, he was thrown into a pit; after Christ was despoiled of human flesh, he descended into hell … Joseph is sold for twenty pieces of silver; Christ is sold for a [similar] amount … Joseph went down into Egypt [which] he saved from want of grain; Christ frees the world from a famine of the Word of God.' *ACCS*, p. 240.

[17] 1 Peter 2:21-23.

simple goodness and righteousness; hated because his father loved him for his goodness. A favourite's suffering, indeed!

Another Favourite suffered. Remember that. 'This is my beloved Son with whom I am well pleased.' 'Yet it was the will of the Lord to crush him; he [God] has put him to grief.'[18] Maybe you have never really suffered. You do not have any or many battle scars. Then humbly thank God for that. But do not forget Joseph. Do not forget either those many believers in other lands who constantly suffer for their faithfulness to Christ. And certainly do not forget our blessed Saviour (to whom Joseph points us), and remember that his suffering is an example to all God's children of how to bear the cross that he asks us to carry.

A Father's Sorrow

Lies are of no account to some people. A number of years ago there were two very different radio programmes on the subject of telling lies. I did not hear the first, but heard a trailer for it; the announcer began, 'We all tell lies.' I wondered how she could be so sure of that. There then followed a clip advertising this particular broadcast and listeners heard a man laughing about the lessons his mother had taught him about truth years before when he was a child; there was unmistakable derision in his voice that he had been brought up to be afraid to tell a lie. The second broadcast—and I heard several minutes of this one—was by a psychologist who had been studying pre-school children. She informed listeners that at the early age of three and four years, toddlers learn deliberately to tell lies.

Lies did not bother Joseph's ten brothers. Deceit came very easily to them. So they tore up Joseph's special robe, dipped it in a goat's blood, and took it back in tatters to their father, claiming they had come across it and would it perchance be Joseph's coat? Of course he recognized it and grieved and wept over his beloved

[18] Matthew 3:17; Isaiah 53:10.

son. And those hypocritical lying ten brothers attempted to comfort their old father, no doubt shedding crocodile tears themselves all the while.

There are two things to be said about this old man's profound sorrow. The first is that Jacob, the arch-deceiver, is now himself deceived by his own sons. Had he not deceived his father, Isaac, who had trembled and shaken when he discovered the deception that his own flesh and blood had practised on him? Recall how Isaac suspected that the one standing before him was not Esau at all but Jacob. Isaac had called Jacob near and smelled Esau's clothes which Jacob cunningly had put on expressly to deceive his father. And Isaac had felt Jacob's hands and neck, which his mother had cleverly covered with kidskin to make them feel rough to the touch of the blind old man to convince him that this was truly his son Esau.[19] And now, equally clever, equally convincing and equally cruel, was the masterly deception of Jacob by his own sons, his own flesh and blood. The deceiver himself deceived!

I suspect that every single one of us thinks that he or she is the one person in the world clever enough to sin and escape the consequences. We hear that the Scripture declares that we reap what we sow.[20] We also hear it said that there is a law, a principle, laid down by God that our actions will one day come back upon us. But we simply do not believe the word of God. Our sin is that of unbelief. We may not call it unbelief. We may argue that we do not always agree with God's word—at least we do not interpret every single word literally. We have our own views which we ingeniously attempt to harmonize with the teaching of the Christian Scriptures; we argue that we have given much thought to it, and have come to our own conclusions. We will admit that God's word applies to wicked people—criminals, muggers and the like. But we consider ourselves to be reasonable people. Thus we secretly disagree with

[19] Genesis 27:14ff.
[20] Galatians 6:7.

God and with whatever his word might say on the consequences of sin and deception.

However, this is not quite the same as the health warning on the packet of cigarettes: 'Smoking can damage your health.' The smoker laughs and tells you about a man who lived to be over a hundred years and smoked twenty cigarettes every day. That may be so. But this biblical principle is different. There are no exceptions. There never ever was a single deceiver who got away with it. Deceit always comes back on us like the proverbial boomerang. Sow the seed and the harvest will surely come. There is no escape, apart from complete and genuine repentance and the blood of Christ to wash and cleanse us from our sin.

But there was another side to aged Jacob's sorrow. Like Mary, the mother of our Lord, he had pondered these things in his heart. Did you notice that in this chapter of Genesis? When he heard of Joseph's dreams, he was angry and rebuked Joseph. But ah! *his father kept the saying in mind* (verse 11). He did not dismiss it entirely. He pondered, 'Could it be? Is God in this? What does God plan for my beloved son's life?'

Because of that comment in verse 11, there is some disagreement among the commentators as to whether Jacob's grief was for the death of Joseph, or for the evil of his ten sons whom he suspected of having somehow disposed of Joseph; that is perhaps unlikely; in this life we shall never know. Nevertheless, we see the grief of the father, his profound anguish and how he could not be comforted, and we have a very faint, shadowy picture of the grief of the Father when his own Son was bruised, beaten and sold for thirty pieces of silver and when his blood was shed because we had hated him, having gone our own way, rejecting the straight path of purity, truth and goodness. The Bible puts it that way.

But the Bible also puts it another way. The Father, Almighty God, whose beloved Son suffered and carried our sins in his body on the cross, now offers his Son to sinners as the way of forgiveness and reconciliation. The Father, who loves his Son more than we can ever understand, now calls us to receive him who endured such torments on Calvary for sinners. But oh, the wrath of the Father when his beloved Son is spurned and rejected! Therefore, let the reader search his or her heart, lest there be a cloak of that most despicable of human failures, hypocrisy, disguising the true condition of our hearts. Consider the waiting Father's tender love as he runs to greet the penitent making his way home, embraces him, kisses him, weeps tears of joy upon his neck and calls for all the company of heaven to rejoice that one who was lost is now found.[21]

[21] Luke 15:22-24.

CHAPTER TWO

'Filled with the Spirit'—Genesis 39 with Ephesians 5:15-6:9

WE come now to Genesis 39, from where I want to pick up certain phrases from the first six verses. They are: *The LORD was with Joseph* (verse 2); *his master saw that the LORD was with him* (verse 3); *the LORD caused all that he did to succeed* (verse 3); *the LORD blessed the Egyptian's house for Joseph's sake . . . the blessing of the LORD was on all he had* (verse 5). Five remarkable commendations of Joseph. Then also notice in chapter 41:38: *And Pharaoh said to his servants, 'Can we find a man like this, in whom is the Spirit of God?'* I want to suggest that when Paul wrote, knowing the Old Testament Scriptures as he did, regarding the attitudes of slaves and masters in Ephesians 6:5-8, he had in mind Joseph who was 'filled with the Spirit'.[1] That possibility has influenced my exposition of this chapter, which is why I am suggesting that Joseph's complete submission to the Spirit of God was the means of the remarkable blessing God bestowed on him and, for his sake, on Potiphar.

The miracles Joseph performed when he was a slave were greater than those he performed when he was a ruler, although the latter made a stronger impression on the hearts and feelings of people. For here there was no outward show in him, no splendour was seen. He went on his way burdened by the labour of domestic

[1] Ephesians 5:18.

government, a pauper and a cast-off, until later that illustrious glory and honour of miracles burst forth. Yet all these things are by no means to be compared with the fact that Joseph was a son of God, and a priest full of the Spirit of the Lord.[2]

Over the years, probably like some who will read this book, I have been in certain churches where those who were leading the meetings claimed that what was taking place was a demonstration of the Holy Spirit's power. I have also listened to people who have claimed to have had dramatic experiences of various kinds. Reflecting on such events and seeking in all Christian charity to evaluate such claims in the light of God's word, I have found myself wondering whether much of what I witnessed and heard had anything to do with biblical Christianity.

Of course, experiences of the Holy Spirit are clearly referred to in our Bibles. In the Old Testament era prophets, priests and kings of Israel were anointed with oil as a symbol of 'special grace'[3] given to them to fulfil their sacred calling. The Spirit of God imparted special abilities of craftsmanship to men such as Bezalel and Oholiab to fulfil with perfect accuracy the instructions that God had given to Moses regarding the furnishings and vessels for the Tent of Meeting.[4] The Spirit of God also came upon Balaam enabling him to utter amazing prophecies regarding the Christ.[5] God gave some of the Spirit that was in Moses to equip seventy elders to share with him the burden of leadership.[6] As Moses drew near to the end of his life, God instructed him to set apart Joshua, 'a man in whom is the Spirit', to lead the people into Canaan.[7]

[2] Luther, Vol. 7, p. 71.
[3] The expression 'special grace' is Calvin's; see *Institutes* II. 2. 17.
[4] Exodus 31:1-6.
[5] Numbers 24:2, 17.
[6] Numbers 11:17.
[7] Numbers 27:15-18.

It is significant that in these and other cases the Spirit was given to enable the Lord's people to fulfil his purposes and the task that had been assigned to them, whether it was the heavy responsibilities of spiritual or civil leadership, the pronouncement of crucial blessings, or manual work requiring unique skills. The focus was invariably upon the ongoing divine commission each one had been given.

In the New Testament Paul states that he had had personal experiences which were intensely private: 'he heard things that cannot be told, which man may not utter'.[8] He also writes that 'the love of Christ *restrained* him'.[9] I know we tend to translate the Greek word there as 'compel' or 'constrain', but that is not the best translation of the verb; it means 'to constrict', 'to shut up close', 'to exercise a restraining influence'. Paul is saying that under the constraint of God's love he deliberately and self-consciously kept the public expression of his experience of the Holy Spirit firmly in check. He further states that 'the spirits of prophets are subject to [the control of] prophets' and that he 'would rather speak five words with my mind in order to instruct others than ten thousand words in a tongue'.[10]

After many years in the Christian ministry and having had close friends who were pastors in congregations where the 'charismata' were regularly practised, I have come to the conclusion that, unless the word of God is given its rightful place and consistently obeyed, assumed manifestations of the Spirit can stray a long way from the divine will and purposes.

Not only is that clearly taught in the New Testament, but in the Old Testament we find this principle exemplified in Joseph and Saul: we see it negatively in Saul who was visited by the Spirit but

---

[8] 2 Corinthians 12:4.
[9] 2 Corinthians 5:14.
[10] 1 Corinthians 14:19, 32.

failed to obey the word of God; we see it positively in Joseph who was full of the Spirit of God and who lived a life of daily obedience.

As we try to see how this was worked out during Joseph's time in the service of Potiphar, I shall attempt to interpret his behaviour and demeanour in the light of Paul's teaching in Ephesians 5 and 6.

We need to begin by asking how the New Testament describes and defines those who are filled with the Holy Spirit of God. In Ephesians 5:18 Paul urges, 'Be filled with the Spirit.' He goes on to offer solid, tangible evidence of how this must work out in the believer's life. First the apostle speaks of the kind of praise that those who are filled with the Spirit will offer to God: adoration, worship, thanksgiving that will encourage and edify others in the Christian fellowship. So the flow of praise from our lips is certainly part of the evidence we are to expect. But the overwhelming weight of evidence of the fulness of the Spirit is along ethical lines, for Paul then directs us to the three main areas of living in order to provide us with tangible evidence of the genuineness of our experience of the Holy Spirit: marriage, home and work.

Let us take Paul's evidence negatively first of all. Think about marriage. Paul deliberately sets the Holy Spirit in opposition to the 'spirit' in alcohol. Imagine for a moment the husband who gets drunk each weekend. Onlookers will see the evidence of his abuse of alcohol very soon in his marriage: there will be violence in the home—fighting, arguing, bitterness and much grief. Undeniable evidence of exactly the kind of 'spirit' he is bringing into his marriage.

Consider Paul's second area of living—home life. The teenager who goes out binge drinking will cause friction in his relationship with his parents. Similarly the parents who abuse alcohol will have children who dread them coming home. I once called on a house and when the woman answered the door, a little boy of about three or four years old saw me and began to scream with terror and scramble up the stairs in fear as he ran away from me. The woman called to him, 'It's alright Jamie, it's not your dad.' She then apologized to me and told me her husband was a drunk and the wee boy was terrified of men as a result. There will be plenty of incontrovertible evidence of the effect of the wrong kind of 'spirit' on home life.

Then take Paul's third area of living—work. In an average year in the United Kingdom, at least fourteen million working days are lost at work on account of alcohol abuse. Again, the evidence shows itself very plainly. The effects of the wrong kind of spirits in marriage, home and work are very clear. Indeed, they are unmistakable.

Now this is exactly the point with the fulness of the Holy Spirit. When a man or woman is filled with the Spirit of God as we are commanded to be in Ephesians 5:18, then there is going to be clear evidence, so clear that it will be impossible to misread or misunderstand it.

It is precisely this scriptural teaching which has caused me over the years to be extremely cautious about subjective and emotional experiences of being filled with the Spirit, of which some churches boast. My Bible tells me to look for evidence within a believer's marriage, home and place of employment.

In the Old Testament, there are various examples of persons who were filled with the Holy Spirit. Two immediately come to mind—Joseph and Daniel. In both of these men's lives the evidence of their being filled with the Spirit of God was confirmed in their work and daily conduct. So we now turn to consider the first of them, Joseph the slave, Joseph the worker.

And our commentary on this young man's remarkable Spirit-filled life we will base on Ephesians 6:5-9.

The Evidence in Joseph's Life

Nothing is recorded about Joseph's personal spiritual life or about his times alone in prayer to his God, though we may assume his unswerving faith was nurtured through personal devotions. Rather, the record we are given of the Holy Spirit filling his life is pointed out to us by a pagan king: 'Can we find a man like this, in whom is the Spirit of God?'[11] The biblical record rather focuses on his work, just as Paul focuses on work in Ephesians 6:5ff. Scripture has already pointed us to his home life; by extrapolation, it will focus later on in this chapter on his sexual life. But in case we have missed the point, we are given clear evidence of the Spirit's reign within his heart and soul and mind. We are taken into one of the divine laboratories of life, and given a demonstration which proves beyond any doubt that this young man was possessed by the Spirit of God.

The setting is unexpected. He has been sold as a slave and an important official of Pharaoh has taken Joseph home to his great household, probably to work there as a kitchen boy. Remember Joseph would not have known the language. He was alone, a stranger, a foreigner and, worst of all, a slave, a scullion. He would have been set to work in a kitchen which would have been unbearably hot, doing all the dirtiest jobs, being knocked about and beaten when he made a mistake through no fault of his own, since at first he could not have understood what was wanted of him.

But we are told that *the LORD was with him . . . and caused all that he did to succeed in his hands.*[12] He did well. Apparently he quickly learned the language, and that must have taken concentration, effort and diligence. Joseph's experience was in the real world. It was not imaginary or mystical; it was not something airy-fairy. His life of faith yielded clear evidence that came out in the way the

[11] Genesis 41:38.
[12] Genesis 39:3, 4.

kitchen was cleaned, the pots and pans scoured, the vegetables prepared, the washing-up done. His master saw and took note. And so young Joseph was promoted. He left the steamy kitchen behind and the other slaves who baited him and who argued and fought among themselves. At length he became the personal attendant of his master, waiting on him at table, running his messages, fetching and carrying.

The evidence of God's presence with him continued, shining out. The Lord's hand was on him; his God was with him. So the promotion continued until he became at length the manager of the whole house, and his master entrusted absolutely everything into his hands, except the elaborate Egyptian religious ceremonial surrounding his food. That is a fascinating detail, for it suggests that Joseph kept himself apart from this man's pagan religious superstitions; he saw to absolutely everything except Potiphar's personal religious scruples.

Being Filled with the Spirit at Work

Consider Paul's words about the work of slaves:

> Slaves, obey your earthly masters with fear and trembling, with a sincere heart, as you would Christ, not by way of eye-service, as people-pleasers, but as servants of Christ, doing the will of God from the heart, rendering service with a good will as to the Lord and not to man, knowing that whatever good anyone does, this he will receive back from the Lord, whether he is a slave or free (Ephesians 6:5-8).

Notice in passing that while his subject is the way a slave does his work, the argument runs from the greater to the lesser, and therefore Paul includes ordinary employees in all he says. We have that at the end of verse 8, 'whether he is a slave or free'. All he says applies equally well to either slaves or employees. Therefore it applies to you and me, whether we are at school, or college, or work in some profession, or at home in the kitchen like Joseph, or wherever. These injunctions include us all.

Paul sometimes uses negatives to drive home his point: he expresses a statement negatively to reinforce the positive. So he tells us not to obey 'by way of eye-service, as people-pleasers'. The NIV translates that as, 'Obey them [your masters] not only to win their favour, when their eye is on you.' In my student days I worked one summer at the wheat and barley harvest. It was in the mid-1950s when smaller farms did not have combine harvesters and I was part of a squad of about half a dozen men working in the old-fashioned way of bringing in the sheaves. Much of the time the men would lounge around until the farmer's car would be seen slowly driving along the edge of the field; then they would begin to work hard, pretending to be industrious and hard at it—idling when he was not watching and then busy when he could see them. That is often the way of the world and of those employees who know nothing of the Holy Spirit. That is probably how other slaves in Potiphar's house worked, always apparently busy when he came along. But that way of behaving never fooled any employer. The person who is filled with the Holy Spirit will not have that attitude at all.

Paul has begun with a positive instruction to explain how the Spirit-filled person will work: 'obey your earthly masters with fear and trembling'. That phrase 'with fear and trembling' is important. The apostle used it to describe his attitude when he went to preach in Corinth. He wrote to them that 'he was with them in weakness and in fear and much trembling'.[13] What did he mean? He certainly did not mean he was frightened of them. Paul was not merely the peer of the Corinthians intellectually, he was vastly their superior. He could stand up to any of them and defeat them in argument with no difficulty. He was not naturally a timorous man. By nature

[13] 1 Corinthians 2:3.

he was as bold as a lion. What then does he mean when he says he came among them 'in fear and trembling'? He means that he was overwhelmed by the high privilege of preaching Christ. He was overawed that his was the task to speak to them of Almighty God and his amazing grace. He was trembling and afraid lest he should fall short in so high a commission. Some young men cannot wait to climb the pulpit steps and preach. Others cannot wait to get up front and tell everyone a thing or two. Not Paul. He went filled with apprehension and trepidation, lest he should fail his Lord, or misrepresent his beloved Saviour.

Now does that give us a clue as to what Paul means about the kind of service we should render to our bosses? There is no suggestion that we are to be afraid of the boss. Not at all. The meaning is that we fear lest the kind of employees we are, and the kind of work we do, should bring any shame on the name of our Lord and Master; we dread lest we should misrepresent our God for whom we are ambassadors. See how central a place Paul gives to *Christ* in his description of how we should work: 'obey . . . as you would Christ . . . as servants of Christ . . . doing the will of God from the heart, rendering service with a good will as to the Lord'.

Put it like this: when your supervisor comes to inspect your work, do you tremble in case he or she will think you are unworthy of the name of Christ, because your work is not really good enough for a Christian? Or when the manager comes round to see how you are getting on, is your chief concern that he will see that your work is of the kind of high standard anyone would expect of a Christian? How is it for you in the office, or in the shop, or on the hospital ward? Is there fear and trembling lest the Saviour should be misrepresented by your standard of work? That is what Paul means.

Therefore as his work was inspected by the chief chef, Joseph's motives were for the honour of his God. For that was being reflected even in the way he washed up, and cleaned the stone surfaces and did the most menial of tasks. The Holy Spirit in him was jealous for God's glory.

There is a further point I would like to draw out of these verses in Ephesians 6. There are three words tucked away in the text which I am sure are used quite deliberately. The first one is 'heart'—'with a sincere heart'; the word 'heart' is important; it is used to describe the centre and seat of our being and acting. The second is 'soul'—doing the will of God from your soul; ESV, AV, NIV, translate the Greek word here (*psyche*) as 'heart', but its meaning is 'the soul'; basically, *psyche* means 'the breath of life'; it can be used both of the *life* lived on earth, and the blessed *life* we will live in heaven. The third is the phrase 'with a good will'—'rendering service *with a good will* as to the Lord'; the phrase is literally 'with a good mind', or a clear mind: *knowing* what God's will is. In other words, Paul is telling us that the Holy Spirit must occupy and control our entire beings; he must be seated, as it were, at the control panel of our thinking, acting and doing, his gracious, loving influence guiding our entire lives.

Of course these three words are the words Jesus uses in the greatest commandment, which tells us to love the Lord our God with all our heart and soul and mind.[14] The point is that Christians at work, filled with the Holy Spirit, are going to give their whole lives to their work, holding nothing back—heart, soul and mind. So let us think a little further about these three words which Paul uses.

First, 'with a sincere heart': this speaks of whole-hearted, joyful, thorough work. We sometimes speak to people at work who are scowling, angry and full of ill-will. Have you ever had a colleague like that? It can be hard going when we work alongside those who complain and grumble that everything is wrong, nothing is

[14] Matthew 22:37; cited from Deuteronomy 6:5.

right. It can be very wearing. But the man or the woman who is filled with the Spirit of God will work from the heart, joyfully and cheerfully, knowing what they are about. What a joy to be with them! Potiphar saw that in Joseph. This young Hebrew slave was so full of joy. Not in a cheeky, impertinent way, but in an attractive, serene way. Is that how we do our work, because the grace of the Holy Spirit fills our hearts?

Second, 'soul': 'doing the will of God from the soul', from your *psyche*, your 'breath of life' or 'life principle' in the sense of 'the mainspring of your life'. That speaks of full commitment. It speaks of those whose obedience is never grudging. There is a kind of obedience which is done with a scowl as if it were a burden. I have a picture in my mind just now of someone saying, 'Alright, I'll do that', and if looks could kill, the boss would drop dead on the spot! Oh dear, with what resentment, anger, and unwillingness she responded! The boss was left wondering how long he could put up with such an employee.

When I was a school teacher a boy would tell me by the way he walked back to his seat what he thought of the instructions I had given. The body language would be very clear. By his walk and manner he could convey an impertinence and unwillingness which in those bad old days (or were they?) gave the teacher sufficient warrant to open the desk drawer and take out the leather tawse.[15] Or, at the very least, to say, 'Alright then, write out that corrected exercise twenty times, if you don't want to lose your sports afternoon and do detention instead.'

It is not only schoolboys whose souls are sometimes not in their work. There are adults too, even those claiming to be Christians. They might even profess to have had an experience which they

[15] A strong, thick length of cow-hide with thongs at one end was used in Scottish schools for discipline until abolished by government legislation. The present writer when a schoolboy in Arbroath was on many occasions at the receiving end of such discipline—usually well-deserved!

claimed had been their infilling with the Holy Spirit. But Potiphar would never have thought that, had he been their employer!

Third, 'serve wholeheartedly': literally, 'serve with a good mind', a clear mind; know what you are about. *Understand* what the will of the Lord is. Paul is speaking about God's will—God's will for a Hebrew slave in an Egyptian scullery. He is not on the lofty level of a mission to Spain or India with an OM[16] team. He sees that we have to learn to prove God's will with a brush in our hands sweeping the floor, or at a kitchen sink washing a greasy frying pan, or clearing up the chairs, or dusting the furniture, or tidying the bedroom.

Remember, we are thinking about Paul's phrase 'serve wholeheartedly' which means using our minds in the way we do our work. To glorify God in our service for him we need to be filled with his Spirit. The Holy Spirit is a Spirit of order. So how can I be blessed by God in my work if I leave behind in my home a bedroom which is dirty and untidy, with soiled washing lying all over, and piles of clothes waiting to be put away and the bed unmade? We need to understand these things. We need to understand what God requires of us. Joseph understood. And whenever Potiphar appeared, his work was all in order, because it was done with a good mind, a clear mind!

Work as God wants you to do—with heart, soul and mind.

We have already noted above how central a place Paul gives to *Christ* in his description of how we should work: 'obey . . . as you would Christ . . . as servants of Christ . . . doing the will of God from the heart, rendering service with a good will as to the Lord.' He states it four times. Is that not very powerful, pointed and challenging?

You may ask, 'But what is the will of God?' It is that we should glorify him in all we do. The remarkable thing about pagan Potiphar

---

[16] A missionary organization known as Operation Mobilization.

was that he saw that the Lord was with this Hebrew slave. Joseph's work made him think of God. Can we take that in? Whatever kind of work did Joseph do that caused a man like Potiphar to think of the Lord? Was it partly that he was so serene, so pleasant, so faithful, so meticulous all the time? Was it partly that everything was so well done, and he was always completely reliable, never breaking his word? Was it partly that he concentrated on his work, and refused to be distracted? Was it also that he was conscientious and wasted no time? Was it because he was scrupulously honest, and wouldn't take even a sheet of papyrus that did not belong to him? I think it was all of these things. He knew the will of God and therefore he glorified God in all he did.

Let us take a modern application of this. I think it would be very wrong for an employee to use up his or her boss's time witnessing and evangelizing—stealing an hour of time in the week that ought to be spent working, but instead is spent debating about Christian things. Quite wrong! The witnessing is worthless because it is coupled with theft—stealing the employer's time. Real witnessing is when our work causes our colleagues and our supervisor to think of the Lord Jesus Christ, and to conclude that he is with us. That is witnessing that will be effective in the long run.

Or, is it not wrong when a student, at school or college, hands in work that is less than his or her best—careless, hurried work, messy and incorrect or incomplete because insufficient time has been spent on it? The Christian's work is the will of God, even if that work is digging a hole, or cleaning out a drain; even if that work is cleaning brass door handles, or dusting chairs.

It is also wrong if the professing Christian is unpleasant as a person. I don't care whether you are a minister, or a doctor or an accountant. Being filled with the Holy Spirit means your clients and your colleagues will see the Lord in you and with you, as

Potiphar saw the Lord was with Joseph, the kitchen slave boy. That is the kind of witnessing that counts.

But the most outstanding test is none of these things. It is not that this young man Joseph was pleasant, reliable and excellent in everything he did. There was an even more remarkable proof that he was filled with the Spirit of God. It was that God blessed his boss for Joseph's sake. I do not want to make any more comment on this other than to say that, as I read the stories of slaves such as Joseph or Daniel and see the blessing of God honouring these and other men and women, bringing blessing to everything they touched, I wonder what has gone wrong with the people of God today? I can only say that I think we must very often be wide of the mark of God's pure and precious truth. For if you and I were in touch with God and filled with his Holy Spirit, then that same blessing would, in some small measure at least, be upon us and with us, and the world would see and know and come to our God, drawn irresistibly by his evident presence among us.

Do we all need to look around our homes? Do we need to review our work and our attitudes to our work, whether it is voluntary or salaried? Do we need to examine our attitudes to everything we do? Do we need to spend some time with God's word open before us at Genesis 39:1-6, and at Ephesians 6:5-9, using Ephesians 5:18, 'be filled with the Spirit', as the fulcrum on either side of which the Genesis account of Joseph and Paul's teaching on work balance each other so delicately?

We need to ask ourselves: Is the glory and blessing of God so evident in our homes and at our work that it can only be so because we are filled with God's Spirit? Will you ask yourself: Am I filled with myself or some other spirit—perhaps selfishness, or laziness, or self-advancement or some other wholly carnal attitude? I believe many of us aim at quite the wrong things. God's will is purity of heart and honesty of life; his desire for us is the obedience of our wills to the prompting of his voice. And his voice comes through his word, not from some airy-fairy dream, but from the clear, down-to-earth word of the living God.

Like Naaman, may we go and wash seven times and be clean.[17] May we also learn to yield ourselves daily to the complete control and infilling of his blessed, gracious Spirit. And may the genuineness of our experience of the Lord be evidenced by the way we live, serving with heart and soul and mind (and, Jesus added, with all our strength[18]). All of this adds up to taking up the cross God chooses to lay upon us and obeying his word, however costly that obedience may prove to be. Who can tell or count the blessings that will be bestowed on those who are faithful!

---

[17] 2 Kings 5:10, 14

[18] See Mark 12:30 and Luke 10:27. '[The heart, Heb. *lebab*] was essentially the whole man, with all his attributes, physical, intellectual and psychological ... and the heart was conceived of as the governing centre for all of these'. B. O. Banwell, article on 'Heart', *IBD*, Part 2, p. 625.

CHAPTER THREE

Joseph Tempted—Genesis 39:7-20

A S we reach the main part of chapter 39, we are confronted with a subject which is not often dealt with nowadays from pulpits or in Bible studies. It is the subject of temptation, but in a very particular sense—the temptation to sexual sin. Satan has many arrows in his quiver, and this is one which he often uses to the most deadly effect. There have been many fine Christian men and women gravely wounded by this poisonous arrow sent with deadly accuracy from the devil's bow: missionaries, ministers, elders, evangelists and ordinary folk like you and me. It is a subject that we must treat with the utmost seriousness: 'Therefore let anyone who thinks he stands take heed lest he fall.'[1]

It is probable that those watching Joseph's progress might have concluded that he had overcome all his problems. Let us assume he was about seventeen when he was sold as a slave into Egypt. And let us also assume he was about two or three years climbing the tree of promotion in his master's house. Now he has been made manager, and we can guess he has occupied this position for some little time, so that during the events which are recorded in this chapter from verse 7 onwards he could have been in his early twenties. Joseph might be forgiven for beginning to relax a little, even to sigh with relief: 'I am still a slave, but I have just about

---

[1] 1 Corinthians 10:12.

come through all my trials. God has been good to me. My brothers would never believe it if they saw me now, manager of this great house and its estate.' Remember, too, that he is now living with a standard of luxury that would be completely unknown back home, for Egypt led the world in affluence at this time.

However, we must all learn that in this life we never graduate as the finished article, the perfected Christian. After all the tears, struggles and trials of the past few years and having done so well, there is another snare, a terrible Satanic ambush, waiting for Joseph, lurking behind the next corner. That is always the devil's method. He will not leave us alone for long. He will be searching through his manual of dirty tricks to see what device he can employ to trip us up and land us with our faces in the mud and filth. We do well never to forget that.

Yes, Joseph had heroically fought some hard battles and by God's grace had won through. But there are always more battles ahead, and this chapter tells us about one of them. Perhaps not all, but certainly many readers of this book, will either have faced this particular battle, or will have to face it in the days ahead. So our God and Guide has given us a clear outline of the ground on which this battle must be fought, and clear instructions as to how the victory can be won.

The Description of Temptation

I do not think there is any intended bias against women here in that a woman is portrayed as the temptress. Later on in Scripture we have a man cast in a similar role. But we should comment that at times men can be a bit direct in their enticements to sin; not always, but generally, a woman may be more subtle and devious. Nevertheless, whether or not that is so, at the end of the day, sin is still sin however cunningly or blatantly it is suggested. And since it all comes ultimately from hell, the devil is quite able to teach a man how to entice and draw away towards destruction his victim with a skill and cunning equal to that of any woman.

It is John Calvin, the sixteenth-century reformer, who understands verse 7 to suggest that for many weeks, perhaps even months, Potiphar's wife looked at Joseph admiringly and appreciatively without sinning. Calvin comments, 'It is not wrong for a woman to look [admiringly] at a man', and I suppose he would say that, *vice versa*, 'It is not wrong for a man to look admiringly at a woman.'

But Satan's method is often to take something which is the very gift of God and distort and degrade it, leading it off along a forbidden pathway. Joseph, we are told in the final clause of verse 6, was handsome in form and appearance. The Latin translation of the Old Testament expresses it well when it says he was beautiful in form and beautiful in features.[2] He had a manly figure and a lovely, handsome face. That was how God had made him.

Step One

We come then to the *first* of five testing points[3] which chart the increasing intensity and pathway of this terrible temptation. Step one is the lust of the eyes.

The NIV is very weak in its translation in verse 7. It has 'his master's wife took notice of Joseph'. But the NKJ has a more graphic translation: 'she cast longing eyes on Joseph'; ESV is similar: 'his master's wife cast her eyes on Joseph'.

In the old days before we had power at the touch of a switch, fire was used far more than today. I remember my father at home taking a shovel of red hot coals out of one fire to light a fire in another room and it usually worked well; it was a bit dangerous, carrying a shovel of blazing embers from one room to another. Now a similar thing was happening with this woman. From her

---

[2] Vulgate: *erat autem Joseph pulcher forma, et pulcher aspectu.*
[3] I have adapted the five points from Palau, pp. 80-82.

eyes to her passions, blazing embers were carried. 'The lust of the eyes', as John calls it in the New Testament,[4] is like a blazing torch carried into the heart, there to set fire to our passions, there to burn with hot desire.

So it is today. Human nature has not changed over 3,500 years. If anything, we are more vulnerable, for today we can be alone at home with just the television or computer for company. Or some magazine might fall into our hands with enough material in it to carry those blazing coals from our eyes to our passions and make them burn ten times hotter. Many of the magazines on sale in the newsagents are packed with sexual 'semtex', which is very malleable and can be easily applied to advertisements, articles and photographs. And this kind of 'semtex' only needs a very tiny detonator to cause an explosion in our passions that is enough to blow us out of the blue skies of pure fellowship with our loving God. That is step one—the lust of the eyes.

Step Two
This second step is subtle suggestions. We might easily miss this out because it does not appear to be in the narrative of Genesis 39. But Calvin again argues that it cannot be doubted that Potiphar's wife began by gently courting Joseph with flattering comments and simple kindnesses. He takes it that this is included in the phrase she 'cast her eyes on Joseph'. I am sure Calvin is right. It will have begun with a smile and a little extra sentence or two. She may have called him more often than was needed, for he was bound to have been at her beck and call. She will have arranged to have him with her or deliberately she would be where he was, putting herself in his way. That is how it will have begun. And in the early stages, there was nothing he could do about that. He was, after all, her slave! I wish we were all as unyielding to these blandishments as

4 1 John 2:16 (NKJ).

Joseph was, because they made no impression on him whatsoever. But how easily many of us succumb.

Not so long ago, a woman told me she had met in a supermarket an old friend from school-days. He had greeted her very warmly, and told her she didn't look a day older. And for starters—let me assure you— that was a downright lie. She was at least twenty-five years older. But she swallowed it. She was absolutely delighted. His attention had flattered her, and I could see she was thinking wistfully about him. He had commented admiringly on her dress and she had been flattered. I must admit, as I listened to it all, it seemed to me all too obvious that the intentions of the former school friend were less than honourable. Step two: subtle (and, very often, not so subtle) suggestions!

Step Three

Next is a shameless proposal: 'Come to bed with me' (NIV). Archaeology discloses that aristocratic Egyptian women were quite shameless and almost always unfaithful to their husbands. Ancient records tell how one Pharaoh searched his entire kingdom for a faithful woman until at last he found one whom he immediately made his queen.

Nowadays I suppose these shameless proposals come with an invitation to a meal out somewhere with a few drinks, and then the invitation, 'Why don't you come back to my place for coffee?' It amounts to the same thing ultimately.

However, we are intended to understand that Potiphar's wife's invitation to Joseph was anything but the language of love. The world calls it love, but it is not; it is lust. And the real difference between love and lust is the difference between heaven and hell.

Step Four

The fourth step was a change in tactics. She saw that she was not going to succeed with this upright young man by using a direct approach. And so she dreamed up another approach. She planned to wear him down little by little. There are two clear hints at that. First, 'Just be with me; come and sit and talk while I do my embroidery; you could pour my tea and have a cup yourself; no harm in that.' Ah, but there was! And Joseph saw perfectly well what she was trying to do, so he refused even to be with her (verse 10). Further, she did not give up but gently persisted. Every day she had some seemingly innocent little ploy to get Joseph to be close to her. Day after day. It was a real challenge to her to make a conquest of Joseph and she seriously set her mind to it.

I have seen this at work again and again. Dallying. Agreeing to go out, but thinking to withstand the seduction. That is a fatal response to step four, this clever change in tactics. He says, 'I know you can't and you won't, and I respect that. But we can just be friends. Nothing wrong with having lunch together.'

And genuinely, sincerely intending to have nothing to do with anything immoral, she goes for lunch and then for dinner for, like Potiphar's wife, he won't give up but keeps on, day after day. And his change in tactics at last works. The fly is drawn into the spider's web, and thereby virtue dies a terrible death.

Step Five

The final step we are given is scheming. Every commentary on this chapter that I have consulted suggests that when the moment came that Joseph and the woman were alone together in the house, it was because she had plotted to create this situation. She had engineered it. It was a deliberate scheme that she was convinced would work. 'Thus the lustful mistakenly assume that others only restrain themselves for want of opportunity.'[5]

How well do you know the book of Psalms? There is many a psalm which speaks about exactly this kind of scheming, about the

[5] Still, p. 174.

person who lies awake at night, thinking and working out how he will accomplish some sin, how he will succeed in getting his way.[6]

And so we have these five awful steps downward into the dark valley of temptation, where Apollyon waits with his coward's blow to bring us to the ground and inflict on us the wound that he intends will ruin our Christian lives and leave us forever as his slaves. It is as real as that. And where would you and I be if it were not for our Saviour? Remember how he said to Simon Peter, 'Simon, Simon, behold, Satan demanded to have you, that he might sift you like wheat, but I have prayed for you that your faith may not fail.'[7]

There we have it, then, very clearly and plainly: the description of temptation.

The Defeat of Temptation

Genesis chapter 39 is far more than an example of superb literary style, though of course it is most certainly that. Its main purpose is to encapsulate a young man's battle against temptation and how he met head-on the hail of darts aimed at his heart, but shielded them off with steadfast resolution. If we are honest, we look into our own hearts and many of us know that in Joseph's position we would have fallen prey to the seductions of sin. Humanly speaking, we would most probably have wrecked our lives, nullified God's purposes for us and been thrown on to the scrap heap. Remember how that was Paul's great dread; he wrote that he feared lest, having preached to others, he himself should be disqualified. And so he disciplined ('buffeted') his body, and kept it under control.[8] He knew the weakness of his fallen humanity and he knew the devil's evil strength. Let us then try and see Joseph's battle against

---

[6] Psalms 10:2; 31:13, 20; 36:4; 52:2; 64:2, *etc.*
[7] Luke 22:31-32.
[8] 1 Corinthians 9:27.

temptation in those five stages, as we follow the pattern of the temptations with which he was assailed.

Stage one was outright refusal.
Verse 8, *But he refused.* That had to be his first defensive action in this battle. Does it surprise some of us that outright refusal is only stage one in a five-round struggle? Yet this is where resistance must begin. Furthermore, I believe that firm and unwavering refusal must begin in the mind. He refused to permit even the suggestion of such an act of adultery to linger in his mind; he cast it out from the start. He did not play with it or turn it over mentally the way we turn over and enjoy a soft chocolate in our mouths; he did not toy with this suggestion. From the start it was, 'No! Never! No!'

Speaking of the spiritual battle in which he was always engaged, Paul wrote, 'We . . . take every thought captive to obey Christ', and again, 'we have the mind of Christ'.[9] You see up to a point Sigmund Freud was right. The sex instinct in all of us is a very powerful drive. It is second only to the instinct of self-preservation. It is always there, even when lying dormant or dozing. It is just waiting to be stirred and when aroused it will spring into activity, like a lion provoked, roaring with menacing fangs. Therefore, unless we settle the matter in our minds, we are in deadly danger. There can be no place for doubt, no wavering. We must be steadfast in our thinking, unswerving and resolute. That is always stage one of the defeat of temptation. Nevertheless, it is the only starting point.

Stage two for Joseph was loyalty to his master.
Now we have to remember that Joseph was not a cardboard cut-out. He was not a moral freak who had a unique immunity to lust. He was ordinary flesh and blood with very human passions and emotions. At this point in his life he was deprived of normal

[9] 2 Corinthians 10:5; 1 Corinthians 2:16.

family affection. He was far from home. He had suffered gross injustice. From the point of view of a Freudian psychologist, he was bound to have been a sitting target for this kind of seduction. So we must break down his firm refusal into its component parts. And the first component was his loyalty to his master.

He spells out in eloquent and moving words the trust Potiphar had put in him and he makes it plain that he would see yielding to Potiphar's wife's invitation as breaking that trust (verses 8, 9). Did you ever ask yourself how our Lord could say that the whole of the Law hangs on love of God and love of neighbour? Here we have the answer vividly illustrated. The seventh commandment on adultery is obeyed when a man truly loves his neighbour in that he refuses to steal or tamper with his neighbour's wife.

There is much here for us all, therefore notice some of the content of this second stage of the fight. Not only would Joseph have been breaking the bond of Potiphar's implicit trust in himself, he would also have been breaking the husband-wife bond created by God. When a man and woman come together physically they are joined together and become one body, one flesh.[10] They belong to each other for the rest of their lives. But let an act of adultery take place and what God has joined together is broken. And this is included in Joseph's words that his master has given him everything in the house except his own wife. That is not to say there cannot be forgiveness and reconciliation. Of course there can. But the point is that love for, and loyalty to, Potiphar ultimately grew from love of God, because the love of God is the fountain-head of love for our neighbour.

When a man or a woman commits sexual sin of any kind, they do so out of love of self. Another name for love of self is lust and that is the very opposite of love of God. Love of God refuses to allow love of self to call the tune. Had Joseph not loved God and had

[10] Genesis 2:24.

he not loved his master in this practical way of being completely one hundred percent loyal to him, then stage one would have been overturned and frustrated at this second stage. He would at length have yielded. But his second line of defence stood firm.

Stage three: the consequences of such a sin
There was a third line of defence. Joseph was aware of the consequences of such a sin. Though still a young man he was wise enough to see that the results of a sexual liaison with this woman would be disastrous. He saw with a clear and steady upward look, unclouded by passion, that he could not commit this sin and get away with it. The secret would ultimately be out, his world forever shattered. And whatever purposes God had for him (remember his dreams) would also be torn apart.

You and I often try to convince ourselves—as King David did over Bathsheba—that we will be able to cover up our sin, keeping it completely secret so that no one will ever know about it. We think we are clever enough, cunning enough, and no harm will come. How often has this argument been used: 'I'm not causing anyone any harm'? Today, with all the modern methods of birth control, that argument is used even more. Yet it is not only the chance of pregnancy (some 9,000,000 terminations since abortion was legalized in the UK in 1967), it is the whole painful tangle of wrong relationships, with the endless complications and the resultant bitterness, heartbreak and destruction of trust and love. But in our modern obstinacy and blindness our society discards all that as if it did not matter. But oh, it does! It is of the very essence of life and living.

Joseph's heart was not obstinate nor his spiritual sight obscured. He saw very well the devastating consequences that adultery with his master's wife was bound to bring in its wake. And so he stood firm behind that sure defence.

Stage four: there are two sides to this 'coin'.

There was the realization of how immense an evil sin is, but also inseparably joined to that there was a holy fear of God. Verse 9, *How then could I do this great wickedness and sin against God?* Joseph's wisdom was to name with total accuracy what the act of adultery would have been—'great wickedness . . . and sin against God'.

We can use all sorts of phrases and words to try and cloak our sins. But there is no cloak or disguise here in Joseph's words. No doubt the woman spoke of love. No doubt she promised complete discretion and privacy. No doubt she spoke of her own frustration—Potiphar had concubines and was not bothering with her these days; it was her right to have a man the same as he had his lovers. But Joseph would have nothing to do with any of that. It was perfectly clear in his mind that the thing she wanted and was urging was both 'great wickedness and . . . sin against God'.

Do we give the correct names to our sins, whatever they may be? And have we this fear of God which gave Joseph the right perspective on the whole situation? Or do we let the internet websites, glossy magazines and the television programmes, which so often joke and laugh about these things, blur our thinking? Joseph was a man who kept God first in his heart and mind. There can be no other way. Christ before me, Christ behind me, Christ above me, Christ beneath me, Christ beside me, Christ within me. That is a stout, impregnable barricade behind which we can find shelter in the hour when the battle is fiercest and the danger greatest.

The fifth and final stage: he ran away.

Verse 12 reads, *He . . . fled and got out of the house.* There is a lovely old Victorian hymn which I have occasionally suggested for funerals because it fits well at the memorial service of a believer. I confess I do not like it for a living, active congregation, for it contains a complete falsehood. It is the old hymn, 'Safe in the arms of Jesus'.

One verse goes like this:

> Safe in the arms of Jesus, safe from corroding care;
> Safe from the world's temptations, sin cannot harm me there.

That is certainly true for someone who has died and is now safe in the Lord's presence. But it is not true for you and me who still have many battles to fight. Even though Joseph was sheltered by his four massive defences of refusal, loyalty to his master, fear and love of God and awareness of sin's consequences, there still remained the further battle of this evil assault, which was the moment when the woman engineered the perfect opportunity to fling herself at him and press her kisses and body upon him. At that point, he was not 'safe in the arms of Jesus'. He was in the most deadly peril. I say again, he was a young, virile man, with his hormones extremely active, stimulating those natural, God-given passions which are such a powerful part of human nature. He was not safe in the arms of Jesus at all, and he was not safe from the world's temptations. That is a serious misrepresentation. He had to run and flee for his very life.

I remember as a student being astonished by a minister who came to speak at our university Christian Union. He told us that on one occasion when he was in a foreign city, far from home, he was solicited by a beautiful young prostitute. He said he had turned and run down the street away from her as fast as he could. I was shocked. I thought he would have witnessed to her and told her of Jesus. But that man knew himself well and he was right to run away.

The apostles implied that there are two kinds of temptation: we might call them 'objective' and 'subjective'. The objective temptations are those from outside of ourselves which we must resolutely resist. We stand firm against them, and say a determined No to them.[11]

---

[11] 1 Peter 5:8-9.

But there are other subjective temptations which touch a chord deep down in our fallen natures, setting our desires on fire and the blood racing through our veins as our pulses quicken; we must run away from those. Paul wrote to young Timothy who was his fellow worker, a pastor and teacher: 'Flee youthful passions'—run away from them![12] I wonder if when he wrote those words Paul was thinking of Joseph running out of that house without even a backward glance?

Have you learned when you must run away? Have you discovered that the time comes when prayer cannot avail anything, when just to repeat the name of Jesus as if it was a mantra is not enough. The moment comes when our resolve will melt and turn to water, our wills will yield and even though our hearts are crying 'No!', our bodies will scream 'Yes!'. Have you realized that the only way to win the final battle in this satanic assault on our morality is to run and get out of the place, putting as much distance between ourselves and the temptation as we can.

And so breathless, clad only in his loincloth, for his cloak had been left behind in the woman's hands, Joseph arrived in his own quarters and flung himself on to his bed, trembling and afraid. There was nowhere to hide, nowhere else to which to run. But he was victorious, that hideous temptation of his passions routed.

Our Defence against Temptation

We need now to gather together the threads of the practical teaching of this incident and so, in conclusion, I offer three simple principles to all who would set their hearts on staying faithful to Christ.

The first principle is this: to our dying day, temptation and sin will remain with us. The root of sin in our hearts is never eradicated in

---

[12] 2 Timothy 2:22; cf. 1 Corinthians 6:18; also 10:14, 'flee from idolatry': 'It is not enough to express disapproval of idolatry; he must run away from it, that is, he must avoid occasions ... that would bring him into direct contact with it.' C. K. Barrett, *1 Corinthians*, 2nd edition (London, A&C Black, 1971, London), p. 230.

this life. When we come to Christ, we repent of our sins and we are washed in the fountain of his cleansing. Baptism speaks of that in a beautiful way—the washing of pure water. God forgives our sins and we rejoice in that. Oh, the marvellous happiness of the burden of guilt falling off our backs and rolling down the hill of Calvary and into the empty tomb of Christ. Because God's forgiveness is forever, the assurance of believers is that they are washed clean by the Saviour.

I wonder if someone reading this knows that the burden of his or her sin has never been lifted. You are still under a dark cloud. The gospel is quite plain: Christ can wash you completely clean and take away all your guilt and fear. With Charles Wesley you can sing with all your heart,

> I woke, the dungeon flamed with light;
> my chains fell off, my heart was free.

There is no need for delay or to continue struggling and toiling under the heavy load of sin's guilt. Jesus Christ is ever standing ready to forgive all who come to him in repentance and faith. 'If we confess our sins, he is faithful and just to forgive us our sins and to cleanse us from all unrighteousness.'[13]

Nonetheless, even though Christ washes us clean, the root of sin remains deeply entrenched within our hearts. It is like a persistent weed that we can never dig down deep enough to root out. Our fallen natures can never achieve perfection throughout our lives on earth. That is the first principle the believer must never forget. We are saved by grace, but we remain sinners saved by grace. To be forewarned is to be forearmed. An army going into battle needs intelligence reports about the enemy, its strength, position, capability and potential. A commander who faces up to his enemy without any knowledge of these things is simply courting defeat.

[13] 1 John 1:9.

Therefore you and I need to know ourselves. We must think soberly of ourselves. We need to know that some of the contents on the internet or the video shop could lead to the very entrance to a direct pathway to hell. We need to know that certain books and magazines have their main office just inside that self-same entrance, and that they will lead those who open and read them to the brink of the pit where the sulphurous fumes of fire and brimstone will choke their lungs. We also need to know ourselves well enough to recognize that we have a keg of high explosive deep down in our fallen natures. And therefore we must be resolved that we will never allow a single spark, let alone a naked flame, near lest a conflagration is ignited and we are seriously burned and scarred for life.

The second principle we must learn is that it is gloriously possible to remain pure. Although it is hard, it is possible. Joseph was no different to us. It can be done. We hear many saying, 'But everyone is doing it nowadays.' That is no argument at all. Would you walk off the edge of a cliff saying, 'But everyone is doing it'? I recall my mother speaking very plainly to me when I was in my mid-teens, and telling me that her great prayer for me was that on my wedding day both I and my bride would be virgins. I thank God for his hand upon me so that her prayer was answered, but I tell you that Satan's aim is always the very opposite.

Will you therefore pledge yourself to God? Will you make a covenant with God, a covenant with your eyes, a covenant with your bodies that, for God's glory and for the freedom and liberty of the Holy Spirit who lives in your hearts, you will keep yourselves pure by Christ's grace?[14] I know that there is forgiveness when a man or woman falls. But the best way, the happiest way, the way of blessing, is the way of purity. It is not beyond our grasp with God's gracious help.

[14] Job 31:1; 1 Corinthians 6:19-20.

Finally, *the third principle* is that the only way to purity is for God to have all of us: mind, soul and heart.

Resisting temptation begins with our minds. Let us daily pray, 'Lord, please guard my mind; Lord, bring every thought captive into the obedience of Christ.' Not only pray that prayer, but mean it by wearing the helmet of salvation and guarding what enters your mind through eye-gate and ear-gate: these are the two gateways into our minds. Keep a pure mind by setting a watch over what you choose to look at and listen to.

Further, our souls must be daily pledged to total commitment to God on the one hand, and to total opposition to wickedness on the other hand. Right from their very depths must our souls belong to our Lord and Master and to him alone. Our Christian commitment must be as in the marriage vow—'forsaking all other . . .'

Mind, soul, but also heart—our love! 'The greatest of these is love.'[15] Love of God and of the things of God. Love of his people, love of his church, love of his praise, love of his word, love of his laws. And love of God goes hand in hand with hatred of all God hates.

> Were the whole realm of nature mine,
>> that were an offering far too small;
> Love so amazing, so divine,
>> demands my soul, my life, my all.[16]

---

[15] 1 Corinthians 13:13.

[16] Final verse of the hymn, 'When I survey the wondrous cross' by Isaac Watts (1674-1748).

CHAPTER FOUR

Joseph in Prison—Genesis 39:20–40:23 with 2 Corinthians 4:7–12

NO one particularly likes exams. It can be wearisome burning the midnight oil, working hard night by night, learning page after page of information or equations or worse still grappling with and trying to master material you have not yet understood, and all this so that you will be able to answer the questions on the examination paper. I wonder if it has ever struck you that God sets examinations for us. Indeed, he sets examination after examination, for until we have learned certain basic lessons, he will not entrust us with important work for his kingdom. Think of a man like Abraham: God taught him to have faith and then tested his faith. Year after year, Abraham waited for the promised son, and year after year his faith was tested as no son arrived. And then, when Isaac was born, God set Abraham a much harder test when he told him to sacrifice his beloved son. Those were hard and difficult examinations.

Or think of Moses: he had an early premonition that his calling was to free the Hebrew slaves from the oppression of their taskmasters. But before God could give him that work to do, he had to spend forty years in 'Bible College', being trained. And the 'Bible College' was a wilderness in the back of beyond, where he humbly cared for his father-in-law's sheep. Or consider David: he knew that God had a great work for him to do. Had not Samuel anointed him and was not he a great warrior? But God had to send him to 'Bible College' as well for many years. He became a fugitive, learned what hunger was like and what it meant to be driven near to despair. But God was training him, preparing him, setting him hard examinations, before at last entrusting him with the special work chosen for him of uniting the chosen people into a coherent kingdom and establishing Jerusalem as their capital city.

That was how it was with Joseph. It is so clear in his life. First he was sold as a slave by jealous, cruel brothers. Then he was forced to work as a scullion in a kitchen and be the lowest flunkey. Having passed that exam and having been promoted, he was then set an even harder test, a physical test, when a beautiful and powerful woman tried to entice him into sin. But he passed that test also. And what then? 'It would be wrong to impugn the gentler sex under the category of Potiphar's wife, although the lengths to which sex-obsessed women will go have to be seen to be believed ... such women (and men), frustrated on the very lip of their desire, grow uncontrollably mad and are ready to hatch the most diabolical plots to avenge their refusals.'[1]

Thus he was thrown into prison. There for several years he was to undergo yet another trial. And it is the testing of Joseph in prison that is the subject of Genesis chapter 40.

Testing

It did not seem to matter what Joseph did—he always had to suffer for it. Back home he had been truthful, honest and reliable. That earned him the envy and hatred of his brothers. He had refused to join in their lying, cheating and stealing, and the reward he got was to be sold as a slave to traders who took him far from home and put him on view in a market, selling him to the highest bidder.

Then he had worked conscientiously, diligently learning the Egyptian language and gradually climbing the slave's career-ladder

[1] Still, p. 174.

until he reached the top and was manager of his master's house. As a slave he could not have got any higher. With what results? Where had his honesty, purity, integrity and obedience to God taken him? He ended up in an Egyptian prison!

In 2 Corinthians 4:8, 9 Paul uses four phrases to describe the trials and testing that may come to God's faithful servants. His first phrase is 'afflicted in every way' ('troubled on every side' AV; 'hard pressed on every side' NIV). A vivid word picture is painted by this phrase. It is the image of someone being attacked by an adversary who is very strong and is driving his victim into a corner, with the intention of leaving him no room to fight back, no room to manoeuvre. While the one being attacked is struggling to resist and ward off his attacker and doing his best to get out of the corner he has been forced into, the onlookers hold their breath wondering if this is this the end of the fight. Has the attacker won and his victim lost because he has been forced into a stance where it is impossible to keep up the struggle? That is what this phrase means, 'hard pressed on every side' (NIV).

The mysterious thing is this: that terrible onslaught and attack only comes to those who are determined to follow God and go his way. If in the face of temptation and trial you just give up, then you will never be hard pressed on every side. Your adversary will have won and you will slip into drifting along with the current. You will not be going anywhere, so spiritually you will get nowhere; your end will be to suffer spiritual eternal loss.[2] But take your stand, resolve to obey God, determine to be true to Christ whatever the cost, say 'No!' to the devil's enticements, and you will find that the battle is on—at school, in college, at work, even within the family. To change the figure, lay your life on the altar and the flames will soon begin licking round the sides of that altar to consume the sacrifice.

[2] 1 Corinthians 3:15.

Paul uses a second term in 2 Corinthians 4:8. Our Bibles translate it simply as 'perplexed'. That is a perfectly correct rendering. But there is also tucked away here a little picture as well. It is of someone whose supplies are almost finished. Humanly speaking, this traveller cannot continue any longer. He has come to an end of his strength and his resources are all but spent.

I have a nephew who served in the Falklands campaign. During the final assault on the Argentine positions around Port Stanley he told me that the British forces had almost run out of ammunition. He was manning a field gun and his gun crew had only two shells left, when a white flag of surrender was hoisted by the Argentinean forces. That was true of almost the entire British force, unknown to the enemy. They had reached the end of their resources, although their orders were to continue the battle until every last shell was used. That is Paul's word here, 'perplexed'; what happens now that we have come to an end of our supplies of strength and can continue no longer? Here is Joseph in prison and verses 14 and 15 spell out how hopeless his situation has become.

> 'Only remember me, when it is well with you, and please do me the kindness to mention me to Pharaoh, and so get me out of this house. For I was indeed stolen out of the land of the Hebrews, and here also I have done nothing that they should put me into the pit.'

He is suffering deeply. 'Why, Lord, why?' His words to the chief butler who will shortly be released contain an implicit pitiful cry for help. The word 'pit' is literally 'a hole'.

In the play, *Fiddler on the Roof,* one of the characters who is a Jew, says, 'I know we are the chosen people', and then, thinking of all the sorrows and trials and hardships of his race, cries, 'But Lord, couldn't you choose someone else for a change?' The exhausted Christian warrior cries: 'Why, Lord?—when we have only endeavoured to serve you? Why, Lord?—when we have only tried to follow your commandments! Why, Lord?—when we have only sought to do your will and obey you! Why should all this happen to us? We are just about finished, Lord. We are through, our strength is spent, we can do no more.' That is the implication contained in Paul's word 'perplexed'.

I remember seeing a film many years ago about someone on the run. His pursuer was relentlessly tracking him. Deeper and deeper into the wilderness he fled. But always his pursuer was there behind him, until at length he found he had taken the wrong route and was trapped. There was no escape. The mountain path ended at a deep gorge and three hundred feet below was a rushing torrent. The game was up! That is our word, 'perplexed'. And that was Joseph. In a hole, a pit, where so many others before him had rotted to death. He had no one to plead for him, no one to speak for him, no one with influence who could have him released. It appeared that this was the end.

Is there someone reading this and you feel that you have reached, as it were, the end of the line and there is nowhere left to go? The outlook is not just bleak—it is worse, it is desolate. Take heart that others have been in that position too, for this godly young man, Joseph, appeared also to have reached the end of the line. It seemed as if there was no one left to help him.

Paul's third word is 'persecuted' (ESV, AV, NIV) or 'hunted'. First he had been persecuted by his brothers. Yet in his slavery it seemed he had escaped like a bird from the snare. Now as a stranger, unknown, unloved, alone, like the bird that had once escaped from the net, he is caught once more in the net and this time it seems there is no way out.

Is this not just how the Lord Jesus said it would be? Indeed, he promised no less. 'Remember the word that I said to you: "A servant is not greater than his Master." If they persecuted me, they will also persecute you.'[3] Often I have heard it said of some well-loved pastor, 'He hadn't an enemy in the world.' But that could not be said of our Lord. Neither will it be said of the one who is faithful to him. I do not for one moment mean that we have to go around like a bull in a china shop, blundering and crashing about, causing offence left, right and centre. Some do that. But that is not what the Lord meant. Joseph's experience shows us exactly what is meant. It was his purity, truthfulness, honesty and goodness which invariably caused him to be persecuted. In Jesus' own words, it was his 'righteousness'.[4] And all who live godly lives will suffer persecution at some time. The vicious hatred and spite this golden youth experienced was of the very same substance as the hatred and bitterness that any godly, faithful follower of Jesus Christ will know. The question for you and me is, 'Are we prepared and willing for it?'

The fourth phrase Paul uses is very vivid: 'Struck down' (ESV, NIV; 'cast down' AV). The fight is raging, and suddenly our man receives a terrible blow, staggers, is almost blinded and falls to his knees. The count begins, 'One, two, three, four, five . . .', but then he gets back on his feet and the fight continues, until again his assailant fetches him another terrible blow that sends him sprawling on his face in the dust; again the count is on, 'One, two, three, four, five, six, seven, eight . . .', but once again he somehow manages to rise to his feet, and those watching hold their breath as he engages in the fight again, his head reeling.

The bitumen pit into which his brothers threw him had been bad enough; that journey in chains across the Sinai desert had been worse; then the humiliation of the scullery of the great house; but now this stinking dungeon, this pit, this hole of a place with its bars and bolts, its narrow slits that passed for windows, its stifling heat in the Egyptian sun; the chains and manacle round his

---

[3] John 15:20.
[4] Matthew 5:10.

neck, as Psalm 105:18 tells us, and the guards. Many a night, I have no doubt, he was struck down and the angels of heaven, watching anxiously, must have thought the fight was over, with Joseph defeated and the life beaten out of him forever.

'Struck down.' I confess that many a time I have been struck down and left apparently unable to continue that fight of faith. And this, reader, is the spiritual test of the soul through which all who would serve Christ must pass before God can bring us through to blessing and fruitfulness. It is the 'Christ-principle': No cross, no crown.

Trust

Here is the wonderful thing: God did not send Joseph to prison, there to learn hard lessons; God went to prison with him, there to teach him great lessons. *Joseph's master took him and put him into the prison . . . But the* LORD *was with Joseph . . . The keeper of the prison paid no attention to anything that was in Joseph's charge, because the* LORD *was with him . . . whatever he did, the* LORD *made it succeed* (39:20, 21, 23). Three times we are told that God was there with this young man who was unjustly incarcerated. And so, for each of Paul's four phrases which give us such clear insights into Joseph's testing, there are balancing phrases telling us that God was at his side, teaching him to trust him.[5]

---

[5] 'Christ also was among unbelievers in the person of the holy apostles, who declared that they carried around in their bodies his scars (*Gal.* 6:17). They did not want to adjust themselves to those things that belong to the world but kept away from any desire of the flesh. Therefore, for this reason they were object of many plots and were oppressed by the slander of those who were accustomed to regard those who wanted to live in Christ as unbearable, so that they fell into tremendous trials and were imprisoned. However, they always bore in mind Christ's saying: "If you belonged to the world, the world would love you as its own. But because you do not belong to the world, therefore the world hates you" (*John* 15:19), exactly as the lustful woman hated Joseph.' Cyril of Alexandria (A.D. 375–444), *ACCS*, pp. 255-56.

'Hard pressed on every side, *but not crushed.*' The enemy never quite managed to keep Joseph hemmed into that corner so he was unable to move. Each time he seemed cornered, there was a way out and Joseph slipped clear of being trapped. So God gave him favour in the eyes of the prison warder. Most probably since Potiphar was the captain of the guard, he was well known in the prison, if not in authority over it. Joseph's story may well have been known to the warder as well. Be that as it may, we are told quite explicitly that there in that pit the Lord was with him; that is why God granted him favour with the warder.

New prisoners may have been surprised to see this smiling young man bringing them their water and bowl of food each morning. 'Not much of a job for this fine young fellow', they may have said to each other when he moved on to the next cell. Then as the days went by they discovered that he was not a paid servant of the crown at all, but a prisoner like themselves. 'Hard pressed on every side, *but not crushed.*'

How we thank God for that word of promise, 'but not crushed'. If it was only 'hard pressed on every side' we would surely give up. The Christian life would be a con. We would be, as Paul puts it elsewhere, though in a different context, the most miserable people in the world.[6] But we thank God for his faithfulness and love which never deserts us, so that we are not crushed. It is like that fire in the house of Interpreter in Bunyan's *Pilgrim's Progress:* Even though the evil-looking man threw pails of water on to the fire, it still leapt up with fresh, renewed flame, and when Christian asked how this could be he was shown behind the fire where there was Another, who was secretly pouring oil on the fire so that it was never extinguished but was constantly revived.

Paul's second word picture, 'perplexed', is answered by *'but not driven to despair'!* Remember that man being pursued by a relentless

[6] 1 Corinthians 15:19.

tracker; he had reached an impasse, and now stood at the top of that gorge. He could hear the sound of his pursuer coming ever nearer. It was now or never, so he threw himself off the cliff into the raging torrent three hundred feet below, and his tracker rushed to the cliff top to see him disappearing into the foam of the rushing water and assumed he must have perished. But quarter of a mile down stream, half drowned he dragged himself to the bank, crawled on to the rocks, and lay vomiting water. Though bruised, gasping and exhausted, he was still alive.

I sometimes wonder how Joseph would have felt when the other prisoners were asleep. I am quite sure that in the silence and darkness of the night he knew that the Lord was with him, strengthening him. Refreshment was brought to his soul and hope was rekindled in his heart. As he did his morning rounds, passing from cell to cell, the light shone in his eyes and there was a serenity on his brow; a friendly word always came from his lips. How he survived, week after week, month after month, year after year, no one knew. 'Perplexed, but not driven to despair.'

Paul's third word picture: 'persecuted, *but not forsaken*'. Years later, Joseph shared with his aged father the trials and testing he had endured, and the trust in God that had burned in his soul through it all. And the old man composed a poem to tell us about it all. He says in his poem that 'The archers bitterly attacked him, shot at him, and harassed him severely, yet his bow remained unmoved; his arms were made agile by the hands of the Mighty One of Jacob.'[7] Jacob's metaphor is of a lonely archer facing impossible odds but incredibly withstanding his attackers because behind him, overshadowing and overarching him, stood another, bending over him, his hands over the archer's hands, his strength flowing into his weakness. 'Not forsaken.' 'When you pass through the waters, I will be with you; and through the rivers, they shall not

---

[7] Genesis 49:23-4; see exposition in Chapter 16 below.

overwhelm you; when you walk through the fire, you shall not be burned, and the flame shall not consume you.'[8]

Do we sometimes think God has forgotten us? At times we think and talk and act as if there was no God, as if we had been abandoned. David Livingstone, missionary and explorer, died on May 1, 1873 on his knees in his tent, alone in the heart of Africa. He was sick from malaria and dysentery and knew he would not see the light of another day. Hundreds of miles from friends and help, he wrote in his diary the words of Jesus, 'I am with you always', and then he added the comment, 'He's never broken his word yet, and there's an end to it.' We must learn to ask, 'Lord, are you there?' His answer will come surging up in our spirits, 'Of course I am. I am with you'—*not forsaken.*

That fourth phrase of the apostle: 'Struck down', is answered by the ringing cry, *'but not destroyed.'* Time and time again, the enemy thought he had downed this man for the last time; he would never rise again. But always, before the count reached ten, he was somehow back on his feet, taking up the conflict once more. Those looking on gasped with amazement that he still had strength to fight on. 'Struck down, but not destroyed.' What was God doing, allowing all this suffering and anguish? Our Bibles tell us very plainly. There can be no dubiety. Joseph's character was being refined. He was being taught to trust in God with the faith of a little child which lies helplessly in its mother's arms.

I think, too, that Joseph's dreams were being refined. Do you have dreams? I am not referring to the silly, confused dreams we sometimes have which are a jumble of unsorted data thrown up from our sub-conscious. I mean aspirations, holy desires to see great things done for God. I mean vision. God needs men and women of dreams in that sense, people with vision, aspirations for his kingdom and glory. Woe betide the day when the people of

---

[8] Isaiah 43:2.

God have no vision for God's glory or for the conquests of the exalted Lord who rides on that white horse, going forth conquering and to conquer.[9] Joseph did have dreams, given to him by God. We noted them in chapter one. But those dreams must be purified.

Rub away at silver, plated on to copper or pewter, and ultimately you will rub through the wafer-thin layer of silver and come to the base metal. But rub as hard as you can on pure silver, even subject it to the flame, and all you will get is silver. As we have already noticed, Psalm 105:19 says, 'He had sent a man ahead of them, Joseph, who was sold as a slave. His feet were hurt with fetters, his neck was put in a collar of iron; until what he had said came to pass, the word of the Lord tested him.' Amazingly, we read something very similar of our Lord Jesus, for in Hebrews it says, 'Although he was a son, he learned obedience through what he suffered.'[10]

God must teach us to trust him with a pure, true faith. Jeremiah expresses it like this: 'For I know the plans I have for you, declares the Lord, plans for wholeness and not for evil, to give you a future and a hope.'[11] In the fires of our trials, we too quickly forget that. But the Lord cannot take us further on until we believe his word with simple trust. We must learn to cling to him and hold fast to him. We must stand firmly upon his word, and have faith that his purpose is not to harm us, but to prosper us; that he really does have a future and a living hope for us! *Not crushed, not in despair, not forsaken, not destroyed!*

Triumph

In 2 Corinthians 4:10, immediately after Paul's four ringing phrases, we read these words: 'always carrying in the body the death of

[9] Revelation 6:2.
[10] Hebrews 5:8.
[11] Jeremiah 29:11.

Jesus, so that the life of Jesus may also be manifested in our bodies.' This is the triumph, that the life of Christ may shine through in everything we do, even when we are hard pressed, perplexed, persecuted and struck down. It is when we are hurting, bruised, even wounded that the glory must shine. This is nothing less than remarkable, but that is what Paul is saying here and what he had proved from his experience.

In the account of Joseph in prison, if we look for it, we can see the glory shining through. We can see that he was victorious, even in that dungeon! Four gentle 'rays of light', so to speak, shine in the prison cell, coming from Joseph's face. The first is that he noticed the anxiety and worry on the other prisoners' faces. He saw they were upset and he was genuinely concerned for them. I think of myself when I am hurting, and how I want to moan to someone and have that person listen to my problems and my grumbling. Not this man! It is quite remarkable. Battered, bruised and treated with cruel injustice, we find him patiently listening while others unburden their hearts to him. And his heart reaches out to them in sympathy. This is victorious living and the first ray of glory from his face—his genuine concern for others.

But there is another shaft of light shining from Joseph. It is that he is so closely in touch with God that the meaning of the butler's dream is revealed to him, followed by the meaning of the baker's dream. The Holy Spirit has not left him. 'If I had cherished iniquity in my heart, the Lord would not have listened. But truly God has listened', says the Psalmist.[12] Those who pray know that God does not answer when we are disobedient and that we have no power with him when we are out of touch with him. But Joseph is clearly in constant touch. There is nothing between him and his Lord. And so the interpretation comes at once and is proved to be the very word of God.

[12] Psalm 66:18.

The third ray shining from dear Joseph's face is his forgiveness of both his brothers and Potiphar's wife. In verse 15, as he tells of his plight, he blames no one. There is no mention of his brothers' hatred and wickedness or of Potiphar's wife's lies and deceit. We find not a trace of bitterness against those who have so deeply wronged him, just the simple statement of his own innocence, without trying to implicate anyone else.

Is that not a very bright ray of glory? Think about it. Do you and I not always try to put the blame on someone? Do we not paint a picture which not only shows how lily-white we are, but how distorted and nasty the other person is? How pride wells up in us as we imply a brother or a sister is to blame. Victorious living? This saintly young man says never a word about the others. There in that stinking place, he breathes no word of accusation. There is no harshness or bitterness in his words. That is surely a ray of heavenly glory.

And the fourth ray of light is that he was faithful with the baker. It was bad news he had for him. In three days' time he would lose his life. Dreadful news, when the butler's news was so good. I am sure that Joseph explained the baker's dream gently, kindly and with sorrow. But he told the truth. He was faithful in his words, leaving nothing out. There was no cover up, no trying to alter the message to make it more palatable. That was a ray of glory too. For while God is love, his love is holy love and he is of purer eyes than to look upon sin.

Testing, trust and triumph! God had great things in store for Joseph, a mighty work for him to do that would affect the whole of the known world. But there was also a work for him to do just where he was. Throughout those years of discipline, when the fires of the divine furnace were refining his soul and the innocence of youth was being burnished until it shone—no longer mere innocence but now virtue, integrity and purity—in all that time the glory of God's presence shone from Joseph's life, and God used him just where he was.

Clearly there are eternal principles of Christian living in all of this. If we are truly and obediently walking with God we will always carry around in our bodies the dying of the Lord Jesus, that the life of Jesus may also be revealed in us. I do not mean this will happen in some mystical way, personal to us alone. Rather it will occur in the most ordinary situations of life: a neighbour in trouble, a workmate depressed, a fellow-Christian carrying a burden. Do we ever notice? Half us of never even wait long enough to look. We are off after the benediction as if there was a heavy fine for staying to say 'Hello' after the service has ended. Or else our neighbour never gets more than the briefest nod and peremptory 'Good morning.' But being a victorious Christian is practical. Walking with the Lord is very down to earth. Though it involves obvious things each day, too often you and I miss them. Our minds are somewhere else. But Christ trod this earth, and walked its dusty and sometimes muddy pathway.

The butler was freed but forgot all about Joseph. So yet again Joseph was left alone. But, as we will see again, the glory still streamed from his face, and he walked humbly with his God, even in that dungeon. And the word of God continued to test him, till his dreams were refined and became the purest silver.

> Though I walk through the valley of the shadow of death, I will fear no evil, for thou art with me ... thy rod to correct me, Lord, and thy staff to support me; Lord, both your correction and your support comfort me.[13]

You have perhaps seen the car sticker that was popular thirty years ago: 'Carpenter in Nazareth wants "joiners".' Here is another motto, less likely to be taken up by the PR pundits: 'Wanted

---

[13] Psalm 23:4.

men and women of silver, tested in the fires of trial, proven to be purified of dross, for use in the hands of the Master Craftsman. Innumerable job vacancies available.'—God help us all!

CHAPTER FIVE

The Final Test—Genesis 41:1-41

WHEN I was a student in London and attended All Souls Church where John Stott was the Rector, one of the stewards who took up the offering was a man called Roger Bannister. His name will not be familiar to many today, because that was over fifty years ago. In those days he was well known as he had been the first person ever to run a mile in under four minutes. His record was achieved on May 6, 1954 during a meet between the British AAA and Oxford University where Bannister was studying medicine. So for us students it was quite something having this outstanding athlete taking up the offering; we thought the world of him, the more so because he was such a humble and gracious Christian man. He went on to become a distinguished neurologist and Master of Pembroke College, Oxford, before his retirement in 2001.

What impressed me about Bannister was that for several years he had worked towards that one race when he would attempt to set a world record by running a mile in under four minutes. For all those years his diet, daily routine, habits, work, leisure—everything he did, including even his sleep pattern—had all been controlled, disciplined and directed so that he would achieve the hitherto unachieved and break the 'four minute mile' barrier.

Of course, there was a fair bit of publicity before he ran the great race. Everyone knew what he was attempting. The media gave the event wide coverage. Sports commentators were being interviewed and asked their opinion as to whether or not he would make it, and the cameras of the world were focused on him. Over 3,000 spectators gathered for the event, but for most of the day of the meet the wind was at twenty-five miles per hour and Bannister decided to wait for another occasion when there was no wind. However, just before the mile race was to be run, the wind suddenly dropped and so Bannister made his attempt. Those watching, whether present at the track or sitting at home in front of their primitive television screens, held their breath, following the race with the keenest of interest. And when the new record was achieved and Bannister was successful, it was generally agreed that it had only been possible because of his single-minded disciplined training, determination and lifestyle over the previous six or seven years.

I well remember at the time reflecting on the lesson of Roger Bannister's four minute mile, a lesson I myself would need to remember all of my life. It is similar to the one that is taught very vividly in Genesis 41, the passage we have now reached.

The Trial of Waiting

In the previous chapter of Genesis, we saw Joseph in prison and we listened in to his conversation with the two prisoners from Pharaoh's palace, the chief cupbearer and the chief baker. We heard his plea to the cupbearer, whose dream he had rightly interpreted as meaning that within three days he would be restored to his position as cupbearer to Pharaoh. And we heard those words of Joseph. 'Only remember me when it is well with you, and please do me the kindness to mention me to Pharaoh and so get me out of this house.'

The Muslims have the story of Joseph in their Qur'an. But they have altered the Genesis account significantly as Muhammad has added a few details. For example, the Qur'an says that when Joseph was thrown into the dungeon God transformed the place, causing a fountain to spring up and a lovely tree to grow just at the door with shady leaves and luscious fruit; but the Qur'an's version goes on to state that when Joseph said these words to the cupbearer, 'Remember me and speak to Pharaoh', the fountain immediately dried up and the tree withered and died, because Joseph had turned from complete trust in God, and looked for help from a mere man.

That supposition is hardly fair as well as being a very serious departure from Scripture. Joseph was human like you and me. By this time we know he was twenty-eight years old. The years were slipping by. He had been a slave since the age of seventeen, eleven years now. How many of those eleven years had been spent in prison it is impossible to guess. But even the bravest and saintliest of people have gone through anguish as they have waited for God. Think of Elijah hiding in that ravine beside the brook Cherith, watching each day as the brook became a trickle, then the trickle became a few drops; all the time Elijah knew a warrant was out for his arrest and a reward had been offered for his capture, dead or alive. Waiting, waiting, waiting . . . The day ultimately came in his life when he at length caved in and cried, 'It is enough; now, O LORD, take away my life, for I am no better than my fathers.'[1] John the Baptist (and remember that the Lord said that among those born there was none greater than John), languishing in prison, getting back occasional reports of Jesus' ministry, began to wonder, 'Was I right? Is this really the promised Messiah? Why am I still in this dungeon? Why isn't the kingdom of God coming in with triumph and victory? What is he doing, pottering about among the villages, wandering from hamlet to hamlet teaching?' And John, greatest of all the prophets, sent a message to ask, 'Are you the one who is to come, or shall we look for another?'[2]

[1] 1 Kings 19:4.
[2] Luke 7:18-28.

So who is any man to point the finger at Joseph and to suggest he should never have asked the cupbearer to put a word in for him to Pharaoh? God often chooses to use some human (even pagan) instrument to work his will.[3] Perhaps the cupbearer had promised to speak to the gardener in charge of the Royal Vineyards, and get him a job there; or maybe he said he knew a secretary in the Egyptian civil service and could get Joseph an appointment there; or maybe he had even thought to himself that he would take Joseph on as a slave in his own wealthy household. And so Joseph waited for the promised help to arrive. And every time he heard footsteps outside, and the key turning in the prison door, his heart leaped, 'This must be it now.' But week after week he waited in vain, and the weeks stretched into long months—waiting, waiting, waiting.

I heard of a woman whose son went off abroad having faithfully promised he would write to her. But he never wrote. The last I heard was that he had been away for ten years, and every single day of the week, she has called in at the village post office to see if there was a letter waiting for her, but still after all those years there was no letter, no word. Is she still waiting, still calling in to see if one has come yet? Many of us have waited for something, therefore surely we can imagine just a little of what it must have been like.

Was the Psalmist thinking of Joseph when he wrote, 'For God alone, O my soul, wait in silence; for my hope is from him'? Such patience and faith are hard to put into practice. We hate to live without someone's sympathy and understanding. We long for the touch of a hand, the sound of a loved-one's voice. As Michel Quoist has put it in his priest's prayer, 'A prayer on a Sunday night':

> It's hard to love everyone, and claim no one. It's hard to shake a hand, and not want to retain it. It's hard always to give without trying to receive. It's hard always to seek others out

---

[3] See *e.g.*, 2 Chronicles 36:22, 23; Ezra 1:1, 2, 7, 8; Isaiah 45:1, *etc.*

and be unsought oneself . . . It's hard to be alone, alone before everyone . . .[4]

But those years of waiting were important for Joseph. He had to learn how frail and forgetful even a good man could be. For he must learn how faithful and constant the Lord God always is!

Are we not at times too frenetic, too impatient? We want things to happen quickly. We set goals and targets, and are discouraged if they are not met by a given date. We argue that life is short and the months are slipping past. I am not despising the setting of goals. But I am thinking of how easy it is to become frustrated because God is not working in the way we want and at the pace we want. When I was in pastoral ministry, I used to look around the congregation, and try to assess where we were going. I had my own hidden agenda. Every minister must have a vision of where he believes God wants to take his people. But the great temptation is to grow tired of waiting—waiting for people to change, waiting for them to see issues as you see them, waiting to see a desire for God growing and blossoming in people's hearts and lives.

We all must take this word and apply it to our own lives as we need it. Here is the lesson: 'Be still before the LORD and wait patiently for him . . . those who wait for the LORD shall inherit the land.'[5] God sometimes has to say, 'Cool it, man; cool it, woman! just lean on me. Wait for me. I know what I am doing. Stop trying to manipulate events to get your own way more quickly. Wait for me. Keep your eyes on me.' Oh, wait on the Lord!

Steps to the Throne

Let us review the past eleven years of Joseph's life. How would you have been feeling if all that had happened to Joseph had happened

---

[4] Michel Quoist, *Prayers of Life* (Dublin, Logos Books, 1966), p. 50.
[5] Psalm 37:7, 9.

to you? Honestly try to put yourself into his shoes: your own kith and kin tearing off your clothes, ripping them up, throwing you into a pit, then selling you to slave-traffickers for about £900; irons being clamped around your ankles and neck, and then being dragged off behind a striding camel, your feet becoming blistered as the slave drivers mock you and crack the whip across your back and legs to make you keep up; being sold in a market as a slave; your work, obedience, diligence and faithfulness rewarded by the lies of a wicked woman sending you into a filthy, dark, Egyptian dungeon; then the one friend you thought you had forgetting all about you—the selfish wretch! How would you or I have been feeling as we looked back? But the reality was that every event had been another step to the throne!

We are so slow to learn. We hear almost every day of tragic events overtaking people. And we sometimes almost shake our fist at the heavens and cry, 'How can there be a God of love to let this happen?' And yet, have you ever known anyone who has truly put their trust in God and who has said, 'God let me down. God was unfaithful. God played me false'? Never! I have often heard those who were stupid and perverse enough to trust the devil saying, like Macbeth in Shakespeare's play trusting the witches with their cauldron of evil spells, that they dared to trade with Satan and thought to gain by it what they most wanted; but at the end they discovered Satan had played them false, and tragedy had been multiplied upon tragedy upon them and their families. Yet out on the streets of our towns and cities each night will be men and women, young and old, hoping that the devil himself will reward them by letting them satiate their passions. I have personally known some who have said to Satan, 'Give me all I want in this life, and you can have my soul.' If ever there was a fool's bargain, it was that. For he always plays his slaves false and, deceiving them, destroys them as well as taking their soul.

In the Egyptian court there would have been scores of young men crawling, wheedling, dealing, licking boots and flattering, offering bribes and making promises, all of them hoping to gain an audience with the mighty Pharaoh to win his favour and secure an appointment as governor of some township or village in the great Egyptian empire. But Joseph's God was going to take him straight to Pharaoh's throne by steps that had been planned in eternity with divinely meticulous care and timing.

However young or old you may be, what is it that you most desire before God? What aspirations and secret hopes find their way into your private prayers? Perhaps to succeed in some profession. Or to find the right partner for life, should that be God's plan for you. Maybe to find the right home. What do we long for and what is the stuff of our dreams? Learn to long for God's will, and not to desire things for yourself. 'Seek first the kingdom of God and his righteousness, and all these things will be added to you.'[6]

God never tells us we will understand all he is doing in our lives. Indeed, the probability is that we will not understand very much of his purposes at the time. My own mother's dearest desire was once to return to Africa where she had been a missionary for ten years; for years she prayed that the Lord would send her back. She rose at four in the morning every day, year after year, with that cry, 'Lord send me back to my black boys and girls again. Lord, why am I still in poor health and unfit for overseas work; please give me back my vigour and heal me!' How hard and persistently she knocked on the door of heaven, pleading to be allowed to return to her first love, the work among those children in the Congo. At last God made it clear to her that he had something else planned for her. And he gave her the sacred trust of thirty-six white boys and girls to bring up for him. Out of those children one has worked all his life in Brazil, two others in Ivory Coast, another in Botswana, and

---

[6] Matthew 6:33.

another in Malawi, another in India, others in the Christian ministry here in Scotland. My mother lived long enough to see this unexpected fruit of God's purpose for her in taking her to work, along with my father, in the small Scottish town of Arbroath, caring for white boys and girls and not those Congolese children she had loved so much.

God has steps marked out for every one of his own children. Pray God our steps may not be as hard and steep and thorny as those Joseph had to tread. But the steps marked out for us can only be ascended by truthfulness, purity and obedience. In these qualities are the little shafts of light that penetrate the darkness of those days of preparation and waiting: the ray of light called truth—to be constant in holding the Lord's hand and keeping close to him; the ray of light called purity—to be pure in our thinking and living; the ray of light called obedience—to be faithful and diligent in all our work, people of invariable reliability. These characteristics of Christian living bring shafts of golden light into the darkest place and illumine the steps just enough to let us see the next one. Surely, we can observe this in Joseph's life. However, we are only promised sufficient light to see clearly the next step—one step at a time. That is all we need.

I have no doubt that some who read this feel that they are like Joseph in prison, waiting, waiting, waiting. Can you not see in front of you the right step just for today and for tomorrow? That is all God has promised. Then step forward, in simple trust holding Christ's hand!

The Final Test

At last God's time came. Pharaoh had his dreams. Notice that the small details of the dream are very accurate in describing Egyptian life and its environment: the cows coming up out of the river, for the cattle love to stand almost submerged in the waters of the Nile to find relief from the burning heat of the tropical sun; the east wind, known as the *khamsin*, comes across the Sinai desert like the blast of a furnace and can wither the sprouting crops as if they had been singed by fire. Also in verses 8 and 24 the word 'magicians' is from the ancient Egyptian language; this civilization was permeated by wizardry and dark arts of all kinds.[7]

So we come to Pharaoh's two dreams. The interpretation was not difficult for someone with spiritual insight and in close touch with God. But the Egyptian magicians and priests had neither the Spirit of God nor the insight the Spirit gives. They had books on how to interpret dreams. Two ancient Egyptian manuals on the interpretation of dreams still survive and are preserved in Cairo Museum. But these books gave the priestly wizards no help. Apparently the manuals speak only about dreams in which events happen to the dreamer, whereas in Pharaoh's dream nothing happened to him at all; he simply acted as a silent witness of events that neither he nor his wise men could fathom. One is reminded of Job's words:

> He leads priests away stripped and overthrows the mighty. He deprives of speech those who are trusted and takes away the discernment of the elders (*Job* 12:19, 20).

Then amid all the fuss and anxiety in the royal court, the chief cupbearer suddenly remembered, reminded by the prompting of God, the young Hebrew prisoner in the dungeon where he had been; he had accurately interpreted both his and the baker's dreams. Alas, he had faithfully promised to try and have the young slave released from prison. So with stammering apologies, the cup-

---

[7] The word is derived from the word for a 'stylus' and was used of those from the priestly caste who occupied themselves with the sacred arts and sciences of the Egyptians—hieroglyphic writings, astrology, foretelling of events, interpretations of dreams, conjuring—and who were regarded as possessors of secret arts. Keil-Delitzsch p. 349.

bearer told his story and the mighty Pharaoh, whose very wish and whim was law in the land, ordered Joseph to be brought from the dungeon.

I doubt that there is in heaven a three-dimensional DVD library containing a disc of Joseph's life. However, if there is in eternity some means of revisiting the lives of God's saints, I would want to watch again and again this hour in Joseph's life! Once more the footsteps sounded outside that prison door, as so often before. Once again, the great key turning and the heavy bolts drawn back. Once again the door creaking open, but this time it was different, this time—could it be true?—Joseph's name was called out and by the command of the mighty Pharaoh, he was led out blinking into the brilliant sunshine. Scripture records no explanation being given him. First a bath, certainly the first since he had been thrown into prison. Then a shave of both his beard and his head after the Egyptian priestly fashion,[8] done with the skill of the royal barbers. His fingernails and toenails manicured. His body scented and clad in perfumed clothing. And all this done most probably with no explanation, no word as to why, but with silent haste by slaves whose lives depended on presenting him within the hour before the throne of Pharaoh, Emperor of Upper and Lower Egypt.

We all rejoice when video pictures are beamed around the world of some hostages being released after being held for some months by terrorists. We watch them walking across the tarmac of the airport runway, supported along by helping hands on either side. But how was it with Joseph, now thirty years of age? Was his step steady and his head clear as he was ushered into the lofty stone-built presence-chamber, lined by slaves with fans, and around the throne a company of ministers of state, advisers and the useless magicians?

[8] Shaving—'a custom which seems to have been peculiar to the priests under the new empire', Skinner, p. 466. See also quotation on shaving and white linen from K. A. Kitchen in Baldwin, note 11, p. 174.

The seemingly impassive Pharaoh[9] speaks: 'I have heard it said of you that when you hear a dream you can interpret it.' Here is the final test in this totally unexpected and astonishing moment in this man's life. What will Joseph reply? Listen! *It is not in me; God will give Pharaoh a favourable answer.* 'I cannot do it',[10] he says. But Joseph, this is your big chance! You are before the mightiest emperor of the world. Fame, riches, power—they are all just within your grasp—what are you saying, man? 'It is not in me; God will give Pharaoh a favourable answer.'

In this final test, Joseph is found close to his God, trusting only in his Lord; his spirit is humble before the Almighty: 'It is not in me.' He has truly undergone that agonizing death to self; the flesh has been crucified; God's years of training for this man have been thorough, each lesson learned through the pain and suffering. He is now an instrument God can use for the saving of his chosen people.

In very different circumstance the boy David had said to Saul, 'The LORD who delivered me from the paw of the lion and from the paw of the bear will deliver me . . .', and then responded to the king's offer of his armour, 'I cannot go with these . . .' To Goliath's taunts he answered, 'I come to you in the name of the LORD of hosts . . . whom you have defied.'[11] David still had his years of suffering and testing ahead of him, but like Joseph he gave early indications that his faith would be in God alone. During his years in 'prison', so to speak, he prayed, 'For God alone my soul waits in silence . . .' The godly man's lesson learned from the history

[9] If the burial mask of Tutankhamun, found by archeologists Howard Carter and George Herbert in 1922 in the almost intact tomb of the young king, gives us any clue as to the appearance of the Pharaohs, as produced by the 'make-up' artists of the day, to be addressed by them could well have been a daunting, even intimidating, experience.

[10] This statement is only one word in the Hebrew: 'With hasty brevity, he points from himself to God as sole revealer'. Kidner, p. 195.

[11] 1 Samuel 17:37, 39, 45.

of the Lord's people was clear: 'It is better to take refuge in the LORD than to trust in princes.'[12] The Apostle Paul had learned the same lesson, as he indicates in his remonstration with the saints at Corinth: 'What we proclaim is not ourselves, but Jesus Christ as Lord.'[13] Indeed, Paul's entire gospel, life and ministry were centred on the risen Saviour.

I have just referred to various released hostages who had been held for a few months by terrorists or Somali pirates. But what of those who have been in prison for years, and have at last staggered from their cells in need of gentle treatment and counselling for many months to nurse them back to health? Yet Joseph, after thirteen years of the most intense suffering required no psychiatrist, no half-way house for phased recovery, no rehabilitation to accustom him to being back in the real world of people. His heart has been resting in his God. His hand has been constantly in the Lord's hand. That is why his first words are so amazing, *It is not in me; God will give Pharaoh a favourable answer.*

Step by step, with clarity of thought, Joseph outlines what will happen. Seven years of full harvests; then seven years of lean, miserable harvests. God was showing Pharaoh what was about to happen. God's word demanded immediate action. God has intimated it; therefore God will do it: *the doubling of Pharaoh's dream means that the thing is fixed by God, and God will shortly bring it about.* 'This is not presented as a judgment for wrongdoing, but rather as an act of God, predetermined, and now announced in advance.'[14] Centuries later God's inscrutable and sovereign will would be revealed and understood as having been deliberately planning the development and salvation of his chosen people through the events in Joseph's life. This is the great theme which Scripture unfolds and which finally found its fulfilment in the birth of Christ.

[12] Psalm 62:1; 118:9.
[13] 2 Corinthians 4:5; cf. Philippians 3:9, *etc.*
[14] Baldwin, p. 175.

Pharaoh and his advisers listen intently as Joseph continues; it is all so clear. Pharaoh must have storehouses built. One fifth of the harvest must be gathered in and stored. Reserves must be built up, so that the seven years of famine will not ruin the land. Pharaoh should appoint a minister for agriculture to supervise this great task.

Then Pharaoh's ministers discussed the interpretation of the dreams, probably with Joseph having been ushered out of the stateroom. They were unanimous; the interpretation was completely credible. More, the course of action outlined was exactly what was required. And Pharaoh himself summed up the deliberations: *Can we find a man like this, in whom is the Spirit of God?* (verse 38). So Joseph was recalled and Pharaoh announced his decision: *Since God has shown you all this, there is none so wise and discerning as you are. You shall be over my house, and all my people shall order themselves as you command. Only as regards the throne will I be greater than you.*

Here is a simple little practical exercise I suggest readers might do for themselves. In your Bibles, colour in or underline the name of God in this chapter of Genesis as often as you can find it. It is there seven times, for God fills and controls to perfection Joseph's heart, mind and will. That is why he is ready, now that God's hour has come. 'It is not in me; . . . *God* . . .', seven times!

Remember how we began this chapter by recalling Roger Bannister's four minute mile—many years of preparation and disciplined training just for one race! God is preparing each of us for the work he has destined and chosen for us. Do we realize that and are we co-operating with God, even though waiting for him to act may often be a trial? The steps forwards and upwards may be hard. But the final test, followed by God's chosen task, will only fully come when we have learned that self must constantly be crucified and Christ Jesus daily crowned as Lord of all in our hearts and minds and wills.

CHAPTER SIX

Joseph, Viceroy of Egypt—Genesis 41:42-57

WE come now in our study of the life of Joseph to the point where he was made what we might term 'Viceroy of Egypt'. Some commentators suggest the title 'Minister of Agriculture', but I think his status was far higher than that. Thinking of the past few decades, Joseph's importance on the world stage might be compared with that of another son of Israel, Henry Kissinger. He was born in 1923 in the city of Fürth in Bavaria, about twelve miles from Nuremburg where Hitler made some of his most infamous speeches to crowds of up to 100,000 people. His name given at birth was Heinz Alfred Kissinger. When Heinz was fifteen years old his father, a local school-teacher, fled with his family to New York to escape the intensifying persecution of Jews by the Nazis. The name Heinz sounded too German in America, so the boy's name was changed to Henry.

Kissinger's rise to power was meteoric and his influence on American foreign policy for the years 1969 to 1977 was nothing less than remarkable. In 1973 the ill-fated Richard Nixon appointed him as Secretary of State and he held that position for a full four years. Kissinger is a contemporary example of a Jew from an obscure family achieving world prominence. But Joseph's experience was one hundred times more amazing, unlikely and unexpected than that of Henry Alfred Kissinger.

The Background

Many years ago, I was given as a Christmas present a beautiful book on Egypt.[1] It is the kind of book which one might find on the coffee-table in someone's drawing room; one needs several hours just to browse through it, for it has scores of colour photographs, diagrams and a clear, well-researched commentary on this former ancient civilization. I have occasionally spent time with the book, gazing at photos of majestic temples, the ruins of great cities, pyramids and palaces. There are buildings five thousand years old which rival St Paul's Cathedral in their splendour and magnificence. Vast halls with arches, pillars, murals painted painstakingly on the smoothly plastered stone. About ten years ago I was able to lead a party of tourists in a visit to Egypt and we saw some of the very places I had read about. In Cairo Museum we saw the golden chariots in which the Pharaohs rode; we saw their jewellery, their golden furniture, carvings from their palaces, wall paintings. We visited as well the temples, the Sphinx and the pyramids of Giza. For me it was a dream come true.

When we turn to the book of Genesis and read the story of Joseph, I can hear some cynic muttering to himself: 'As if the mighty Egyptian Pharaoh would promote an unknown slave to the highest office in the land. It's a good story, but a tall one. It's much too far-fetched to warrant belief. You don't expect me to take that stuff seriously, do you?'

However, as we study the careful histories that have been built up and reconstructed by archaeologists and Egyptologists, a fascinating picture emerges. During the time of Abraham, more than a century before Joseph, Egypt was in her Golden Age and at the height of her power and cultural development. Her literature, art and architecture had reached its zenith. But it is the old, old story:

[1] Barocas, *Monuments of Civilization: EGYPT*.

the luxury and affluence brought in a flabbiness, a decline in moral fibre, a loss of discipline. Thus the way was laid open for her downfall.

Brought into Egyptian society during this Golden Age were many slaves, culled from the Middle East and Asia Minor by the inevitable slave traders, young men such as Joseph. One ancient inscription lists the names of no less than seventy Semitic slaves in an aristocratic Egyptian household. But these Semitic slaves belonged to a highly intelligent ethnic group known as the Hyksos; and as the Egyptians themselves became more degenerate and decadent, Hyksos slaves were promoted to positions of power and influence within the Egyptian civil service. At this time, the Pharaoh himself was struggling against his powerful nobles, and increasingly he began to trust his civil service which was more and more controlled by Hyksos slaves. Then the inevitable happened—yes, you have guessed—there was a coup, and one of the Hyksos slaves seized power and made himself Pharaoh.

This new Hyksos dynasty held power in Egypt for about an hundred years until they were driven out by a kind of Egyptian nationalist political faction. However, the story of Joseph slots in very well into this Hyksos period of dominance. A line of Pharaohs who came from a slave civil service would understandably promote another Semitic slave to a position of power, especially one who had been imprisoned by one of the Egyptians. The imprisonment of the chief cupbearer and baker suggests a period of intrigue, plots and counter-plots. And then, a generation later, when the Hebrews in Egypt were themselves made slaves by 'a new king over Egypt who did not know Joseph',[2] there is the suggestion of a complete change of dynasty, back to the Fourteenth Dynasty and the overthrow and subjugation of the Hyksos, who inevitably took the Hebrews with them back into slavery.

[2] Exodus 1:8.

One of the characteristics of these slave rulers of Egypt was that they adapted quickly to Egyptian culture. They took Egyptian names and followed Egyptian practices, all of which accords very well with our passage from Genesis 41, as Joseph takes up the reins of office as viceroy of the empire. Little details in the story have been confirmed by historical research. For example, Joseph was dressed in robes of fine linen and had a gold chain placed round his neck. *The Illustrated Bible Dictionary* carries an illustration from an Egyptian painting of a viceroy, clothed in linen, having a gold chain hung round his neck in the presence of Pharaoh.[3] Horses and chariots were actually introduced into Egypt by the Hyksos, which again fits in with Joseph riding in state in a chariot.

These details offer a fair bit of credibility to those doubters who too often dismiss Old Testament biblical history as mere folklore and legend. We Christians should be grateful to those who have painstakingly researched the archaeology of Egypt. For far too long the sceptics and mockers have held the stage. Unbelief has been systematically taught in our schools and universities and I believe it is important to point out, especially to young people, how much archaeological authentication there is of the Bible's accuracy.[4] So much, then, for the briefest of glimpses into the background of our passage.

Joseph's Work

Joseph took an Egyptian name, Zaphenath-paneah. The scholars cannot agree on the meaning of the name. Some say it means

---

[3] The Investiture of Paser as vizier of Sethos I; from a carving in the tomb of Paser, Thebes c. 1300 B.C. *IBD*, Part 2, p. 814.

[4] I would not want to be understood as here implying that Christians depend on or need extra-biblical historical evidence in order for them to accept the Bible as the inspired word of God; rather, I am suggesting that when evidence which authenticates biblical history becomes available, it can be encouraging for believers to be made aware of it.

'Supporter of Life', others, 'God and he lives', yet others 'He who knows things.'[5] But what is certain is that it was an Egyptian name. Joseph married. His father-in-law was priest of On, a city later named by the Greeks as Heliopolis or 'City of the Sun'. This man, Potiphera, was therefore most probably a priest of the sun-god Ra; his name means 'He whom Ra has given.' The priesthood of Egypt constituted the aristocracy of the land. So Joseph had made a thoroughly Egyptian marriage and thus secured a place for himself in one of Egypt's proudest families.[6]

He at once began his new task by travelling throughout the land; twice the narrative tells us that (verses 45 and 46), suggesting he began by getting to know both Upper and Lower Egypt, visiting the farms, towns and villages, seeing firsthand all that was happening and estimating the size and potential of the harvests. I doubt whether we have ever seen successive Secretaries of State travelling around Scotland in their early months, trying to learn for themselves what is happening, and getting their fingers on the pulse of our national life in all its aspects. I cannot remember any of our Secretaries of State who have ever bothered to do that! Occasional public relations (PR) visits here and there, yes, but no personal survey of the country for which they have been made responsible. I know that when I lived in Northern Ireland, the Ulster people strongly suspected that some Secretaries of State who were appointed by the Westminister government were unwilling to learn anything at all about the Province, but came with their minds already made up about the situation. Not so Joseph. He

---

[5] See Keil-Delitzsch, p. 351; Leupold, p. 1035. However, K. A. Kitchen gives little credence to these suggestions in his article on 'Zaphenath-Paneah', *IBD*, Part 3, p. 1673a.

[6] The name of Joseph's wife, Asenath (41:45), is well attested in the Middle Kingdom and Hyksos periods of Egyptian history, corresponding to the times of the Patriarchs and Joseph. 'Asenath' means 'she belongs to thee' which could be referring to either of her parents or else to some Egyptian goddess.

went through all the land. He would have talked with the farmers, met local officials and assessed the situation firsthand. He involved himself in Egyptian life day after day.

We have seen how diligent he was in Potiphar's house. Now we see him just as diligent in his high office of state: choosing sites for storehouses, giving orders for their architectural design, consulting builders, always efficient and painstaking; no doubt he personally reported to Pharaoh all that was happening. I guess that he managed his work with such industry and care that his authority and standing increasingly became secure.

Here we are touching on one of the most central teachings of our Christian faith, the incarnation of Jesus Christ who was made flesh and 'pitched his tent among us'.[7] Joseph was completely identifying himself with the work God had given him to do and with the people among whom he found himself. He was adapting to a new situation, new challenges, new demands. That is the great principle behind the whole life and work of the Lord Jesus Christ in his complete identification with men and women in this world of need to which he came.

So there is surely a clear word to all believers about our involvement in the work to which God has called us, whatever that work may be. A church should be known as a place where people come to meet with God, there to be delivered from their past shame and sin. But alas, there are some congregations which people enter and leave without any interaction at all. So many professing believers find anonymity in a church as they stay on the periphery of the fellowship and, with the skill of wily foxes eluding the huntsman, they avoid any personal involvement. They have one foot in and one foot out. As you think of Joseph, consider also the Lord Jesus. Our Saviour's example of total involvement cannot be clearer or more pointed.

---

[7] John 1:14; the literal meaning of the Greek, ἐσκήνωσεν ἐν ἡμιν *eskenosen en emin;* also as translated by J. B. Rotherham in *The Emphasized New Testament.*

Of course, it all comes down to what God wants of each of us. The trouble with so many is that we have never given this any thought or prayerful consideration. Little wonder then that we have the vaguest idea of what God might be asking of us. It may be that during Sunday worship we have only ever thought about ourselves. God's work, Christ's church, the great divine mission to the world entrusted to the Lord's people have never entered our minds. Had we languished in a dungeon for years, we would have been compelled to ask, 'Why is this happening to me? What is God doing in my life? What does he want of me?' But we belong to a society which is chronically self-obsessed, in which people are madly infatuated with themselves and with the material things surrounding them. Consequently the will of God and the destiny he has for his Son's church, to say nothing of the burning need of others, are all blatantly ignored. Little wonder then some churches become somewhere to get lost, instead of somewhere to be confronted with the crucified and risen Saviour whose command is that we should deny ourselves and take up the cross and follow him.[8]

As we read this section of Joseph's life, we see a man who was endlessly busy in the work he had been given. We observe him as someone who gave all his energies to the task before him. I watch him working, constantly soiled with the dust and sand of the land, his hands often dirty and his eyes and hair full of sand as he gave himself unstintingly to his endeavours. Joseph's involvement could not have been greater. He spared himself nothing, as he threw himself into the massive responsibility he had been given, for he had been called to save a nation and its adjacent neighbours from famine and death.

But we also see him as an example for every Christian man and woman. Is that not our calling too? Do we not live in a world

[8] Mark 8:34.

which faces spiritual famine? Does God not need Josephs by the thousands to toil ceaselessly and tirelessly in his church towards that divine objective of sharing spiritual food with a dying world?

All of us should take Joseph as a model for our work for God, not least because his life clearly anticipates and foreshadows the ministry of Jesus. His industry, toil and the application of his whole strength to his God-given task clearly reflect the One who was to come centuries later and who would say, 'My food is to do the will of him who sent me and to accomplish his work.'[9] In that, Joseph reflects Christ. Should we not, therefore, reflect Joseph and, through him, reflect One greater by far than the grand vizier of Egypt?

His Family

Joseph married an Egyptian woman. He took an Egyptian name. His manners, his dress, his whole way of life became Egyptian. That becomes evident as the story continues. I am convinced he was right. Those who go to foreign lands as missionaries have to identify completely with the culture in which they now live. It is a terrible mistake to attempt to establish a western enclave out in Africa and behave and live as if Jesus had been a Scot, or an Englishman, or an Ulsterman, or a Welshman, or an American. The church of God is designed for every nation and every culture. The gospel is a sweet wine that will flow into any vessel whatever its shape or colour. And Joseph's Egyptian way of life was completely appropriate.

Notice, however, something else about Joseph and his family—the names he gives to his two sons, Manasseh and Ephraim. They are Hebrew names, not Egyptian names. There is a genuine paradox in that because Manasseh means 'making to forget' (verse

[9] John 4:34.

51),[10] and Joseph was saying that God had caused him to forget his trouble and his father's house; yet he retains his Hebrew identity both in his faith in God and in the Hebrew names for his children. We are bound to conclude, therefore, that on the one hand there is a sense in which he does forget, but on the other hand a sense in which he could not and must not forget.

Once again, we are face to face with an important aspect of our Christian faith: the gift of forgetting. We might be more familiar with it as the principle of forgiveness. It is not just that God forgives us. Inextricably bound up in God's forgiveness of us must be our forgiveness of others. And what has God done with our sins? It is like the domestic rubbish collection. You wheel your bin on to the pavement outside your house, and it is then emptied and you never see that rubbish again. It is taken away and buried somewhere in a land-fill site and you are grateful to get rid of it. God's forgiveness of us is like that: the Saviour died to remove and bury forever all our sins, mistakes and failures. How we thank God for that!

But then we must ourselves learn to bury the sins of others against us.[11] We too must learn to forget. That is one of the hardest demands of the gospel. Joseph had suffered appallingly. We have traced his torments and sorrows. And now he names his child with a Hebrew name to help him to remember that he has forgiven and forgotten; he has buried the past with its injustice, hurt and cruelty.

Consider this. Can any Christian fellowship or individual Christian function effectively unless this lesson has been learned? Indeed, this is one of life's hardest lessons. We deceive ourselves if we think it is easy. And we are naive in the extreme if we think Joseph found it a small matter to forgive and forget all that his brothers

[10] Ephraim means 'making fruitful' (41:52).

[11] Matthew 6:14-5, 'For if you forgive others their trespasses, your heavenly Father will also forgive you, but if you do not forgive others their trespasses, neither will your Father forgive your trespasses.'

had done to him. How would we have felt? Slavery? Loneliness? Prison? And for thirteen long years? Our hearts go out to those whose daughters are raped and murdered, or whose little children are abducted and abused and then killed by paedophiles. But I doubt if any of them will ever say with Joseph, 'Manasseh'—God has caused me to forget the wrong done to me. That can only be done by a miracle of pure grace.

What ugly scars there are in many hearts! What deep, deep hurts! I know just a little of the brave resolution that enables wounded souls to stand firm in the face of suffering inflicted on them by others. But Joseph's forgetting was more than just brave resolution. It was a divine work of grace in his heart. It may be that some readers have deep scars on your souls because you have suffered at the hands of someone, somewhere. There is still an ache which causes pain, a secret wound still infected by poison which you keep carefully bandaged so that no one can see it. Only a divine work of grace can bring you truly to forgive and forget. That divine work involves the cross. Not just emotionally, but nails into our hands and feet, as it were, and death to our pride; and the tide of Christ's cleansing forgiveness to drench us so that we may learn to forgive and forget, as he has done for us. Manasseh: God has caused me to forget.

The second boy was Ephraim. This name means 'God has made me fruitful in the land of my sufferings.' I have often heard it said that God does not demand success of his servants, only faithfulness. Of course God demands that we be faithful in the work that he has given to us. But God has promised fruitfulness as well. The Lord Jesus said to the Twelve, 'You did not choose me, but I chose you and appointed you that you should go and bear fruit and that your fruit should abide.'[12]

[12] John 15:16.

So what task has the Lord given to you? Is it to share Christ's love with a neighbour—just by your smile, helpfulness and understanding? Or with a colleague at work, in order that by your life you become known as a genuine Christian? Or is it by working with children, or visiting some housebound person? There are literally thousands of darkened souls living all around us, and unless God works a swift miracle (and, by definition, miracles are extremely rare events), it may take months, even years, of patient 'silent' witnessing to see a genuine change in someone's life. But if you are faithful, the day will come when that neighbour or colleague or elderly person asks you, 'Can I have what you have? Could what has happened to you also happen to me?' That situation may arise through an illness, or through a family tragedy or even through a family joy. Some opportunity will come and if you have built a good foundation, and that family has come to know, trust and respect you, the word will then be Ephraim—'God has made me fruitful'! For the Spirit of God will do his quiet, unseen work and a gracious change will become apparent. That is one reason why Jesus Christ has called you and appointed you: to make you fruitful in the work of his kingdom.

And so the seven years of good harvests slipped past. Joseph worked. One fifth of each harvest of plenty was gathered in during those seven successive years. The two boys grew and Joseph enjoyed the love of his wife and sons. Then, just as God had said through Joseph's interpretation of the dreams, during the eighth year famine struck. And there was desolation and misery throughout the land. The people cried out to Pharaoh, who sent them to Joseph, and the great storehouses were opened and there was enough for every need.

God has given to you and me his living word, the very bread of life. Have we storehouses ready with a full supply when men and women are crying out in their spiritual need? Not just enough for ourselves, but enough and to spare for any who will come with a genuine spiritual hunger? May our objective, both as individuals and congregations of the Lord's people, never ever be only to look after ourselves. God save us from that! Yet it is all too easy for churches to fall into such sterile barrenness and to think that because we make ends meet, annually balance the books and keep our buildings in good repair, we have done our duty and fulfilled all that God desires of us!

We hold in our hands both the bread and water of life, not just to eat and drink ourselves, but to offer freely to all who are hungry and thirsty for God. May that vision never dim. May our fellowships be great storehouses, whose doors have been opened wide, with scores of eager hands and hearts ready to give and give and give what God has freely and lavishly given to us.

> God fills the soul that it may pour
>   the fullness on another heart:
> not that those filled with good may store
>   the good God giveth to impart.
>
> God fills us with the finest wheat,
>   that, strengthened in the inner man,
> We may attempt some noble feat,
>   the starved and hungry never can.
>
> He fills us that our souls may rise
>   above the lower earthly things:
> Mount upwards to the cloudless skies,
>   arising as on eagle's wings.
>
> Hast thou this filling? Give thy store!
>   Speed onward! Hoist thy every sail!
> Made strong, put forth thy strength the more,
>   rise high above earth's misty vale.[13]

[13] I have been unable to trace the author or source of this poem.

CHAPTER SEVEN

Steps to Repentance—Genesis 42

T HE book of Genesis is full of steps. There were many steps that Abraham had to climb—steps of both faith and patience—before at last the promised son was born. Then there were the steps from heaven to earth in Jacob's dream; thereafter, what a long, testing climb for Jacob as he ascended the steps from earth to heaven—and the story of Israel here in Genesis is not finished with the old man yet. There have also been the steps which Joseph has had to climb, and what gruelling, steep steps they have been, 'steps to the throne' we have called them, until at last he stood before the mighty Pharaoh's throne. The steps Joseph had to tread first led down into dark places before ascending into temporary sunshine when he became manager of Potiphar's house and estate; but they then went down into deeper darkness than before into prison until at last they took him steeply upwards into an altogether new life of brilliant sunlight, luxury and immense responsibility.

Now in Genesis 42 we come to a very different stairway with steps which lead down into the valley of repentance. Descending this stairway we will find Joseph's ten brothers, men who were hardened rascals, immoral, cheating and villainous—some worse than others, but all complicit in each others' sins. Nevertheless, God had a plan for these men. He was not going to thrash the living daylights out of them, as we say; rather he was going to corner them until they had no other option than to descend those steps down into repentance.

Step One: Unexpected Events Bring Unexpected Memories

I vividly remember a three-month drought in Scotland: in 1961 there was no rain from early April right through to the second week of July. Angus, my home county in Scotland, is a fruit-growing area and the farmers were crying out for rain. Day after day the sun shone down from a cloudless sky until the very grass was burned brown! Everyone—gardeners, fruit-growers, the Water Board—all were praying for rain. At last their prayers were answered, but unfortunately for Lorna and myself the rain came on our wedding day. It was not at all what we had been expecting!

However, in that second year of famine in Egypt and the neighbouring countries, for a year and six months there had been no rain, and consequently only the meanest of harvests. The ground was baked hard as iron. Food supplies were almost gone. Water was precious and every drop was being counted. Only here and there, around an oasis, were a few date palms still green. Because the famine was all over the known world, Jacob sent for his ten sons. *Why do you look at one another?* he asked them. *Behold, I have heard that there is grain for sale in Egypt. Go down and buy grain for us there that we may live and not die.* So the brothers packed their meagre supplies and made their way south until they turned west to cross the Sinai desert along the selfsame route that those Ishmaelite traders had taken Joseph twenty-one years earlier.

As long as their daily lives had been much as before, with their store-chests full and the home-fires burning each evening as their womenfolk cooked the evening meals, and as long as it had been work as usual, they had been able to forget—at least to repress the memories of their wickedness towards their younger brother. Only their aged father continued to grieve for his beloved son; only he shed tears into his pillow night after night. The ten brothers still laughed and joked. They were alright. There was nothing to disturb their daily routine. Not, that is, until something completely unexpected happened and they found themselves following the road along which they had sent Joseph in chains, to be sold as a slave in the very land to which they were now travelling. As they sat round their camp fire each night, did one of them ever let slip what must have been in all their minds, 'This is the route our brother took all those years ago'?

God sometimes comes to disturb our lives. When he does, it is not that he wants to inflict on us any needless hurt. Rather, it is because he knows what lies hidden and repressed beneath an outwardly quiet, calm exterior.

When I was a boy my parents told me of nasty little insects in the Congo which could sting the bare feet of someone walking along a forest path. After that initial slight sting, nothing seemed wrong. But the sting consisted in several hundred microscopic eggs being injected under the skin, which a few weeks later hatched out into tiny maggots; and those maggots fed off the flesh inside the sole of the person's foot, and as they fed, they grew larger until the foot became swollen and very painful. When the skin was at last punctured, there was a seething mass of maggots waiting to emerge into the world and metamorphose into the insect that had originally stung its victim. 'Jiggers' was the name the Europeans gave these nasty little brutes![1] At the time, those ten brothers had been 'stung' by their sin, but they had been able quickly to forget the momentary pain. However, hatching out beneath their apparently calm

---

[1] *Tunga penetrans* is known as the chigger, jigger or sand flea; see www.jigger-ahadi.org/jiggers.html

appearances were dark memories, growing, squirming, poisoning and irritating them however hard they tried to repress those awful recollections. To change the figure, I have often listened to a wife's story of her husband's life-threatening illness: 'I knew he was ill, but for months he point-blank refused to go to the doctor; now this has happened, and he's been told that if he'd gone to see about it sooner they would have been able to help him.'

Those ten brothers drew back from the pain and shame of bad consciences that should have been taken to the great Physician. But God was now going to cause them to turn to him, and as they travelled that desert road to Egypt, he was stirring up their memories, and doing the totally unexpected in their hearts and souls. Can you see what a significant sub-plot this is within the wider panorama of the Joseph story?—a sub-plot that points clearly to the universal rejection of God's grace in Jesus Christ by fallen humanity.[2]

Let us use some common-sense imagination. As the party of brothers entered Egypt and asked directions for the grain stores where supplies were being sold, I have no doubt they would have often passed squads of slaves at work on some building site or new road. As they heard the crack of the task master's whip, and as they saw sullen slaves labouring under the burning sun, did they look anxiously at each other, and even more anxiously at those squads of slaves, half-expecting to see their younger brother among the gang of sweating men? And did they heave a sigh of relief when at last they reached the crowds milling round the grain stores—relief that among the hundreds of slaves they had passed, none of them had recognized Joseph? One may have said quietly to the others, 'He couldn't possibly be still alive after more than twenty years. Those slaves can't live long. Did you see how hard they were driven?'

But their consciences had been awakened and the pain of their guilt revived. The Holy Spirit was beginning his particular work in

[2] John 1:11; Romans 3:19; Ephesians 2:1-3, *etc.*

them. They had inadvertently found themselves on the first step of the descent to brokenness and contrition. Unexpected events were bringing back unexpected memories.

This is always the pathway back to God for the person who has been for years 'on the run' from him. Peace of mind goes as memories of past sins begin to rise up in the mind from the depths of the subconscious where they have long been concealed and repressed. Unexpected events can bring a sense of unease and anxiety. 'This should not be happening to me', says the one in whose life the Spirit is silently at work. 'Nothing has changed. That all took place ages ago. It's in the past. No one knows about it. Stop worrying. There's no need to become nervous after all these years.' And he does his best to persuade himself everything is perfectly alright. But, that cannot be true—'For the Lord disciplines the one he loves, and chastises every son whom he receives.'[3]

Step Two: An Unexpected Reception from an Unexpectedly Hostile Ruler

I suppose there was a considerable crowd of foreigners waiting to buy corn. The brothers probably had a long time to wait, maybe even two or three hours. They had watched buyer after buyer paying their money, then having the grain weighed and handed over. They had seen the precious supplies loaded on to beasts of burden and the grateful recipients setting off on their journey back to their own land. By the time it was their turn they knew the routine; they had their money ready and knew exactly what to ask for. Things were going their way. 'We'll soon be on our way, lads!', they will have said. 'It's us next.'

But as their grain was being weighed, the unexpected happened. The ruler himself appeared. Anyone could see half a mile away

---

[3] Hebrews 12:6.

that he was a man in highest authority. He was clothed in spotless white linen and there was a gold chain and medallion round his neck. The people all bowed before him. As he stood in front of the ten brothers, they knew what they must do and they too bowed to the ground before him (verse 6). What they did not realize was that he had already seen them waiting and had been watching them carefully. Now he deliberately appeared when it was their turn to be served, knowing perfectly well that they would never recognize him.

Someone asks, 'How did they not know it was Joseph when he knew at once they were his brothers?' The answer is easy. Their dress, beards and hair would have been unchanged and told everyone that they were humble herdsmen from some neighbouring land; on the other hand, Joseph's head would have been shaved, his scalp oiled and his face and eyebrows painted with cosmetics as befitted his status as an Egyptian aristocrat; his immaculate dress would have indicated his lofty office as ruler of the land. The scent of the world's most expensive perfume on his body would have been far stronger than our modern aftershave lotions! The brothers had been looking for Joseph among the sweating gangs of labourers; they would never have dreamed that this Egyptian of such presence and power who spoke in a language they could not understand was their own kith and kin—their long-lost brother!

As Joseph saw his brothers bowing down before him with their faces to the ground, he *remembered the dreams he had dreamed of them* (verse 9). This detail is important and stands in contrast to the meaning of the name he had given to his first-born son, Manasseh: 'God has made me forget all my hardship and my father's house.'[4] Those dreams had been God's word to him and now the Holy Spirit brought them to his mind and he understood it all—the

---

[4] Genesis 41:51.

events of the intervening years had been in direct fulfilment of the Lord's purposes for his life. His brothers 'meant evil against [him], but God meant it for good'.[5] Calvin here draws a parallel with the women who found the tomb empty that first Easter morning and were told by the 'two men in dazzling apparel ... "Remember how he told you ... that the Son of Man must be delivered into the hands of sinful men and be crucified and on the third day rise." And they remembered his words.'[6]

An older commentator makes a plausible suggestion regarding Joseph's thoughts as he recognized his brothers, *remembered the dreams* and said to them, 'You are spies' (verse 9). He speculates that twenty-one years earlier when Joseph had at last found his brothers at Dothan, and they had seized him and torn off his special coat, they had then said, 'So you've come to spy on us, little brother, and you'll stay with us for a few days and then run off home and tell our father all about our deals. Well, we'll see now what comes of your fancy dreams, you dirty spy!' The suggestion is that it was those last words they spoke to him which now triggered his first words to them at this unexpected meeting, *You are spies, and you have come to see the nakedness of the land.*[7]

Be that as it may, the accusation was perfectly reasonable. This was a charge that travellers in the East often encountered. We know that the Egyptian frontiers were fortified and closely watched. Records from this period of all foreigners entering and leaving Egyptian territory still survive in a Cairo museum. Therefore a band of ten men would naturally arouse some suspicion. The brothers' reply that they were *all sons of one man* implies that surely it was obvious ten brothers would never be so naive as to enter the land together as spies.

---

[5] Genesis 50:20.
[6] Luke 24:4-8; see Calvin, p. 341.
[7] Meyer, p. 72.

Speaking in the Egyptian tongue with its very different cadences to their language, Joseph's voice was well disguised. Of course as the interpreter translated his words into Hebrew, he listened to their replies, heard their conversation between themselves and understood it all. Then they said to one another, *In truth we are guilty concerning our brother, in that we saw the distress of his soul, when he begged us and we did not listen. That is why this distress has come upon us* (verse 21). Notice their double use of the word 'distress': Joseph's distress so long ago was now being visited upon them. Events have moved round the full circle and come back on to their heads.

In Shakespeare's play, *Hamlet, King of Denmark,* Hamlet's father is murdered by the uncle, the king's brother. Hamlet knows the truth, so he arranges for the royal players to re-enact the murder before his guilty uncle and his mother, the queen. The uncle cannot take it and has to hurry away from the play, saying, 'Oh my offence is rank, it smells to heaven!' Likewise, when Joseph declares, *You are spies . . . you* [will] *remain confined, that your words may be tested'* (verses 14, 16), they can cloak their guilt no longer as their dark secret rises up like a ghost from the past to haunt and fill them with fear.

Modern medical science has taught us just a few of the marvels of the human brain. Apparently our brains contain about ten billion cells, and each cell can act as a microscopic disk on which is recorded the memory of an event, and along with that memory the actual emotions felt at the time. Obviously, we can only consciously recall a very few of these millions of memories stored in that vast disk 'library' of the brain; but whether we are able to recall them or not, nonetheless they are still there. You must have experienced this, if you think about it: something happens which causes you suddenly to play back a 'recording' of some event decades before which you seemed to have forgotten, but which is still there in the brain's library, deep down in your subconscious. It is a bit like opening a filing cabinet where some document has been lost for years and you unexpectedly come across it again.

When our sins are forgotten, but not forgiven, they remain there in that 'filing cabinet' or, to return to the brain's vast storage system, there on a microscopic disk, so to speak, in our brain's library of memories. Each unforgiven sin, never repented of and therefore never scrubbed clean, is there waiting to be recalled by some unexpected occurrence. The day then comes when something downloads that memory from our subconscious and brings it into the forefront of our consciousness, exposing it to the open and into the light of the clearest recollection. Awful, shameful records which you and I thought had been erased by the passing of the years and so lost forever, actions and words and even thoughts executed privately in secret places but still filed away—they are all still there. A whole past, years and years of life, all preserved in those recordings. Things we have done in distant places far from home that happened among people we believed we would never see again, and indeed have never seen since—and never want to see again—the memories of such deeds are all there; for a few hundred miles, or a few thousand miles, or a decade, or four or five decades, will never wipe those disks clean. There they remain, long concealed, but waiting that awesome moment when (to change the figure) those skeletons in our mental cupboard will rattle their bones and stare at us from empty eye-sockets, and point accusing fingers which silently say, 'Guilty! You are guilty!'

There are countless illustrations of this which many, if not all of us, can cite from our experiences. What of Richard Nixon who did his best to withhold, and even to scrub, those notorious tapes on which were recorded his illegal plans to discredit his political rival? You may remember that he did manage to have some of the tapes erased, but that others remained with sufficient evidence on them to have him shamed and impeached. Nevertheless, with those recordings of our lives there can be no erasing by mere human powers. Only the blood of Jesus Christ can wipe those disks clean and empty the trash from that vast filing system of our memories. And oh! the blessedness of that fountain filled with blood drawn from Immanuel's veins, where sinners, plunged beneath that flood lose all their guilty stains!

That is not to say that the devil cannot himself bring up evidence of past sins and accuse us. His very name Satan means 'accuser' or 'slanderer'.[8] But we have nothing to fear from his accusations. We simply answer his intimidating suggestions, 'Get out of my life and my mind! I am ransomed, healed, restored, forgiven!' 'Resist him, firm in your faith'[9] and he will flee from you. James gives us the secret of how to resist him: we must first submit to God, for it is only when we have surrendered ourselves to his control that we will have both the desire and the will to resist Satan. 'Submit yourselves therefore to God. Resist the devil and he will flee from you. Draw near to God and he will draw near to you.'[10]

Back then to Joseph's ten brothers. But this time it is not the devil who is evoking the memory of their past sins. It is the Holy Spirit. And, like all those under conviction of sin, they are finding this a devastating experience. They are being drawn, in spite of themselves, into a deep, dark valley where the shadows of evil images come to life and where the eerie echoes among the rocks become the distressing cries of a seventeen year old brother as his clothes are torn off his back and he is clamped with shackles and dragged off crying out for pity and mercy. And mingled with those cries of distress echoing in that desolate valley of sinful deeds are their own cruel jeers and mocking laughter. Now

---

[8] Revelation 12:10; cf. Job 1:9-11.
[9] 1 Peter 5:9
[10] James 4:7, 8.

confusion and shame fills their hearts and Joseph, witnessing it all, hearing their confession, is moved to tears and slips away to weep, for he still loves deeply the brothers who so wronged him (verse 24).

There are other details recorded for us that we should notice. Joseph kept his brothers in suspense for three full days. All of them were put into custody and the threat hanging over them was that nine of them would stay there until the one released returned to Egypt with their youngest brother (verse 16). The fact that he appeared to change his mind when *he took Simeon from them and bound him before their eyes* should not cause us to charge him with indecision. There can be no doubt that he intended them to face the prospect of weeks, if not several months, of incarceration in order to awaken their consciences thoroughly to the wickedness of their betrayal. When three days later they were released, in his hearing they began to make full confession of their sin—notice that they used the word 'sin' (verse 22). His careful strategy had been effective.

There is often a reluctance today among preachers to bring before the minds of their hearers the heinous nature of sin in the sight of God. Perhaps in the past such attempts have been too censorious and even tinged with both sadism and Pharisaism on the part of the preacher, with the consequence that in our generation the pendulum has swung to the other extreme. When Robert Murray M'Cheyne was told by Andrew Bonar, one of his ministerial colleagues, that he had preached the previous Lord's Day on the subject, 'The wicked shall be turned into hell', M'Cheyne responded, 'Were you able to preach it *with tenderness?*'[11] I like to think that all Joseph said and did at this time was executed with underlying tenderness. Nevertheless, his love for his brothers was a

---

[11] Andrew Bonar, *Memoir and Remains of the Rev. R.M. M'Cheyne* (Edinburgh: Banner of Truth, 2009), p. 43.

tough love, and he did not shrink from ensuring they were obliged to face up to their past and acknowledge their corporate wickedness.

Step Three: An Unexpected Time of Waiting and Reflection on Their Past Sins

After the three days in custody they were brought out, blinking in the brilliant Egyptian sunshine, to face the all-powerful potentate who had accused them of evil intentions. Before their eyes Simeon was bound and taken off to prison on the strict understanding that he would only be released, and that when they returned they would only be permitted to buy fresh supplies of food, if their younger brother were with them (verse 24).

Think of them on their journey home, their feet and hearts heavy as lead. Think of their fear when at their first stopping place, as one of them opened his sack to get fodder for their donkeys, he found the money he had paid was there in the top of his sack. Consider, too, their safe arrival back to old Jacob's settlement, and having to tell their father that Simeon was incarcerated in an Egyptian jail, and that they had been accused of being spies, and that one of them had found his money in his sack. Think too of their renewed fear when the other nine brothers began to unload their sacks and each of them also found his money in his sack. Years before they would have gloated that they had somehow cheated the Egyptians out of so much cash!

It was such a different situation now. They had many months to reflect on their evil past, knowing that Simeon was desperately waiting and longing for their return with Benjamin, so that he could be set free—yet, as far as they knew, Joseph had never been set free. But what they did not know was that the powerful ruler before whom they had trembled and bowed low had abruptly left that final confrontation to weep. Yet Joseph's love was wise enough to resolve to find out how they would treat their youngest brother, also a favourite with their father as he himself had been. They did not know either that Simeon had been held in Egypt as an incentive for them to return, or that their money returned in their sacks had been Joseph's generous provision for them in those days of severe famine. Joseph was in no hurry, as is evident as we watch his careful strategy unfolding. He was content to take his time and allow the grace of repentance to work in their lives little by little.

At times we can wince when God's hand is heavy upon us. David wrote about this correcting rod of God: 'my bones wasted away through my groaning all day long. For day and night your hand was heavy upon me; my strength was dried up as by the heat of summer.'[12] Did David merely feel the pain of a wounded conscience, or was he also dimly aware of the grief and sorrow in the Lord's face as in his later prayer of contrition?[13] I wonder if he ever realized how deeply the Lord yearned that he would make a full confession and, with true repentance, have all the poison of sin purged from his heart and mind, so that he could be clean, healthy and right with God once again? Certainly, as the weeks and months passed for these brothers, although the Spirit was convicting them of their past sin, they did not have any idea of how that Egyptian ruler yearned for them to return or how anxiously, day after day, he eagerly waited and looked for them with a brother's true love.

So what of the heavenly Father's love as he longs for us to return to him by way of descent down those steps of repentance? How stubborn and hard many of us can be! We may go through all the motions of following the Lord; we attend our places of worship, sing the psalms and hymns, bow in prayer and listen to the word of God; we talk like good Christians and even dress and look like Christians; we know how to play the part. But is the truth that we

---

[12] Psalm 32:3-4.
[13] Psalm 51:4.

have bolted and barred an innermost door within our souls and the Saviour is not allowed to enter that most secret place? For weeks, sometimes for months, many are inwardly sick with deeply troubled consciences.

Some years ago I knew personally a man who had at one time been a bright and committed believer; but he had become so spiritually paralyzed through conviction of some secret sins that for several years he had been unable to face the other members of his fellowship or to attend worship on the Lord's day. I recall the anguish he endured until at length the love of Christ broke through again into his benighted soul. He had found those steps of repentance very hard, even too difficult, to tread until the Lord came and, having first caused him to descend into the humiliation of genuine contrition, then took his hand and gently enabled him to ascend into the dawn of a new day. In my pastoral work I have met with tortured souls whose past betrayals of Christ have never been drenched in the cleansing fountain of forgiveness; how hard and excruciatingly painful it has been for them to prostrate themselves before a grieving, yet forgiving, Lord.

If you are ill, you need a doctor. If you have an abscess in your mouth, you need a dentist. If you have a detached retina, you need an optometrist. If you have a burden of guilt, you need a Saviour. So the Spirit of God uncovers to us our sin so that he can come and cleanse us. We read in the next chapter that those nine brothers delayed and procrastinated as long as they could; true, Jacob himself was reluctant to let them take Benjamin away. But the time came when it was either death by starvation or face the Egyptian overlord once again.

So what of those who clutch tight hold of their sin and guilt, refusing to let go and pour it all out before the Lord?

> Nay but much rather let me late returning,
> Bruised of my brethren, wounded from within,

Stoop with sad countenance and blushes burning,
Bitter with weariness and sick with sin:

So to Thy presence get me and reveal it,
Nothing ashamed of tears upon Thy feet,
Show the sore wound and beg Thine hand to heal it,
Pour Thee the bitter, pray Thee for the sweet.[14]

[14] From the poem, 'St Paul' by Frederick Henry William Myers (1867).

CHAPTER EIGHT

Joseph Reveals Himself—Genesis 43-45

B ECAUSE the quantity and quality of the fodder being fed to the animals was being cut back more and more, they were becoming ever thinner and their ribs were sticking out of their sides. Bread on the family tables was increasingly scarce. The last remaining stores of grain that had been brought back were being grudgingly eked out. Yet down in Egypt there was grain in abundance. But the problem was this: the Egyptian ruler had said to Jacob's sons that they would not see his face or be allowed to buy any more grain unless they brought Joseph's younger brother, Benjamin, with them. But Jacob, who loved his youngest boy dearly—he was the only surviving son of his beloved Rachel—refused point blank to allow him to make that long journey across the Sinai desert; he feared lest he should lose him as he had lost Joseph.

However, the point came when the large family's supplies of food could only last another two or three weeks at most, and so the old man's unwillingness to let Benjamin go was finally overcome by Judah who laid his own life on the line as a pledge of Benjamin's safety. So at last Jacob tearfully agreed. He insisted they return double the money that had been found in their sacks, and that they also present a modest gift to placate the all-powerful viceroy, *a little balm and a little honey, gum, myrrh, pistachio nuts and almonds*

(43:11f.). And so, with a heavy heart and earnest prayers, Jacob bade a sad farewell to his sons, including Benjamin, as they set off once again for Egypt.

This episode in the story is about the overcoming love and power of divine grace. It is also about the stubborn struggle of men and women as they try to resist the will of God invading their lives. It is about that 'trench warfare', so to speak, during which people dig themselves in as they attempt to fight off the constraints of the love of God. That makes this narrative one of the most self-evidently contemporary parts of Scripture (though it is part of the oldest stratum of the sacred history) because men and women are still afraid of God's will for them and so still blindly struggle against his hand in their lives. Yet we might as well attempt to stop the incoming tide as King Canute is reported to have done; I suppose that foolish king could have had some kind of a dam built to keep back the sea from a little stretch of the seashore, just the way we often try to keep back from God an area of our lives for our private use. But we are blind, proud fools to attempt such a futile refusal of his mighty love. For, with irresistible waves of grace, his tide of mercy ultimately encroaches on our personal, petty stretch of beach. Yes, the Lord's call to those on whom he has set his love is an effectual call.

Thus God won with Jacob as he was soon to win with his recalcitrant sons. Perhaps the old man ultimately prayed about the Egyptian ruler's demand. (Certainly he sought the Lord in prayer and had an historic encounter with the Almighty before he himself finally left Canaan to travel to meet Joseph in Egypt.[1]) Be that as it may, he at last surrendered and bowed to the inevitable. So let us join the brothers and walk along with them as they make that dreaded journey once again down into Egypt.

---

[1] Genesis 46:2ff.

The Hospitality

Joseph had been expecting them for some weeks and would have been watching out for their appearance. Had he given orders that when nine Hebrew herdsmen entered the grain market, he was to be notified at once? If so, he was there to see them as they joined the queue of those who had come to buy supplies. To their astonishment they were at once ushered into the vizier's private apartment. They quickly assumed that they were going to be accused of theft for not paying for the grain they had taken away on their earlier visit. However, the steward reassured them that all was well: *Peace to you, do not be afraid. Your God and the God of your father has put treasure into your sacks for you. I received your money* (43:23). Simeon was then released from where he had been held and joined them. Their astonishment soon increased as they discovered they were to eat in the ruler's luxurious home. When he appeared they bowed low before him.

Joseph *enquired about their welfare and said, 'Is your father well, the old man of whom you spoke? Is he still alive?'* They said, *'Your servant our father is well; he is still alive.' And they bowed their heads and prostrated themselves.* Seeing Benjamin, his mother's son, he asked, *'Is this your youngest brother of whom you spoke to me? God be gracious to you, my son'* (43:29).[2] Then, overcome by deep emotion, Joseph hurried from the room to be alone to weep. He undoubtedly clearly recognized how God was fulfilling those predictive dreams of decades ago![3] He had missed his family and his blood-brother, although he knew that in the divine providence his separation from them had been part of the cross laid upon him that had so totally directed his life. At length he pulled himself together,

---

[2] Some of the early church Fathers are insistent that when Joseph's gaze fell upon Benjamin it was as if Christ himself mystically looked upon Paul and loved him; so Ambrose (A.D. 333–97) *ACCS*, p. 285. See below, Ch. 16 and the Blessing of Jacob on Benjamin.

[3] Genesis 37:5-11.

returned and ordered the food to be served. The eleven brothers sat together while Joseph ate apart by himself, and senior members of his staff by themselves, *because the Egyptians could not eat with the Hebrews, for that is an abomination to the Egyptians* (43:32).

The mystery deepened as they were seated according to their age and birthright; inexplicably, Benjamin was given five times more than his half-brothers. But nonetheless, they ate and drank, relaxing and thoroughly enjoying the very best food that Egyptian chefs could provide. It would appear that as night fell they were shown to sleeping quarters somewhere near at hand. It is unlikely that they would have been in Joseph's own house, for that might have raised questions and suspicions in the brothers' minds that would not have served Joseph's private agenda. Next morning they found their sacks filled with grain and their donkeys ready for them, and they departed with light and gladsome hearts. Little did they know that Joseph had ordered his silver cup to be placed in the top of Benjamin's sack (44:1-3).

It had been a bizarre situation, having a fine time and enjoying lavish Egyptian hospitality with someone they did not know. They had been royally entertained. Surely they must have had some sense of the immense privilege of it all, and some awareness of the quite inexplicable nature of those hours in the ruler's own gracious residence. Nevertheless, they did not yet have any inkling of what was happening. This paradoxical situation was quite beyond their comprehension because one simple factor in the equation was missing—the real identity of their host by whose grace and favour and at whose expense they had been entertained.

There is another feast which is both awesome and enveloped in mystery. Those who sit down to eat are aware that this is no ordinary occasion; there is something unique and special about it, something quite marvellous. What that 'something' is, some only darkly understand; it remains a mystery to them because one simple factor in the equation is missing—at whose expense and by whose grace and favour are they participating in the sacramental banquet? Oh yes, the brothers knew that the vice-regent of Egypt was a great and powerful man. What they did not know and never guessed as they ate his bread and quaffed his wine was that he was the one against whom they had sinned; he was their brother. Had they known that, the meal would have been completely different.

Think of the supper to which Christ invites us. Those who partake surely know that he is great and powerful. But how many truly recognize him as the one against whom we have sinned, and that he is our heavenly Brother?[4] Do we know the One who, through his representative, breaks the bread and gives it to us, the One who passes us the cup saying, 'This cup is the new covenant in my blood'? The question is not whether we know about him, rather it is whether we know him for ourselves. Do we know him the way we know a human brother, parent, husband, wife, or friend? Do we know what our sins brought upon him? Do we know it was we who 'sold him into slavery', so that he bowed his back to carry the guilt of our wickedness? It was on account of our sin that he descended into the darkness of death, having been betrayed by us and nailed to the cross. Do we know that? Have we discovered that the One who invites us to his sacred table is the very One we have tried for years to ignore? Or do we still, like those eleven brothers, eat and drink in total ignorance of who it is presiding over the feast?

The Test

Joseph quite deliberately had instructed his steward that Benjamin should be given greater honour than the others at the feast, for he was resolved to find out whether these men were still nursing hatred in their hearts against Rachel's (remaining) son. Were they

---

[4] Romans 8:29; Hebrews 2:11.

still willing to get rid of their father's favourite, even if it meant killing him? Were they still cruel felons? Or had they undergone some change of heart during those intervening years? In other words, had the grace of repentance begun its work within them? That was why the silver cup from which Joseph had drunk the evening before was now concealed in the top of Benjamin's sack.

Therefore as they had not gone far on their journey the next day—as we have just noted 'with light and gladsome hearts' and with full supplies of grain sufficient to last for another year—they were unexpectedly overtaken by the imperial guard. Now they found themselves accused of base ingratitude in stealing the vice-regent's precious cup after enjoying his bountiful hospitality. A search by the guards at length found the silver cup in Benjamin's sack, and so the scene was set for the final test of what truly was in their hearts.

So confident were they of their innocence that as the search had begun they had said, *Whichever of your servants is found with* [the cup] *shall die, and we also will be my lord's servants* (44:9). Now brought back as prisoners and arraigned before Joseph, for the third time they prostrated themselves to the ground in his presence. In the deeply moving dialogue between Joseph and the brothers (44:14-34) Judah made an implicit confession of their sin against their long-lost brother: *'What shall we say to my lord? What shall we speak? Or how can we clear ourselves? God has found out the guilt of your servants'* (44:16). And when Joseph reassured them and told them that only Benjamin would be arrested and made his life-long slave while they would go free, then they were confronted by their very worst nightmare—returning home to their aged father without his beloved son.

In effect, they were saying: 'Sir, we have a dark past about which you can know nothing. God is now visiting our sins upon our heads. How this situation has come about we cannot understand, but we deserve all we are getting. Only, please, please, please let our younger brother go free, and take as your slave any or all of us, but not Benjamin.' Joseph interrupted them and said, *Far be it from me that I should do so! Only the man in whose hand the cup was found shall be my servant. But as for you, go up in peace to your father.* Judah then stepped forward and pleaded with deepest pathos and moving eloquence that he should be allowed to stand in as Benjamin's substitute and be enslaved for life so that his youngest brother might go free. Before they had set out to buy grain, taking Benjamin with them, their aged father had said, *If you take this one also from me, and harm happens to him, you will bring down my grey hairs in evil to Sheol* (44:29).

The test was now complete. Gone was their hatred, cruelty and hardness of heart. Each was willing to face the dire consequences as long as Rachel's son was allowed to return to his father unharmed. Their profound concern for Jacob was manifestly genuine. A change of heart had taken place within them. The transformation was evidently genuine.

We must pause and attempt to assess the reality of this apparent change in them. Many churches are populated by what the late William Still used to call 'half-converted Christians'. He meant there are too many professing believers who make light of what God calls us to be in Christ. A Christian is not someone who merely nods assent to a creed or to one of the great Reformation confessions. Nor is a Christian someone who has felt an emotional warmth somewhere in the *solar plexus* and has been moved by an emotional account of Christ's suffering. When the Holy Spirit does his work in a person's life, there is an about-turn which is as revolutionary and far-reaching as it was in the hearts of these ten men. The Scriptures call that revolution 'repentance'. It reaches the most personal and the most secret places in our souls. Deep resentments, bitter grudges, rock-hard resistance—all these begin to be broken down. Festering in the hearts of us all are pride, hypocrisy and carelessness about spiritual things together with self-idolatry, self-righteousness and self-justification; all this and more is the warp and woof of our fallen natures. When the grace of real repentance visits us, these awful sins begin to be exposed and then crushed by the love and mercy of God. We are told that when there is a nuclear explosion the very elements dissolve and turn to radio-active particles. But when repentance comes the gentle power of Christ reduces to dust and ashes the proud monuments to self that have long stood, sphinx-like in their stony arrogance, within our hearts. Then at last we kneel before the Lord and with tears cry, like these ten men, 'We are guilty before you, O holy Lord, we are guilty!'

There is a truth tucked away here which is extremely important for our understanding of the relationship between the Old and New Testaments. It affects what we believe about baptism, the Holy Spirit, the doctrine of the Christian church and indeed about Scripture itself. A commonly held view among some Christians is that, during the Old Testament era, to be a member of the church of God, one simply had to be born an Israelite and that all members of that ethnic group were automatically members of the people of God. But (so this view goes) when Jesus came to earth, he changed all that; he abolished that Old Testament dispensation of membership of the church through physical birth into the ethnic community of Israel, and he inaugurated a new dispensation of membership of the church through spiritual rebirth—being 'born again'.[5]

Though this view at first seems quite plausible, it is, I believe, quite erroneous. Those who hold it must go on to say, 'Because being born again only came in with Jesus, entry into the kingdom of God only came in with Jesus. His life and ministry initiated an

[5] John 3:3ff.

entirely new era. There are no gospel continuities from the Old Testament into the New Testament, only discontinuities.' Those who think like that also must assume that repentance and conversion were first spoken of by Jesus to Nicodemus.

How mistaken such an assumption is! Did not the Lord say to that member of the Jewish ruling council, 'Are you the teacher of Israel and yet you do not understand these things?'[6] 'What things?' you may ask. That the only way to enter the kingdom of God is through a second birth by the Holy Spirit. All teachers of Israel ought to have known that perfectly well, because it is taught in the Old Testament Scriptures, as here in the account of Joseph's brothers. It is also taught repeatedly elsewhere in the Old Testament. What the prophets clearly saw was that only a remnant of ethnic Israel were true men and women of faith; they had been spared the awesome judgment of God and they would share in the blessedness of his kingdom; they were the regenerate.[7]

Be that as it may, centuries before the Psalmists, Isaiah, Jeremiah and Malachi, ten men who became the founding fathers of the people of God were transformed from being the miserable sinners that we all are, into being sinners who had been bathed in repentance and the forgiveness of God's grace.

So has the touch of the divine finger of grace reduced to dust those granite battlements that your pride has built up around your soul? Has the Spirit of God worked within you to bring you to bow in contrition and brokenness before the Lord? 'The sacrifices of God are a broken spirit; a broken and contrite heart, O God, you will not despise.' 'I the Lord search the heart and test the mind, to give every man according to his ways, according to the fruit of his deeds.'[8] This was the test of these ten men.

---

[6] John 3:10.

[7] See, *e.g.*, Psalms 23, 32, 43, 51; Isaiah 35:8-10; Jeremiah 33:8-11; Malachi 3:16-18, *et al.*

[8] Psalm 51:17; Jeremiah 17:10.

The Reconciliation

Come near to me, please. I am your brother Joseph, whom you sold into Egypt. And now do not be distressed or angry with yourselves because you sold me here, for God sent me before you to preserve life (45:4f.). The brothers were speechless! But more than merely speechless; they were distressed at this disclosure, dismayed, unable to say a word!

How the situation had changed! Now it was no longer an apparently overbearing, all-powerful ruler whom they saw and heard, but a brother whose face shone with love and whose voice overflowed with compassion. They stood amazed, listening to one who was making promises of help, provision and protection beyond their wildest dreams; one who was in full control of events and who now issued them with instructions which they must obey.

> It would not have been strange if they had died with terror and joy at this word . . . This is a very beautiful example of how God deals with us. For when he afflicts [us] and conducts himself as a judge who wants to destroy us, he says at last in his own time and at a suitable hour, 'I am the Lord your God' . . . Therefore we Christians must learn that Scripture teaches this humbling everywhere . . . In the same manner Joseph also disciplines and humbles his brothers that he may exalt them.[9]

I wonder how you think of the Lord? I spoke with a man some years ago who said to me, 'You'll never ever see me in any church', and there was bitter antagonism against God in his voice and body-language. Yet when I read this story of Joseph weeping before his astonished brothers, I think too of Jesus weeping over the city with a sorrow and anguish far greater than Joseph ever knew or felt. 'O Jerusalem . . . how often would I have gathered your children together as a hen gathers her brood under her wings,

---

[9] Luther, *Lectures*, Vol. 8, pp. 3, 4, 5, 6; he also cites 1 Samuel 2:6: 'The LORD kills and brings to life; he brings down to Sheol and raises up.'

and you would not!'[10] I doubt if anyone who truly by faith has seen the Lord's sorrow over our sin, and witnessed his love in dying in our place, can ever be the same again.

I am Joseph. Fifteen centuries later another man who had been motivated by bitterness and hatred at length also bowed himself to the ground and asked, 'Who are you, Lord?' Was there at that moment an echo of Joseph's words as the answer came to him, 'I am Jesus'?[11] 'All that has happened to me has been in God's perfect plan', was the message Saul of Tarsus began to understand. 'It was my Father who sent me to die for you so that I might have the authority and the right to bring you into the real promised land, which Canaan only foreshadowed.'

I recall a time in my student days when worldly ambition took over my thinking. I began to plan my life and decide what I would like to do, putting God to one side. He had to deal with me. In his own way he brought me to my knees. I was in my third year as an undergraduate and I vividly remember the evening when, alone in my room, like so many countless straying believers before me, I bowed before him in total submission. 'Who are you, Lord?' I wept. 'I am Jesus', came the answer, 'against whom you have been struggling and fighting. I am the Lord! Come near . . . come near!'

Have you ever read the story of Augustine of Hippo? His life straddled the fourth and fifth centuries of the Christian era. He was a brilliant young man with a dissolute, pagan father, but a pious, praying mother called Monica. He was born and brought up in North Africa, in the area which today is Algeria. To his mother's distress, he forsook the Christian faith and became a Manichean, a popular religion with some similarities to contemporary Buddhism. A wealthy man paid for him to study in Carthage where he distinguished himself in the skills of rhetoric. After nine years

---

[10] Matthew 23:37.
[11] Acts 9:5.

there, he went off to Rome, leaving behind his mother, grieving over his godlessness. In the great capital city he was disappointed with his students, most of whom disappeared when they were due to pay him their fees for his instruction. However, through the influence of his Manichean friends, at the age of thirty he secured the prestigious chair of rhetoric at the imperial court of Milan. He had tried all the vices he could but had always been disappointed.

While in Milan Augustine went to hear the godly Ambrose preach, for he had heard he was a brilliant rhetorician. It was through Ambrose's exposition of the Bible that he underwent a dramatic change. He had studied many of the philosophies of his day and been disillusioned by them all. At last, he turned to the New Testament documents, finding Paul's Letter to the Romans. By the time he had reached chapter 13, Christ had taken him by surprise. He came to the final verses of the chapter: 'The night is far gone, the day is at hand, so then let us cast off the works of darkness and put on the armour of light. Let us walk properly as in the daytime, not in orgies and drunkenness, not in sexual immorality and sensuality, not in quarrelling and jealousy' (these words described the kind of life he had been living), 'but put on the Lord Jesus Christ, and make no provision for the flesh, to gratify its desires.' As he read, he heard the voice of One saying to him, 'Come near', and, trembling in deep conviction of his sin, Augustine drew near to Christ and was locked for ever in his loving embrace.

As his terrified brothers backed away in their fear Joseph said, *Come near to me, please* (45:4). And soon his brother Benjamin was locked in his embrace and he kissed his ten half-brothers and wept for joy at this long-awaited reunion. In the same way, we 'who once were far off have been brought near by the blood of Christ'.[12] We had been aliens, strangers, but now have become brothers and

---

[12] Ephesians 2:13.

sisters, members of the family of a great Lord and Ruler over all. *Come near to me, please,* he says. Had it been Simeon who had suggested murdering him all those years before? He embraced him. Had it been Issachar and Asher who had received the silver from the Midianite traders as the price for him? He embraced them. Had it been Gad who had dragged the coat off his back and torn it up? He embraced him. Had another brother helped to put the shackles on his neck and ankles? If so, he embraced him too.

Our Lord has been through all this with those who have been his debtors. As often as a man or woman hears his invitation, *Come near to me, please,* the reconciliation takes place all over again. For when a hell-deserving sinner (as we all are) bows before him in contrition, he once again says, as he said to Saul of Tarsus, 'I am Jesus.'[13]

---

[13] Commenting on the mystical presence of Christ in the person of Joseph as symbolized in verses 5 and 13, Ambrose (A.D. 333-97) writes: 'Jesus is the same who spoke before in Joseph and afterward in his own body, seeing he did not change even the words. For at that time he said, "Be not grieved . . . Go up to my father and say to him, Thus says your son Joseph, God has made me master of the whole land of Egypt." And in the gospel Christ says, "Do not be afraid. Go, tell my brothers to go into Galilee, and there they shall see me" (*Matt.* 28:10).' *ACCS*, p. 291.

CHAPTER NINE

Father and Son Reunited—Genesis 46

I understand from conversations with both psychiatrists and pharmacists that an increasing number of our nation's population are being prescribed sedatives and anti-depressants.[1] Of course, there are bound to be very different reasons why people require that kind of medication and many readers may have benefited from a much-needed course of such treatment. However, there are those who require tranquillizers because they are oppressed either with a sense of failure or worthlessness or else by a guilt-complex. It is even possible that some genuinely strive to be better Christians but suffer from depression because they feel they cannot live up to the standard Jesus Christ has set for all who would follow him.

It may be that you have repeatedly tried to do the right thing and live Christ's way. But you constantly seem to fall short and fail dismally, in spite of your best resolves that next time you will behave differently. You have probably prayed earnestly for God's help. Yet, alas, down you have gone into the dust and mire once again with the result that you feel you are not merely a feeble disciple of Christ but even worse, a total failure.

I was once asked to speak to a university Christian Union on the subject, 'Coping with failure'. It was not an easy address to

[1] An official figure published in the UK on April 7, 2011 is that 47% of all doctors' prescriptions are for anti-depressants.

prepare because it not only involved looking into Scripture to see how different believers had coped in their times of failure, but it also required that I search my own heart and life and re-examine the many failures and set-backs littering my past. The prospect of failure can haunt us—failing at our work, failing exams, failing in marriage, failing to find a life-long partner, failing with our children, failing as a friend, failing financially.

While I would never want to encourage unhelpful introspection, it can sometimes be wise to ask ourselves how we have coped with failure. Because to feel that one has been a failure can have a deep effect on our sense of wellbeing and our ability to relate spontaneously and lovingly to those around us. Those who feel they are failures can become withdrawn and lonely; they can cease to aim higher and instead sink into mediocrity. In other words, they do not function as the whole, healthy persons God intended them to be, because they are overwhelmed by a debilitating sense of disappointment.

We should consider a few very simple things about this. First, God knows all about our failures and, wonder of wonders, he still loves us as his children. When we make a mess of being Christians, he does not 'go off' us the way some fair-weather friends might do. In fact, it was while we were at our very worst that he loved us and gave his Son for us.[2] The love of God and of his Son—these two are mysteriously one love—are the most firm anchorage in all the world, and no furious, raging waves of failure can ever dislodge them. At our very worst the Lord loves us more than we can ever comprehend.

Second, our failures, the mess we make of following Christ and the resulting guilt, make absolutely no difference to God's eternal purposes for each of us—that we should ultimately change into mature Christian men and women. When young men and women

[2] Romans 5:6-8.

are training to be pilots with Royal Air Force, unless they prove themselves able to fly solo within a certain limited time, they are rejected as too slow to make fighter pilots. But that is not at all how God works with any of us. He does not take a few weeks with us until our lack of progress causes him to give up on us; he does not even give us the benefits of a few years to change. Rather he takes a whole lifetime, so that long after your psychiatrist, doctor, wife, husband or friend has despaired of you and given you up as a bad job, God still continues to work patiently in order to produce in us just a few grains of love for himself and the first rudimentary promise of the fruit of Christian character.

Why say all this? Because Genesis 46 contains great encouragement for us all. After a long lifetime of blunders and shortcomings, attempts to change that never really succeeded, after over one hundred years we find frail old Jacob a truly transformed man. Although it took almost a whole lifetime, God was willing patiently to wait to fashion Jacob into the kind of person he ought to be. And if the Lord did that for Jacob, is he not willing and able to do it for you and me?

In Jacob's Life There Were New Fears

Jacob had always been rather a timorous man; perhaps he had inherited his timid nature from his mother. Remember how he had been afraid of Esau's anger and had fled to escape from him. He had also run away secretly from his uncle Laban, afraid of him and his sons. He was terrified too of meeting up again with his brother and devised a cunning plan in the attempt to appease his anger. Further, since Joseph had been taken from him, he was afraid that the same might happen to Benjamin.[3] He had been a man prone to very human fears which to a certain extent controlled his actions and thinking. But now we find that Jacob has

[3] Genesis 27:41ff.; 31:1f.; 32:3ff.; 42:38.

altogether new fears, godly fears which cause him to seek the mind and will of God.

Let me explain. The old man has at last heard the almost unbelievable news that Joseph is alive and well; even more incredible, he is the ruler of all Egypt. He has seen the wagons and abundant supplies sent to enable him and his extended family to make the journey down into Egypt, there to be succoured by his beloved son during the remaining years of the famine. And now, his family having packed up all their belongings, their tents, clothes and cooking utensils and having loaded them on to the provided transport, he has begun the journey to leave the land of Canaan with his entire household of seventy persons (46:27). The company of nomadic shepherds has reached Beersheba, near the southern extremity of the promised land. Here they set up camp as they prepare to make the gruelling journey across the Sinai desert and into Egypt.

But Beersheba was a place redolent with memories for Jacob who knew well his family's history. It was here that his grandfather Abraham had gone wrong, also leaving the land of promise during a time of famine; he had deceived Pharaoh, and Sarah had been exposed to the hazard of shame and dishonour.[4] It was here also that his own father Isaac had sought refuge from the troublesome Philistines, and here that God had appeared to him and assured him of his continued blessing on him right there in the land of promise: 'Fear not, for I am with you'; then peace had been made with Abimelech.[5] Now it was here that he had altogether new fears: was he right in departing from Canaan? Canaan was the promised land, the land of the covenant made with Abraham, renewed to Isaac and confirmed to him. Was he falling into a trap? Was he leaving his God behind as he ventured into foreign territory?

---

[4] Genesis 12:10-20.
[5] Genesis 26:23-33.

The aged Jacob had been at prayer: *He came to Beersheba, and offered sacrifices to the God of his father Isaac* (46:1). Now when the others were all asleep, we find him wide awake. Was it because he truly feared that he might be stepping out of God's will and acting in disobedience to the terms of the covenant of divine grace? 'The fear of the Lord is the beginning of wisdom',[6] and Jacob had learned the wisdom of fearing God lest he disobey and depart from his will, however plausible and desirable the reason might seem to be. He had learned to cultivate in his heart an altogether new fear.

I wonder if you suffer from fears? I do not mean childish phobias such as fear of the dark. I mean adult fears: fears of what the future may hold; fears that you might be left with insufficient income to live on; fears that you might be bereft of your loved ones and be left friendless; fears that you might lose your reputation. There are very different fears that people may have—about work, or next week, or the family, or the children.

While I was doing pastoral visitation some years ago, I recall speaking with a woman who confided in me that her whole life had been overshadowed by various fears. It did not need a psychiatrist to see worry written all over her face and to recognize that she was pathologically afraid; her features were etched with years of anxiety and fear. Indeed, in the worst case scenario I have known some who have been hospitalized as the result of fears which have taken them over and which have prevented them from being able to function normally as human beings.

I am not suggesting that anyone reading this is obsessed by fears. Nevertheless, the Scriptures do teach that without God as our rock and defender, it is surprisingly easy to slip into a mind-set of fearfulness. There were events when the prophet Isaiah was living which had thrown people all around him into genuine panic of what the future would hold. So God spoke to him to tell him that

---

[6] Proverbs 9:10.

he must not have the same fears as the people of his day—fear of losing their homes and possessions at the threat of imminent war. 'Do not call conspiracy all that this people calls conspiracy, and do not fear what they fear, nor be in dread. But the LORD of hosts, him shall you regard as holy. Let him be your fear, and let him be your dread . . . I will wait for the LORD . . . and I will hope in him.'[7] When God is our Lord, all that the world fears becomes irrelevant; our lives, our future, our destiny are entirely in his hands. So the fears and terrors that possess the minds of many are pointless for the believer. Those whose faith reposes in their God fear him with a loving, filial fear; that is, with the deep respect and reverence a good son has for a wise, just and righteous father.

When Potiphar's wife tried to seduce Joseph, remember the fear that he had of his Lord: 'How can I do this great wickedness and sin against God?'[8] Joseph feared to step outside God's strait and narrow way into no-man's land where the ground is mined by the tempter in order to inflict serious life-threatening injury on those who depart from the paths of righteousness. This must always be the godly fear of the Christian—to step out of the realm of God's protection by wandering away from the Lord.

Now this is the lesson old Jacob has learned. That is why he was now trembling at the prospect of travelling beyond the borders of Canaan and going down into Egypt. Calvin agrees with Luther that he feared perpetual exile and the loss of the promise. 'There is no doubt that he was afraid that he would lose the promise, which was based on the land of Canaan, the land he wanted to leave. Undoubtedly he was deeply disturbed.'[9] Thus God came to him *in visions of the night and said, Jacob, Jacob.' And he said, 'Here I am.' Then he said, 'I am God, the God of your father. Do not be afraid to go*

[7] Isaiah 8:12, 13, 17.
[8] Genesis 39:9.
[9] Luther, vol. 8, p. 78.

down to Egypt, for there I will make you into a great nation. I myself will go down with you to Egypt, and I will also bring you up again, and Joseph's hand shall close your eyes' (46:2-4). O that our lives were always controlled and governed by such fear of God, the godly fear which is the beginning of wisdom. Aged Jacob had now learned that wisdom.

In Jacob's Life There Was also a New Faith

There was something in this man's life from which he had always been running away, but somehow it had invariably managed to catch up with him. You will guess straight away what it was: it was his cheating nature. He was Jacob, the 'Supplanter'.[10] Perhaps when he fled from Esau almost a whole lifetime earlier, he had thought he had left his old nature behind. But it followed him to his uncle Laban's house. Perhaps when he had run away from his uncle, he thought that this time he had left it behind. But no, when he met up with Esau once again, it was still close on his heels.[11] I have no doubt that over the years he manfully fought against that wretched nature of his, but just when he thought he had overcome it, it reared its ugly head again. Even though at Peniel God had given him a new name, Israel, he continued to be called Jacob.[12] Was that because he had never managed to shake off the 'Jacob' in himself?

Do you know anything of this kind of inner spiritual struggle? Can you empathize with him? Have you discovered you have the same kind of fallen nature as Jacob had, though your sinful bias may show itself in very different ways?

[10] Jacob was born clutching the heel of his elder twin Esau (*Gen.* 25:26). 'Jacob "supplanted" (this is a nuance developed from "to take by the heel, to overtake") his brother, first obtaining the birthright of the elder son by taking advantage of his brother's hunger and then beguiling Isaac into giving him the blessing.' *IBD*, Part 2, p. 727b.

[11] Genesis 31:17-21; 33:12-17.

[12] Jacob's new name: Genesis 32:27-28. Still mainly called 'Jacob': 33:1, 5, 8, 10, 13, 17, 18; 35:20, 21, 22, 27, *et al.*

For many years of his life, this man had two names, and my understanding of those two names, Jacob and Israel, is that they reflected two natures—the old nature of the cheat, and the new nature which God was working lovingly and patiently to form within him. This is the same principle we find unfolded in Romans 6 and 7 and again in Galatians 5. An inner spiritual conflict is going on in every believer as the flesh (our fallen sinful nature) struggles against the Spirit (who implants the new divine nature in us) and likewise the Spirit struggles against the flesh. Those who know nothing of that inner conflict cannot be, it seems to me, truly in Christ. For

> And they who fain would serve Thee best
> Are conscious most of wrong within.[13]

So what has happened in his life that the old man should be any different now? For over twenty years he has mourned the (assumed) death of his dearest son. There was a sense in which Jacob himself had died. His natural way of extricating himself from trouble had formerly been to outsmart others and, in outwitting them, to emerge unscathed, so he thought. But in this profound grief he could not do that. To him Joseph had died and with that bereavement had come another death—the death of the old way of doing things. Jacob's self-esteem and self-sufficiency had drained away, and he had been left like a bird with a broken wing. There was only one recourse remaining to him and that was to cling by the tips of his fingers to his God. He had, in effect, bowed his neck to this severe discipline from the hand of God and he had submitted to the divine will. His final struggle had been to permit Benjamin to leave home and make the hazardous journey down to Egypt.

Out of that death there has come a kind of resurrection: the son who had been assumed to be dead was alive, he who had been lost

---

[13] From the hymn by Henry Twells, 'At even, ere the sun was set' (1868).

has been found. Jacob's spirit had revived and he at last had entered upon the final stage of his long life with God's loving assurance that all was well and that nothing that had happened had been by bad luck or misfortune, but through the mysterious purposes and providence of his God.

I wonder if you remember the story of General Charles de Gaulle who during the Second World War led the French resistance to the Nazis from the United Kingdom. However, at the end of the war the French nation rejected de Gaulle and so he retired to the country, virtually forgotten. Then twelve years later when France was in deep trouble during the 1958 crisis and was leaderless and divided, the cry went up, 'Bring back General Charles de Gaulle!' And back the General came to restore to his nation her dignity and greatness as a world power. He founded the Fifth French Republic and was its first president for ten years. He is still affectionately known in France as *Le Général*.

At times it may seem as if God has retired from our lives. He often delays in answering our prayers as he waits for his time. His timing is often occasioned by our unwillingness to surrender our wills wholly to his and submit ourselves completely to his control and direction. So the sovereign Lord waits patiently, seemingly in obscurity, so to speak, until our lives are ordered according to his purposes for us and we are ready to hear and obey his voice.

I love this little cameo of God speaking to Jacob while the others slept and he was quite alone with God. (That is what had happened at Peniel: 'And Jacob was left alone.'[14]) Now God reveals his love and faithfulness, and as Jacob is able at last to catch a glimpse of the panorama of the divine purposes, his faith rises and pulsates with renewed strength. My guess is that the next morning his sons and daughters-in-law along with his grandchildren saw a change in his face and bearing. I like to think that there was a new serenity,

---

[14] Genesis 32:24.

a quiet confidence, a calm poise which they had not seen before. His faith had finally found a steadfast anchorage in his God.

Have you noticed that from chapter 43 onwards the new name Israel begins to be used much more frequently than his old name Jacob? Can you see the significance of that? A changed name in the Scriptures should always be noted carefully.

So how about you? We all have problems and burdens; that goes without saying. But we must not delude ourselves. Have you ever been tempted to think that God has forgotten about you, or is not greatly concerned about your trials? Is it possible that he is waiting for you to learn to trust him wholly? Can you not see that there is something beautifully simple and childlike about this old man's renewed faith in his God, purer and truer than it had ever been before, even immediately after Peniel, where he had wrestled with God and prevailed?[15] Now, like a little boy holding his father's hand, Jacob takes up the journey away from Canaan, across the Sinai desert and into Egypt, knowing the Father is with him, leading him to his beloved son.

In Jacob's Life There Is Final Fulfilment

[Joseph] *presented himself to him* [Israel] *and fell on his neck and wept on his neck a good while. Israel said to Joseph, 'Now let me die since I have seen your face and know that you are still alive'* (46:29f.). That was not a morbid statement. He was rather expressing deepest

---

[15] Genesis 32:28: 'But the question now occurs, Who is able to stand against an Antagonist, at whose breath alone all flesh perishes and vanishes away, at whose look the mountains melt, at whose word the whole world is shaken to pieces, and therefore to attempt the least contest with him would be insane temerity? But it is easy to untie the knot. For we do not fight against him except by his own power, and with his own weapons; for he, having challenged us to this contest, at the same time furnishes us with means of resistance, so that he both fights against us and for us ... Inasmuch as he supplies us with more strength to resist than he employs in opposing us, we may truly and properly say, that he fights against us with his left hand, and for us with his right hand.' Calvin, p. 192.

peace: he now knew that because all was well he was ready to depart this life at any time, as God should choose. In fact he still had left many years and lived to make some of the greatest utterances and prophecies in the entire Bible. He also lived to bear testimony before Pharaoh to God's great goodness towards him. I would venture to suggest that his final years were his happiest and most sublime because he knew beyond any shadow of doubt that the mighty purposes and promises of God were true, steadfast and eternal.

On December 26, 2004 we heard with shock of the tsunami which swept over the coastline of Sri Lanka and some of the Indonesian islands, bringing death and destruction to thousands. But God's purposes for his beloved people are no tsunami, no devastating, fearful wave of destruction. Rather, the divine purposes are worked out carefully by a Master Planner who takes into full account all our weaknesses and failures. He silently weaves into our lives those golden threads that lead to ultimate fulfilment; the promise of God to all who fear and trust him is that all will work together for good.

However, his promise is also of a transformation from what we despise about ourselves, from being failures who constantly fall short of God's glory as we follow the Saviour so feebly and imperfectly. This fulfilment which takes a lifetime is directed to our becoming more like Jesus Christ and showing in our lives the fruit of his own nature. Perhaps you think to yourself, 'I can't ever see that happening in my life, though I would love it to be so.' But God will wait for years, even throughout our whole lives, until at length the pale reflection of his Son's face can be seen in those who truly are his children. Then others who meet with us, work alongside us, or share our homes, may find themselves quite unintentionally thinking of Jesus Christ; they are reminded of him because of the kind of persons we are.

It is recounted that one afternoon Robert Murray M'Cheyne was visiting a children's ward in a Dundee hospital—and hospitals in those days were like barracks, places of tragedy, suffering and death. As he slowly moved along the line of beds speaking to each child, one little boy at the top end of the ward watching him said to his mother who was sitting with him, 'Mother, is that bonny man Jesus?' What higher compliment could be paid to any man or woman?

We admire a friend's little child and comment on her looks. 'Isn't she like her father?' we say, 'She has his eyes and smile!' God's purpose for us is that others looking on should say, 'Isn't he like his heavenly Father!' or, 'Isn't she like her Lord and Master!' When that does happen, those of whom the comment is made will be totally unaware of any such likeness, but without their ever realizing it, they will be bringing glory to God and pleasure to his fatherly heart.

CHAPTER TEN

The Greater Blesses the Lesser—Genesis 47:1–12

T HE main theme I want to consider from these twelve verses is the blessing which the aged Jacob bestowed on Pharaoh. But before we come to that we should notice a significant phrase in 46:34: 'for every shepherd is an abomination to the Egyptians'. A question jumps out at us: when Joseph presented five of his brothers to Pharaoh and they were asked, *What is your occupation?* Joseph told them to answer, *Your servants are shepherds, as our fathers were.* Would their reply not bring shame upon themselves when they admitted that their occupation was one which was 'an abomination to the Egyptians'? Indeed, we wonder if it would not also have besmirched Joseph's own reputation. Why walk straight into such a cultural minefield?

It is probable that Egyptians would have regarded shepherds in rather the same way that some in past generations regarded tinkers. In Joseph's day herdsmen rarely had a change of fresh clothing, far less a regular bath; after all, where was there to bathe in the Judean wilderness where they lived? From their handling sheep and cattle they would have retained something of the smell of the livestock they worked with. The fastidious Egyptians who had the deep, clean waters of the Nile in which to bathe would have found shepherds and herdsmen extremely undesirable. Anyway, there has always been an antipathy between town-dwellers and nomads or gypsies. So what are we to make of this detail in the story?

Notice a couple of points. First, it was a wise move on Joseph's part to select Goshen for his family as that area of the Nile delta was ideal for livestock and apparently at this time had few inhabitants. The delta area would enable the Hebrew people, all seventy of them, to live apart from the main areas of Egyptian population and therefore keep themselves separate as the chosen people of God. Second, arising from that, living in Goshen would also enable Jacob's family to maintain their ethnic and religious distinctiveness; they would not be exposed to the paganism of the Egyptian culture. The way their request was presented to Pharaoh (verse 4) 'is a good model of straightforward, peaceable dealings between a pilgrim people and the temporal power'.[1] If we are right in our earlier suggestion that the dynasty ruling Egypt at this time was that of the Hyksos, the shepherd clan of Israel would have been less objectionable to this Pharaoh than if he had been an indigenous Egyptian.

What becomes clear, therefore, is that here is the important principle which develops throughout the Old Testament and is so explicit in the New Testament: followers of Christ are a pilgrim people for whom this earth is only a temporary home; their gaze is fixed by faith on the heavenly 'city that has foundations, whose designer and builder is God'.[2] Further, we must be willing to be separate from the world, perhaps despised as well; the call is to 'go out from their midst and be separate from them',[3] for we are to be temples of the living God.

I remember a student mission that was held in my home town of Arbroath in the early 1950s. One of the divinity students came to preach at the Town Mission. He was absolutely astonished by the number of young people worshipping there—about sixty or

[1] Kidner, p. 210. Cf. 1 Peter 2:11-17.
[2] Hebrews 11:10.
[3] 2 Corinthians 6:17.

more—and also at the deep Christian commitment they clearly exhibited. The singing during the services lifted the roof, and it was clear there was an ardour for Christ burning in the hearts of this great crowd of teenagers. I recall how he asked the Town Missionary what the secret of such devotion was. He received the reply that these young people were so ardent in the Christian faith because they lived separated lives. The divinity student agreed, and as one of those young people at that time, I also must agree. The great majority of those five dozen or so teenagers were not following the Lord half-heartedly with one foot in the world. For them it was, 'All for Jesus, all for Jesus!'[4]

Someone may object to this principle of separation from the world and certain objections may well have some validity. But we have to be directed by the New Testament's careful balance. It is not that we are taught to practise a kind of monasticism, cutting ourselves off from daily contact with anyone who does not follow Christ. There have been deviationist movements that have advocated such separation. Paul clearly teaches that while we must not be *of* the world, we cannot but live *in* the world. Indeed, living as we must within our society, we are called to 'be blameless and innocent, children of God without blemish in the midst of a crooked and twisted generation, among whom you shine as lights in the world'.[5]

Here is a surprising thing. During the four hundred years Jacob's descendants spent in Egypt, they did not shift their faith from their forefathers' God of the covenant. Rather it was the Egyptians who changed. About two hundred years after the Hyksos domination ended and this ethnic group had again been subjected to servitude, Egyptologists tell us that a new religious movement started

---

[4] First line of hymn by Mary B. James, *Redemption Songs* (Scottish Bible & Book Society, Glasgow), No. 833.

[5] Philippians 2:15.

in Egypt. The Pharaoh of that time initiated a monotheistic religion, that is, belief in one god. The new god who was worshipped was the sun, but so strong was this religious movement that the royal capital was re-built to accommodate this radical change. Further, so all-absorbing was this new religion that Egyptian power in the middle east began to wane. We are left wondering whether, after the Hebrews escaped from slavery under Moses' leadership, the Egyptians then tried to imitate the belief in one God which the Hebrews practised, a God whose power had been so remarkably demonstrated.[6] Quite apart from that, Scripture records that when the slaves finally departed from Egypt 'a mixed multitude [of Egyptians] also went up with them'.[7] That surely was a significant indication that a faithful, separated life can be an extremely effective testimony to the grace and power of God.

One other point should be noted. Joseph was not ashamed to be associated with his shepherd-brothers, even though their occupation was so despised by the Egyptians. There he was, married into the Egyptian aristocracy, ruler of the entire land, all bowing the knee before him; yet he takes this momentous step of embracing, welcoming and letting it be publicly known that he comes from the very lowest class in ancient society. We will never know what was said about him behind closed doors by the proud nobles and the upper classes. But for us today does Joseph not remind us of our Lord who is not ashamed to call us his brothers and sisters? Indeed, we read that Christ has so identified with his people—

[6] Amenhotep IV (1352-36 B.C.) destroyed the temple of his parents' god and developed further a monotheistic strain which had existed for some time in Egypt. For him, the essential nature of the godhead consisted in 'the force of all life' with its centre in the sun. He removed his capital from Thebes to the new city of Akhet-Aton. The famous 'hymn to the sun', which gives expression to this new belief, contains themes and turns of phrase similar to those found in Psalm 104. See *New Atlas of the Bible* (Collins, London, 1969), p. 48; also website on Amenhotep IV, http://interoz.com/egypt/18dyn10.htm

[7] Exodus 12:38.

sinners saved by grace, former strangers and enemies of God—that he even sings our praise in the midst of the congregation, and he points to us, saying, 'Behold, I and the children God has given me.'[8]

Here, therefore, is one of the ways in which Joseph typifies our Lord and Saviour. There is a spiritual sense in which we belong to that group of nomads, shepherds and cowherds, the lowest of the low in the world's estimation. And as we confess that 'we have become, and still are, the scum of the world, the refuse of all things',[9] Joseph foreshadows Christ in that he was not ashamed to own his brothers and sisters before the whole world.

Jacob's Testimony before Pharaoh

In my years of ministry I have made literally thousands of visits, many of which have been to frail old people. Sitting chatting to some of the elderly can occasionally be an unhappy experience; especially when they tell some of the saddest of stories. Then the pain of their lives can be read in their faces. On the other hand I have visited many old folk who were absolute saints. I recall one blind old lady who was not merely housebound but also confined to her bed; visiting her put fire into my bones and I always left both humbled and elated (forgive the deliberate oxymoron!).

First, notice Pharaoh's question to Jacob as Joseph presented his father to the potentate of the great Egyptian empire: *How many are the days of the years of your life?*

We are all aware that there tends to be a kind of 'magic' number with regard to our age. For many decades we prefer to keep our age a secret; indeed, it is considered to be rather rude to ask a lady how old she is. But after we pass that 'magic' number, our age becomes almost like a university doctorate. 'I'm eighty-seven', she says with a smile touched with a little pride, and of course the usual answer

---

[8] Hebrews 2:11-13.
[9] 1 Corinthians 4:13.

is, 'I can't believe it—you look about seventy-five.' I have always tried to be honest and I confess I have occasionally seen disappointment in someone's face when they have told me their age and my look has betrayed that I already guessed it and even thought they were ten years older than that! I recall one unfortunate *faux pas* when after a service I had conducted I spoke to a man who was wearing the university tie of my own alma mater: I made the serious blunder of saying that he would have graduated well before I had done, only to discover he was about eight years younger than myself; he was most offended by my obvious implication that he looked much older than me!

The sight of this aged man standing with his snowy-white hair, his weather-beaten face, his slow steps, his bowed shoulders, all of which spoke of a great age, caused Pharaoh to ask, 'How many are the days of the years of your life?' I suspect the question was put with some reverence and gentleness. Clearly, Pharaoh was impressed by the old man's antiquity and dignity. Advanced years are still regarded in the east today with immense respect.

For believers there is a much more penetrating estimate of age than mere years of 365 days. It is not for one moment that I am suggesting any lack of respect for old age. Not at all: 'You shall stand up before the grey head and honour the face of an old man, and you shall fear your God: I am the LORD.'[10] These words from Leviticus clearly mean that reverence for God, 'the Ancient of Days',[11] will lead to honour for the elderly, and that is something our godless society in the west is increasingly losing.

The truth is that too many professing Christians have spent much of their lives submerged in the froth of selfishness and indulgence. A former generation sought to live sacrificially, but many of our present generation of believers revel in eating out in the very

[10] Leviticus 19:32.
[11] Daniel 7:9, 22.

best restaurants, regardless of the expense; they spend four or five times more money on their holidays than they give to the work of God; they have enough clothes in their wardrobes to last several lifetimes. If John the Baptist were living today he would be saying to them, 'Those who have two outfits or two suits, give one of them to someone who has none.' Far too many of the Lord's people live ninety percent of their lives for themselves and only ten percent for God. So the 'years' they have lived are only a few lines in the record containing the days of their lives, only a brief paragraph here and there in the lengthy book recording their deeds.

The huge scrap yards, which are in effect car cemeteries, have giant crushers. When a large, flashy limousine is fed into that massive crusher, out comes a relatively small cube of metal ready for the smelting furnace where it will be recycled. I wonder what will happen to some of us whose years appear to have been very impressive with much achievement? When those days and months and decades are fed into the fires of divine judgment, how much will emerge unscathed so that it will last for all eternity? The wood, hay and stubble will all be reduced to ashes; only the gold and silver and precious stones will endure.[12]

Harold Hughes was born in 1922 in Iowa; he served in the United States army in the North Africa campaign during the Second World War. Arraigned before a court martial for assaulting an officer he was punished by being sent to serve in Sicily where the judge expected him to be killed on the frontline. But he became ill and was unable to take part in the Anzio assault, when the landing craft he should have been in was blown up by an enemy shell and all the occupants, including Private Walter Thomsen, his replacement, were killed.

Back home after the war he became a dropout from college and soon had a jail record. In 1946, when he was only twenty-four years

---

[12] 1 Corinthians 3:10-15.

old, his young wife filed an order for him to appear before the Ida County Sanity Commission to have him declared insane on account of his chronic alcoholism. At length when he was thirty-five years old he resolved to take his life. He climbed into the bath with a gun to blow his head off (doing it in the bath, in his own words, would be 'less messy for those who would have to clean up'). But before he committed the deed he thought he should first try at least to make his peace with God and so there in the bath he knelt and asked God's forgiveness. In that moment, the Holy Spirit came upon him and he was totally transformed.

By the time he was forty, Hughes had been elected governor of Iowa where he served for the next six years. He was then elected as Senator where he served for a further six years. He was the one who exposed Richard Nixon's illegal wire-tapping of his political opponents. He retired from the Senate in order to give himself full-time to Christian service, particularly to working with alcoholics and drug-addicts. His autobiography, *A Man from Ida Grove: A Senator's Personal Story*, tells of his wasted years and then of his opportunities to serve Christ. But my point is this: his first thirty-five years were squandered, whereas his remaining thirty years were spent in honouring Christ in all that he did and was. Today Harold Hughes is still revered by Democrats in the State of Iowa.

Very few Christians have the squandered years of Harold Hughes; but think of all he achieved for his Lord in just half of his lifetime. One half of his life totally wasted, the second half invested effectively in God's service. When Hughes became Governor of Iowa, he asked if he could see all those serving life-sentences in the state prison. There he met one aged man who had been inside for forty years. When Hughes asked him if he would like his freedom, the old man broke down and wept. Alas, he died before that pardon was processed; another wasted life. Amy Carmichael wrote these words:

Give me the love that leads the way,
The faith that nothing can dismay,
The hope no disappointments tire,
The passion that will burn like fire.
Let me not sink to be a clod:
Make me thy fuel, Flame of God.[13]

So how are we using our years? What is our true age, not in terms of days, weeks and months, but in terms of the time we have invested in our Lord's service? Like gold dust being blown away in the breeze so the wind of time passes over our lives.

Second, notice Jacob's answer to Pharaoh's question. *The days of the years of my sojourning are 130 years. Few and evil have been the days of my life, and they have not attained to the days of the years of the life of my fathers in the days of their sojourning.*

The principal rule of understanding the Bible is to interpret Scripture by Scripture. Our New Testament literally grows out of the Old Testament, gathering, as it does, from these inspired accounts of the patriarchs a whole body of teaching on the Christian life. That is why we should take note of a vital word repeated twice in Jacob's reply—*sojourning*. (The AV, NKJ and NIV translate it 'pilgrimage' while the RSV and ESV translate it 'sojourning'.) The word refers to Jacob's nomadic lifestyle, for in this world he had no continuing city but looked and waited for the heavenly city whose designer and builder is God. And so we have the seed of the New Testament teaching that believers are exiles here on earth, waiting for the return of the Lord to bring us into our eternal home.

When writing of these great men of the book of Genesis the author of Hebrews says:

[13] Amy Carmichael, *Toward Jerusalem,* 'Make me thy fuel', verse 3 (London, SPCK, reprint 1953), p. 94.

These all died in faith, not having received the things promised, but having seen them and greeted them from afar, and having acknowledged that they were strangers and exiles on the earth. For people who speak thus make it clear that they are seeking a homeland. If they had been thinking of that land from which they had gone out, they would have had opportunity to return. But as it is, they desire a better country, that is, a heavenly one. Therefore God is not ashamed to be called their God, for he has prepared for them a city.[14]

This is a cardinal truth believers must never forget, for when we do neglect it we become focused on earth as if we really did belong here. The danger is that we then live as if we do belong here, and are not pilgrims at all, on our way to heaven. Robert Leighton, at one time Episcopal Bishop of Dunblane Cathedral, wrote in his commentary on 1 Peter 1:1, 'to those who are elect exiles', that the Christian in this world is like a traveller who stops off at a comfortable wayside inn; he enjoys the log fire, the good meal set before him, the comfortable bedroom and the hospitality of the innkeeper. But he does not fix his heart on that wayside inn, for he knows that the next day he must depart and continue his journey.

Few and evil have been the days of my life, and they have not attained to the days of the years of the life of my fathers. The word 'evil' in AV, NKJV, RSV, ESV, the NIV translates as 'difficult', the NRSV as 'hard'; I prefer Calvin's understanding of 'evil' here as meaning 'labours and troubles'. Recall how Jacob had fled from his home after he had deceived his father and cheated his brother; also how he had worked like a slave for his uncle Laban—fourteen years with no payment other than the problem of two sisters as wives who quarrelled bitterly with each other. Then there was Laban's constant cheating of him, in spite of his faithful, costly service for

---

[14] Hebrews 11:13-16.

him. Remember too Jacob's terror at the approach of Esau and the way he again deceived him and broke his word that he would meet up with him again. And what of the shame that came on his sons through their massacre of all the men of Shechem? Nor must we forget how Jacob grieved for more than twenty years over the assumed death of his beloved Joseph. And what of the insult to his person the incest of his eldest son, Reuben, had been, to say nothing of his son Judah's disgraceful conduct towards his daughter-in-law, Tamar! His life had indeed experienced much 'evil', many troubles and hardships. Jacob had never had his sorrows to seek, as we say.

The pilgrim way for this man had been up the steep mountain of difficulties and down into the dark valley of humiliation; many had been his 'labours and troubles'. Yet was that all he had known and experienced? Esau had had his 'wine, women and song', as the saying goes, but had his been a better life? No, not for one moment! As Joseph presented his father to the king, in the normal nature of things it was Jacob who should have bowed before Pharaoh! But see how aged Israel lifts his hands and blesses Pharaoh, one of the most powerful monarchs in the world at that time; see too how Pharaoh bows his head to receive and accept the blessing. Who is it who blesses another? Surely the greater blesses the lesser: 'It is beyond dispute that the inferior is blessed by the superior.'[15]

Pharaoh was a royal person in the eyes of the world; Jacob was a royal person in the eyes of God: 'Your name shall no longer be called Jacob, but Israel, for you have striven with God and with men, and have prevailed.'[16] As we remarked in the previous chapter he still had some years left to him and from his lips would flow some of the most amazing prophecies in the Christian Scriptures. Be that as it may, I suspect that the most beautiful aspect of this

[15] Hebrews 7:7.
[16] Genesis 32:28.

meeting between Israel and Pharaoh was the way in which the patriarch's godliness and spirituality were so unaffected: they were so natural and gentle. I think too that the only person present who was unaware of the grace shining forth from him was the old man himself. I doubt if it ever occurred to him that this was truly a momentous meeting or that it was utterly bizarre that he, an 'abominable shepherd', should presume to bless a king. But Jacob gave not a second's thought to that as he bestowed the blessing which was within his power to give. The holiness of his character could not be concealed. How could this be?

Third, consider the explanation of Israel's remarkable poise and spirituality, evident even as he engaged in self-depreciation. Two factors need to be noted.

1. *Jacob had had life-changing encounters with God.* It had all begun in a barren rocky place where the only pillow he could find had been a boulder. There in the loneliness of his flight from Esau, in the solitude of the night and in the consciousness that he had acted deceitfully towards his father and brother, God had met with him. His dream of the angels ascending and descending a ladder between heaven and earth, with the Lord standing above it, had been his first (recorded) encounter with God.[17] A new factor had come into his life from that night on. Doubtless he had heard of God from his father and had been present when Isaac had called on the name of the Lord. But now this same Lord had spoken to him, and confirmed to him the covenant first made with his grandfather Abraham.

Throughout Scripture and the subsequent history of the church countless numbers of men and women have encountered God as Jacob did. For some it has been a clear voice calling their name in the night, a call for them alone and not for others near them,

---

[17] Genesis 28:10-17.

just as Eli had heard nothing when Samuel's name was spoken.[18] For others it has been like the voice of Jesus sounding across the raging waves of the storm on Galilee, 'Take heart; it is I. Do not be afraid'.[19] For a few it has been like that blinding light and shining presence that came to Saul of Tarsus, throwing him to the ground.[20]

Down the long years God had continued to intervene and intrude into Jacob's life. How could any person remain the same when God perseveres with them as he did with this man?

2. *There was also Jacob's suffering.* His cheating, sly nature has become legendary; we all know about this despicable side to his character. But God was not going to permit him to remain the same crafty, calculating man, so he brought suffering into Jacob's life. The deceiver was himself deceived—many times over. Laban deceived him over his marriage; how that must have cut painfully into his soul. Then he was deceived over the death of Joseph; what anguish that brought to him for many years. But God's chastening of him was not, 'Serves you right! Now you know what it's like to suffer!' For whom the Lord loves he disciplines.[21] The Lord was preparing and training him for his coronation as a prince of God.

We have already noticed how, when his sons broke the news to him of Joseph's exalted position as lord of all Egypt, though at first he was stunned and unable to believe their story, his spirit revived. Fresh life came into his body and soul, as there was born from the ashes of his sorrows a living hope, grounded in his God.

If for you and me the cross stood alone and isolated, then we would have no good news; there would be no gospel. But near the cross is the empty tomb, the stone having been rolled away; he who died is risen. Likewise any cross we are given to carry and any

---

[18] 1 Samuel 3:1-14.
[19] Mark 6:50.
[20] Acts 9:4-7.
[21] Proverbs 3:11-12; Hebrews 12:6; cf. Psalm 94:12.

sorrows sent by God into our lives are never complete until there is also a resurrection or restoration that brings new life in altogether new radiance.

So how do you see yourself? As a poor slave, ill-clad, ill-fed, faint and ready to die? Or are you among those who once were slaves but are now redeemed; not only redeemed, but born into a royal family, bearing on their souls the hallmarks of our destiny? Have we known that encounter with God, and the life of communion with him that flows from it, together with the discipline of suffering that issues in resurrection life?

Jacob Blessed Pharaoh

Twice we are told, *And Jacob blessed Pharaoh* (verses 7, 10). You might wonder how this godly old man could bless a pagan king. Is that biblical? Yes it is. Do you recall Jeremiah's letter to the exiles in Babylon? He wrote to them: 'Seek the welfare of the city where I have sent you into exile, and pray to the Lord on its behalf, for in its welfare you will find your welfare.'[22] Paul gives us much the same instruction: 'First of all, then, I urge that supplications, prayers, intercessions, and thanksgivings be made for all people, for kings and all who are in high positions, that we may lead a peaceful and quiet life, godly and dignified in every way. This is good, and it is pleasing in the sight of God our Saviour, who desires all people to be saved and to come to the knowledge of the truth.'[23]

These Scriptures, along with Jacob's blessing of Pharaoh, are very different to that narrow Hyper-Calvinism which restricts the blessing of God to a small, select group of the elect. Indeed, some so emphasize predestination that they refuse to offer the grace of God indiscriminately to others in case any who are not elect hear it and respond! What a perversion of the Bible's teaching. As Paul

[22] Jeremiah 29:7.
[23] 1 Timothy 2:1-14.

said in his address in the Areopagus in Athens, 'God . . . commands all people everywhere to repent'.[24]

So Jacob was quite right to call upon God to bless this pagan ruler, for in the welfare of Egypt lay the welfare of the people of God. He is the God whose compassion is over all his works and extends to all he has made.[25] Does Christ himself not even command us to pray for those who hate and persecute us 'so that we may be sons of our Father who is in heaven. For he makes his sun rise on the evil and on the good, and sends rain on the just and on the unjust.'[26] In blessing Pharaoh Jacob demonstrated that he was a true child of his heavenly Father!

But take this from a different angle. How many there are in this world who need someone to come alongside them with the spiritual power to bless and pray for them. Not that you or I have anything of our own to impart, but that we may pass on to others that which we ourselves have received as an unmerited gift—the blessing of God which makes rich and adds no sorrow with it. In my earlier pastoral work members of our congregation have conducted visitations from door to door asking if people had any requests for prayer; were there any serious problems or domestic situations or personal anxieties for which we could pray and ask the hand of God to intervene? (That was by no means to neglect the need for sinners to repent and seek the Saviour's forgiveness.) Do too many Christians today fail to grasp the opportunities that are right there on their very doorsteps? Although many invariably

---

[24] Acts 17:30.

[25] Commenting on Psalm 145:9, 'The Lord is good to all, and his mercy is over all that he had made', Calvin writes: 'God "makes his sun rise on the evil and on the good" (*Matt.* 5:45). Men's depravity does not prevent him showering his benefits upon them, even though they are not aware of it. However, only believers enjoy a reconciled God (*Psa.* 34: 5, 8); nevertheless, his mercy is over even a fallen world.' *Commentary on Psalms, Abridged* (Edinburgh, Banner of Truth Trust, 2009), p. 646.

[26] Matthew 5:45.

treat believers with contempt, some will respond; they will ask for prayer, for we will come across those in whose lives God has already been at work.

Think of Samuel's words to disobedient backslidden Israel: 'As for me, far be it from me that I should sin against the Lord by ceasing to pray for you.'[27] What does that say about our lethargy and coldness of heart in the prayer meeting? What does it say about those voices that are silent and the spirits that are heavy and drowsy or those whose thoughts are far away during our prayer times? Dare we say that it would have been failure on Jacob's part not to have invoked the blessing of God on Pharaoh? Certainly we can say that it is sin against the Lord when you and I fail to pray for the town in which we live and for men and women whose hearts are hard. I do not know of a single instance of revival that has come without there having been one or two lonely, faithful souls crying out to God for his blessing—some of them for years. For the prayers of God's people are his divine decrees beginning to work.

---

[27] 1 Samuel 12:23.

CHAPTER ELEVEN

Joseph's Administration—Genesis 47:13-26

WE had an old clock at home which had been sitting on a side-board for about fifteen years. But it was only an ornament, because apparently it was broken. It had belonged to my wife's mother, and so for sentimental reasons we never threw it out. Then our daughter asked if she could have it. She thought it would suit her little house and fit in well. So one afternoon I decided to try and repair it. Years before a friend who was an expert on clocks had given me a couple of hints about trouble-shooting with the movement of an old clock. I remembered what he had said, and began by detaching the movement from the case. I had never looked at a clock movement in my life before. So I was interested to inspect this one. It was French, and the movement had a series of wheels driven by the main spring. I soon saw how it functioned. The main spring was encased in a brass cylinder, from which the various cogs were driven, passing through a kind of restraining, or balancing mechanism. This was the delicate part of the movement that needed attention to get the clock to go. I admired the ingenuity of clockmakers and their skill. Having made a slight adjustment, I put the clock together again and—believe it or not—I had it going, and it has been going ever since.

Clocks are mechanistic. They can be cleaned, oiled and set right, and will do exactly what they are designed to do. But people are very different. If we try and treat a person as if he or she is just a cog in a movement, we are in big trouble. We cannot do that with people because the skill needed to guide forward someone's destiny, and ultimately human history, is infinitely greater than the skill of the clockmaker.

As we read the account of Joseph's administration in Egypt during the seven years of famine we might ask, 'Why is this aspect of Joseph's work in the Egyptian famine recorded for us in the Bible?' As we attempt to answer that question we must remember that Joseph and the Egyptians were real people, living in our same fallen world with its pain, demands, opportunities and temptations. In this world often the unexpected happens and human plans go astray. Meanwhile each minute ticks on with inexorable certainty. And with each hour, day, week and year, the secret purposes of God move relentlessly forward. Nothing goes wrong with God's plans. The mysterious 'clock' of his inscrutable working is always exactly on time—to the second! Each stage of the divine will is achieved with faultless precision. I admired the movement of a little French clock. But oh! the movement of God's purposes, involving as it does unpredictable and fickle humanity, is far more amazing, so amazing that when we catch the smallest glimpse of that silent, hidden movement, we are drawn to marvel and adore so great a God.

The Administration of Egypt Needed a Strong Character

Here was a man, Joseph, who belonged to a peculiar race. His great-grandfather, Abraham, had resolutely turned his back on all the fashions and fads, idolatry and iniquity of his generation. He had gone into the Judean wilderness to live a separate life. Joseph's grandfather, Isaac, had also been true to that strict, upright way of life. So had his father Jacob. Joseph too, unlike ten of his brothers, early on in his teens had determined that he also would live as Abraham, Isaac and his father had lived; their God required honesty, purity and truth.

Not for one moment am I suggesting that Joseph was perfect. Nevertheless, his story makes it quite plain that he lived a godly life. Sex, drink, honesty, truthfulness, work—in these areas of living he could not be faulted. Even though he was put on the rack, so to speak, and spiritually tortured by the temptations that came to him, he clung to God and God kept him pure. We have seen how the biblical account records his remarkable story. Why then does Scripture give such a clear picture of his righteous living? It is to let us see the kind of a person who would remain faithful and unsullied by the responsibilities of power, along with the great wealth and influence lavished on him. In the account of his years of hard work administrating the nation's resources we are given an insight into the character he is shown to have had, and how he handled a nation's life alongside his own privileges and authority. Without the full story of his slavery and imprisonment, his treatment by his brothers and then his treatment of them years later, we could not fully understand the lessons of his extraordinary life.

When I was in my twenties and thirties, I had a little motto on my desk, *'As now, so then.'* I believed that the kind of people we are when we grow older depends on the kind of people we are when we are young: 'As now, so then.' We look at people with plenty of this world's goods and we may think how lucky they are and how easy life must be for them—but how hard it is for us! If we had their money and their job, we would be so happy; such thinking is wrong and twisted. It is not like that at all. A few years ago a survey was done of thirty people who had won the football pools and been landed with a million pounds or more. Out of the thirty, twenty-eight told how their pools wins had wrecked their lives, and they cursed the day the news of their supposed good fortune had been broken to them. Their homes had been ruined, their marriages broken and their lives made unbelievably bitter. Twenty-eight out of thirty longed to turn the clock back to the days when life was normal, and they had had to work for their living. The truth is that wealth is a great responsibility and it is far easier to be relatively poor than to be fabulously wealthy.

Now I suspect that most readers do not believe that. You may be among those who think that you would be the exception, you would be one of the five percent who could handle being a multi- millionaire. Statistically the vast majority who think like that are quite wrong. We had a family friend whose father owned a huge national company whose products were (and still are) on the shelves of every grocery store and supermarket. This young man was a committed Christian and he used to say that, when his father passed on, he intended giving away to the Lord's work half of his inherited wealth. In time his father died and left his fortune to him. My own father had the effrontery to ask him about his oft repeated resolve of shedding much of his inheritance by giving it to God's work. This is what he said in reply: 'I didn't have the money when I said that.' Now that the wealth was in his hands he was not going to let go of it!

What is significant about the account of Joseph is that he undoubtedly was one of the five percent who could steward wisely and well his unlimited wealth. Yes, he had a Rolls-Royce chariot, chauffeur driven; he had probably even entered his chariot in the Egyptian Grand Prix and carried off the championship. Yes, he had a villa on the shores of the Mediterranean. And he had a retinue of servants who maintained his lovely home. Nevertheless, he remained uncorrupted and incorruptible. How did he manage? *As now, so then.'* He had learned discipline and holy living in those days when he was a kitchen boy. When the other slaves had been carrying on behind their supervisor's back, and stealing from the wine cellars in Potiphar's house, Joseph had refused to join in. When they had been experimenting with sex, Joseph had kept himself chaste. When they had tried to get away with sloppy work, Joseph had done his work with meticulous care. He had not been ashamed to admit that he belonged to a peculiar family who would be despised by the majority of the population. He had the courage and determination to keep himself clean from deceit, theft and dishonesty. That is precisely why he had been promoted again and again until he was in complete charge of his master's house and estate. Nevertheless, though he was still a slave, the temptations had come to him. Although he had not only lost his job on account of his integrity, and had been thrown into prison and abandoned with no one to plead his innocence, he had remained steadfast, faithful to his God. Now, as the money poured in for the corn, flour and dried fruit, he gave the same meticulous account of every coin paid, just as he had always done. Not a groat was missing. Not a figure was out of place in the audited accounts. Because Pharaoh knew he could still trust him, Joseph's power and influence continued to grow until he became not merely a national figure, but an international celebrity.

'As now, so then.' If we are weak Christians now, we will be weak Christians then. If we are easily swayed now, we will be easily swayed then. If we are soon deflected from obedience to God now, we will be soon deflected from obedience to God then. If we are weakly ensnared into ungodliness now, we will be weakly ensnared into ungodliness then. Those readers who are still young, how do you spend your money? Largely on yourself, or is a biblical proportion given to the Lord's work? In other words, how spiritual are you in stewarding the little you have now? How honest are you with your parents and family? Do you deceive them now? Do you think that you will be honest in five or ten years' time if you are a liar now? Are you as weak as water, afraid to take your stand as a follower of Christ Jesus now? Then what sort of slob will you grow to be when you leave the influence of your parental home? The corruption, temptation and exposure to moral pollution does not get less as we grow older. It increases. And if we do not resolve to stand firm and true to Christ today, we will end up compromising with his enemies tomorrow.

Essential to the secret purposes of God and the silent movement of his will are men and women who are like Jesus Christ, as Joseph was like his Lord; his was a godly character! And compared to Joseph, being faithful for us is much easier, for he had no fellowship, no young adults group in a nearby church, nor—as far as we know—even a single godly friend. He was completely alone, far, far from home. When others were out abusing their bodies, he was left alone. When others were pilfering, he stood alone. When others practised deceit, he alone remained trustworthy.

What pathetic, spineless creatures some of us are, almost ready for the local authority's civic amenity site already;[1] nor have we even begun to face the real heat of battle 'against the cosmic powers of this present darkness, against the spiritual forces of evil in the heavenly places', in short, 'against the schemes of the devil'.[2] Some ought to be hiding their faces in shame, instead of masquerading

---

[1] My reference is to *Gehenna*, in NT times a dump for waste matter. The Gk word *Gehenna*, usually translated 'hell', originally was used of the Valley of Hinnom (*Neh.* 11:30); it was near the entrance into Jerusalem by the Potsherd Gate (*Jer.* 19:2). 'Under Ahaz, Manasseh and Amon it was made the scene of the cruel rites of heathen worship, idolatrous Jews passing their children through the fire there to Molech (*Jer.* 7:31) . . . after its pollution it became a place of horror to the Jews, and is said to have been made a receptacle for bones, the bodies of beasts and criminals, refuse and all unclean things . . . fires said to have been kept burning in it to consume the foul and corrupt objects that were thrown into it, made it a natural and unmistakable symbol of dire evil, torment, wasting penalty, absolute ruin. So it came to designate the place of future punishment.' Hastings, Article on 'Hell', Vol. 2, p. 344b.

[2] Ephesians 6:11-12.

as Christians, when the truth is they are spineless lay-abouts, with feet of clay. Such people have not yet surrendered themselves— mind, body and soul—to God for him to begin his work of changing them into men and women of integrity, righteousness and holiness.

My point from this passage in Genesis 47 is that the administration of Egypt needed strong character. Any service for Christ, be it ever so humble and menial, also needs strong character, the kind of strength which our blessed Lord had during his earthly ministry. For Joseph constantly points us to Jesus Christ.

The Administration Carried with It Enormous Influence

Many scholars have debated the ethics of Joseph's handling of all the corn, flour and dried fruit stored in those great warehouses that he had built during the seven years of good harvests. Let us remind ourselves of what he did.

To begin with, as the harvests failed and the stored supplies were sold, he transferred little by little virtually all the nation's money into the royal exchequer. Next he transferred from private ownership (what would some of our contemporary politicians say about this?) all the livestock in the land into state ownership—cattle, flocks, horses. He then he took over all the land in exchange for food. Finally, the people sold themselves into servitude.

As I have just commented, the ethics of all these policies has been debated at length. But let me attempt to summarize what all this adds up to. I offer four considerations arising from Joseph's decisions.

First, the implications of the people selling all their land, livestock and themselves to Pharaoh were actually very simple: they now had to pay income tax to Pharaoh. That was all; *a fifth* (verse

24) is simply a tax of twenty percent across the board.[3] Until this time, monarchs gained their income from their own lands, which were worked by slaves. But now a regular revenue into the state exchequer was secured. If we are inclined to ask if Joseph's fixing of the rate of tax at twenty percent was high, bear this in mind: in the time of the Maccabees, the Jews had to pay to the Syrians thirty-three percent of the value of their corn and fifty percent of the value of their fruit; in Persia, the peasants paid seventy-five percent; in other Arab lands, fifty percent. So Joseph's twenty percent rate of tax was actually very moderate and even accords with the present lowest rate of tax in the United Kingdom today.

The *second* effect of Joseph's work was to break the power of the old aristocracy. Egyptologists tell us that there had been a powerful and ruthless aristocracy controlling the nation's wealth and laying heavy burdens on the poor. Joseph's policies completely swept away this privileged class, and there ensued a wholesale restructuring of society. It was a bloodless revolution which over seven years created a totally new formation in Egyptian society. 'Old school tie' influence, as we say, vanished and every person stood shoulder to shoulder.

The *third* effect was to bring stability to the monarchy. If we are right in thinking that the Pharaohs of this time were from the occupying Hyksos tribe, theirs would have been a precarious power-base. We have already suggested that a Hyksos Pharaoh would have been more likely than an indigenous Egyptian monarch to promote Joseph, a former slave, to the position of Prime Minister. But this kind of 'foreign' dynasty would have been very susceptible to overthrow by a *coup d'état* (as ultimately happened). Genesis 47:21 reads in the ESV and NIV, *As for the people, he made servants of them from one end of Egypt to the other*. But this

---

[3] See article on 'Joseph' by K. A. Kitchen, *IBD*, Part 2, p. 815a; also, Keil-Delitzsch, p. 379-80.

translation follows the Septuagint; although that may well be true, it is not the reading of the Hebrew text. The Hebrew says (as the marginal notes in both ESV and NIV indicate, and as both AV and NKJV render it), 'And as for the people, he moved them into the cities, from one end of the borders of Egypt to the other end.' I prefer the Hebrew reading and therefore understand the text to be saying that, in order to make accessible the widely scattered supplies of stored food, Joseph arranged for whole areas to be repopulated, and certain less well-served areas to have their populations reduced. It would appear that the reason for this wholesale resettlement was most probably to make the supply of food easier; but it also brought a political stability to the Hyksos dynasty, which consequently for several generations remained secure and strong. We gather then that, as the years of famine continued, Joseph was confronted by what could have been a national disaster; certainly it was a nation-wide emergency which called for wise and firm action to keep the population alive and well. Joseph's policy averted this potential widespread chaos.

Fourth, the final effect of Joseph's policies was to give Egypt a leading role on the international scene, for the nations around Egypt also came to buy food; that has been referred to earlier in the narrative. The seven years of the famine were quite extraordinary and remarkable in their consequences, for the record gives no indication whatsoever that the people were in any way resentful of the enormous changes that took place in the whole structure of their society, economy and foreign policy. On the contrary, they were profoundly grateful to Joseph who was seen as the saviour of the nation and whose wise planning had improved their lot and brought them more secure and fuller lives

The Administration Furthered God's Secret Purposes for His People

If we can say it reverently, God went to enormous 'trouble' with Joseph. Joseph might not have thought so at the time when he was a slave and then in prison, but later he understood it all so clearly: patiently and with the consummate skill of the divine psychologist, God had prepared him for the great weight of responsibility that now lay on his shoulders. I might add that, though you and I seldom realize it at the time, God goes to a great deal of time and 'trouble' with all of us. Some of us kick against what he is doing; at times we try to throw off his loving hand from our shoulder and push him from us; we even try to run away from him. What fools we can be! God's plans for us are for our good, happiness and fulfilment.

Having prepared his man, having put him in place as ruler of a great empire, giving him full freedom to use his native intelligence, energy and creativity to do the phenomenal work we have been studying—yes, and also to enjoy the good things of life lavished on him by a grateful king—we see God's plan silently unfolding. Joseph himself saw just a little of it. But, like the iceberg, the greater part of what God was concerned to do lay concealed beneath the surface. I mention just two points to elucidate this.

First, there was the need to preserve this little tribe whom God had chosen to be the foundation of his church in the world, and to whom he would reveal and entrust the oracles of his truth. Joseph's great-grandfather Abraham, together with Isaac and Jacob, were all part of that founding of the church. It was from their stock that the Saviour would be born. They, however, had been called to a little strip of fertile land called Canaan, already inhabited by various tribes. Life there was not easy because at that time there was not much room for them to expand. Abraham had been obliged to live in rocky barren areas; Isaac had moved from place to place, often in trouble with the inhabitants of the land; Jacob had faced similar problems. So God had deliberately withdrawn them from Canaan, and settled them in a fertile area that was allocated specially to them. There they were to multiply and grow strong. There they would be provided for and preserved. There they would prosper until they became a substantial race, ready for the task of possessing the land promised to them.

Second, what of the various ethnic groups already in Canaan? We have already been told of God's long-distance purposes for Canaan. In Genesis 15:12-16 God had spoken to Abraham in a vision and told him that his descendants would be strangers in a country not their own. There they would become slaves and be ill-treated. But ultimately they would return to Canaan. Then we get this awesome, foreboding statement: 'And they shall come back here in the fourth generation, for the iniquity of the Amorites is not yet complete' (NIV 'the sin of the Amorites has not yet reached its full measure'). In other words, God had withdrawn Jacob and his family from Canaan for four generations, to give the people of the land full and just time to mend their ways, to change, to turn from evil.

God's judgment of nations is never hasty. Before his hand falls in judgment he will allow years, even a century and more, for a wicked nation to repent. Thus the depraved peoples of Canaan were being given the chance to repent. Their consciences knew what they were doing was wrong, just as those engaged today in child abuse, not only in the United Kingdom but on the continent and in other countries, know perfectly well what they are doing is both evil and perversely wicked; secular society knows that. Beneath all the paedophiles' and perverts' excuses and specious arguments there is a full awareness of sin, yet there is also a hatred of God and a rebellion against his holiness; believers recognize this is so. Thus, while the population of Israel was quietly growing, the clouds of judgment on the Canaanites were slowly gathering.

At length the exodus from Egypt would take place, the Red Sea would be crossed and the land re-entered and purged of wickedness. The deeper, underlying divine purpose was that the church should be established, and a place prepared for Almighty God to bow the heavens and in the Person of his Son gather himself as a new-born baby into that animals' feeding trough that he might reveal his merciful lowliness, his mighty meekness and his unfathomable grace.

What matters most to Christ's people in our day and generation? I suggest something that ought to be right at the very top of our priorities—the will and purpose of God for our lives. It is of paramount importance that we should reflect upon and enquire of Christ, 'Lord, what are you doing in my life? Lord, what do you want me to do?' Because the movement of his mysterious purposes is both amazing and beautiful. It is infinitely more intricate, delicate and wonderful than my little nineteenth-century French clock. For the wheels and the balancing mechanism of the divine will relate in perfect synchronism with the spring and summer, autumn and winter of each of our lives. God's will is concerned with our weekend leisure, our evenings out with friends, as well as with our worship on Sundays. If you are still at school, his will is concerned with your prep and homework assignments; if you still live at home, it has to do with your relationship with your parents; if you have your own home, it is to do with your families and children and the work to which you are called. And all these aspects of living must be integrated with divine precision to God's people and their witness and influence throughout your town or city—and the influence of the church in the wider world. (How much more could be added about that, both negatively and positively!)

In the final analysis Joseph reflects and foreshadows the Lord Jesus Christ. He was sold for twenty pieces of silver while Jesus was sold for thirty. He was betrayed by those who ought to have been his friends; Jesus was betrayed by one of his own disciples and rejected by his own people. Joseph was a slave who suffered; our Lord took upon himself the form of a suffering servant. Joseph was then brought up out of prison as the Lord was brought forth from the very grave. Joseph was finally exalted and given a name above every other name in the whole land; before him every knee had to bow, not least those who had betrayed him, until at last the people said, *You have saved our lives; may it please my lord, we will be servants to Pharaoh.* The people of the land had so learned to love Joseph because of all he had done for them, that they yielded to him gladly, selling themselves into life-long servitude and handing over to him all they possessed. And so Joseph foreshadowed him who has been given a name above every name that at the name of Jesus every knee should bow and every tongue confess him Lord.[4]

So how much do we love our exalted Lord and Master who has redeemed us and saved our lives? If we truly love him, gladly will we submit to him. If we have surrendered ourselves unreservedly to him, we will long to be gathered up into his mighty purposes of love. The Apostle Paul wrote, 'I appeal to you therefore, brothers and sisters, by the mercies of God, to present your bodies as a living sacrifice, holy and acceptable to God, which is your spiritual worship. Do not be conformed to this world, but be transformed by the renewal of your mind, that by testing you may discern what is the will of God, what is good and acceptable and perfect.'[5]

---

[4] Philippians 2:10-11.
[5] Romans 12:1-2.

CHAPTER TWELVE

Jacob Blesses Ephraim and Manasseh—Genesis 47:29–48:22

I wonder if you have ever paused and thought about verse 5 of that great hymn attributed to Francis of Assisi, 'All creatures of our God and King'? The verse goes like this:

> And thou, most kind and gentle death,
> Waiting to hush our latest breath,
> O praise Him;
> Thou leadest home the child of God,
> And Christ our Lord the way hath trod,
> Alleluia . . .

If you have reached the stage in life of taking a few moments to contemplate your death (sooner or later you most certainly will), and you have considered the inevitable fact that either your body will be interred in the earth or else your ashes be scattered to the four winds, do the words of Francis of Assisi express what you feel about such a prospect? In other words, does your opinion of what happens to you when you die accord with the Bible's teaching rather than that expressed in the hymn? Not many think of death as kind and gentle; after all, it is 'the last enemy'.[1]

---

[1] 1 Corinthians 15:26. 'Death shall reign until the resurrection. Then men shall never more be subject to its power. Then death shall be swallowed up in victory.' Charles Hodge, *First Corinthians, Geneva Series* (Banner of Truth, Sixth Edition, 1959) p. 331.

Chapters 48 and 49 of Genesis are about the death of old Jacob. Undoubtedly they are two of the most noteworthy chapters in the Scriptures. They are quite magnificent. In these two chapters we reach heights of inspiration which find their place among the most awesome prophecies in the whole of the sacred record. Yet the scene is that of a deathbed as an old man faces his imminent departure from this life and the end of his earthly pilgrimage. None of us know how we will die. When our time comes it would be good to pray that the Lord might grant that we pass from this scene of time as full of a sense of God's sovereign purposes as Jacob was.

A Significant Request

The account begins towards the end of chapter 47. Jacob calls Joseph and makes him take a solemn oath as he placed his hand under his father's thigh.[2] *Do not bury me in Egypt, but let me lie with my fathers. Carry me out of Egypt and bury me in their burying place* (47:29). We must ask if this request came from a meaningless superstition or if in fact there was genuine significance in it.

Every schoolboy knows that the Egyptians were very much into burials and preparations for some afterlife in which they believed; they embalmed and mummified the bodies of their dead. More, they had cities built specially for the dead to live in. I have been to Egypt and visited the famous City of the Dead and the Valley of the Kings. Some of the tombs are built of solid stone. When I say 'solid stone', I mean just that. The kings' palaces are not four walls with a space inside where someone could enter, go into and walk about. They are solid right through, because the ancient Egyptians believed that spirits could pass through solid walls, and did not need any empty 'space' to live in.

As well as building a stately city for the dead the ancient Egyptians also constructed great ships in which the dead could sail the

---

[2] An ancient and solemn way of making a binding promise; cf. Genesis 24:2.

uncharted seas that lie beyond the grave. One of these burial ships survives today, and can be seen by visitors to Cairo Museum. And of course school children also know that the pyramids of Giza were built to keep safe the treasures which the Pharaohs were to take with them into the next life. I am told that there are enough stones in one of those pyramids to build a two metre high wall round the whole border of France. Remember too that in the days when the pyramids were built, they had no mechanical diggers or cranes. It was all done by human muscles and hands.

The point I am making is simple and obvious: the Egyptians were into the business of burials in a big way. Therefore we might have expected Jacob to say, 'How fortunate I am that I shall die in Egypt. Better to die here where there are cities for the dead to live in, and boats to take the departed safely to the other side.' A little bit like someone moving from the country to a large prosperous town and saying, 'It's much better for the children here; there are good schools, a well-equipped leisure centre, lots going on. We're glad we've moved here.'

Instead, we find Jacob saying something very different. He asks Joseph to promise most solemnly that, when he dies, his remains will be taken back to Canaan and buried there in the family tomb. Then he gives the reason for this request. *God Almighty appeared to me at Luz in the land of Canaan and blessed me, and said to me, 'Behold, I will make you fruitful and multiply you, and I will make of you a company of peoples, and will give this land to your offspring after you for an everlasting possession'* (48:3-4). Therefore, he must be taken back there to sleep beside his fathers. More, Rachel was buried there, and he tells Joseph, *As for me, when I came from Paddan, to my sorrow Rachel died in Canaan on the way, when there was still some distance to go to Ephrath, and I buried her there on the way to Ephrath (that is, Bethlehem)* (verse 7). His unshakeable conviction is that his sons and their descendents shall share the inheritance of the land (verse 6).

I know that it would be another 1,700 years before the Saviour would be raised from death and so open the door to eternal life. Nevertheless, it is impossible to deny that in some way we may not understand, Jacob saw himself as inheriting, even after his death, the promises God had given him. For him death would not be extinction, but rest or sleep along with his father Isaac and his grandfather Abraham. One day he would meet up again with his beloved Rachel. Christians have a name for that kind of conviction: we call it *faith*. And these two chapters breathe that simple faith. Although Jacob peered into the future, seeing the fulfilment of the promise only dimly because of the mists of time, he unquestionably believed that there was a future beyond the grave.

What was the ground of his faith, the reason why he believed in something far better, still to come? It was God's word, his promise. That is all. *God Almighty appeared to me . . . and blessed me, and said to me . . .* And what God had said was the whole foundation of his life. He lived in the faith of that divine word. No attractions of Egypt's impressive city for the dead, or their fleet of ships to carry him into the next life. No dazzling glitter of this country whose civilization was probably more than one thousand years ahead of poor, impoverished little Canaan, could ever shake or deflect old Jacob's trust in the living God who had spoken to him. He could say with Paul, 'For I know whom I have believed, and I am convinced that he is able to guard until that Day what has been entrusted to me.'[3]

Today, apart from one burial ship which has wonderfully survived by being buried for a few thousand years in the sand, nothing remains of that gloomy fleet in which Jacob's bones might have set sail to nowhere. The stately city of the dead is now little more than a ruin, inhabited by vultures which nest among the tombs, and hyenas and desert foxes which skulk by night among their

[3] 2 Timothy 1:12b.

empty streets; yes, and it is visited by sight-seers like myself. By contrast, for all the conflict of the centuries that left the dust of the holy land stained with blood, Jacob's Canaan remains as the cradle of the Saviour. It was the site of Calvary and the empty tomb of Easter morning; it was the location of the Upper Room where the Lord's Supper was instituted and where the Holy Spirit was poured out upon the church and fell upon the apostles; it was from here that the church of Jesus Christ has spread across the whole world.

In what do we trust as we grow older and death draws ever nearer? We may be fortunate to live in a country with modern hospitals, and—in spite of all the criticism and carping—to have available to us an excellent health service. We are blessed to have up-to-date facilities, skilled practitioners and consultants. But in what do you and I trust? In the spiritual sense, we have no more and no less than Jacob had, for he had the word of God. That is the foundation of our faith too. 'I go to prepare a place for you', said Jesus. 'And if I go and prepare a place for you, I will come again, and take you to myself, that where I am, there you may be also.'[4] We cannot prove to the sceptic that the tomb in which Jesus was laid was empty that first Easter morning, apart from discarded grave clothes. It is still just the word of God that tells us our Lord was raised from death.

True, what for Jacob was very dim in the mists of time,[5] is now far clearer and fuller in outline for us in the bright light of Christ's

[4] John 14:3-4.
[5] Referring to the gospel set forth in the Old Testament through types, symbols and shadows, ultimately fully illuminated in the Person and Work of Christ, B B Warfield wrote, 'The Old Testament may be likened to a chamber richly furnished, but dimly lighted: the introduction of light brings into it nothing that was not in it before; but it brings out into clearer view much of what is in it but was only dimly . . . perceived before.' *Biblical Doctrines*, rev. ed. (Banner of Truth, Edinburgh, 1988), pp. 141-2; quoted by Sinclair B. Ferguson, *The Holy Spirit* (IVP, Downers Grove, Illinois, 1996), p. 29.

revelation. By faith we can see the Saviour's form, the empty cross and the stone rolled away. But we are still left with only the word spoken to us by the Lord. And we have to set that word against all the philosophies, cleverness, arguments and theories of our day, in the same way as Jacob had to set God's word against the sophistication of Egypt in his day. Like him we lay hold on God and cast ourselves on him, *God Almighty* (verse 3), the God whose power is greater far than anything in this world, even when man is at his strongest and most arrogant.

A Special Blessing

We can easily work out the ages of Joseph's two sons. They are called 'boys' in verse 16 in the ESV, and 'lads' in the AV. But by this time they were both over seventeen years old, because they were born before Jacob arrived in Egypt and we are told that Jacob had been seventeen years in Egypt when the time came for him to die.[6] Today they would be considered to be young men, eligible to vote, drive or join the armed services. Now they come with their father who, we must not forget, is the most powerful and wealthy man in the land, second only to the king. Joseph brings them to visit their aged grandfather who is shortly to die. We should notice that as the old patriarch puts his hands on them to bless them, he claims them as his own sons: *Ephraim and Manasseh shall be mine, as Reuben and Simeon are* (verse 5). What was the meaning of that?

I doubt whether teenage lads have changed all that much, if at all, since the seventeenth century before Christ. These two young men had been brought up in a wealthy home with servants and the Egyptian equivalent of several fast cars, the best of everything, clothes, books and the latest gadgets. Their appearance most probably would have been in the Egyptian style, and they may well have been wearing the best Egyptian clothes. They would also

[6] Genesis 47:28.

have been educated in Egyptian schools and were probably ready for entrance to higher education. But they had cousins who were, frankly, the equivalent of local tinkers, who looked after cattle, sheep and goats. In Egypt, only slaves did work like that. The two boys' uncles were also cowherds with tangled beards, dressed in the oddest long clothes. Instead of fast chariots, they had ancient old cattle transporters, and instead of riding on sleek horses, they rode ridiculous little donkeys, their feet trailing on the ground as these bizarre looking animals awkwardly walked along.

The contrast between their father's home, wealth and way of life could not have been more stark and vivid compared to the homes of their uncles, cousins and grandfather. Ephraim's and Manasseh's way of life was aristocratic, for they lived with all the privileges of princes. The rest of their family, no doubt still clinging to their former way of life in Canaan, lived in Bedouin tents. And now here is this old man in his peasant's clothes, with his long hair and even longer beard, claiming these two young men in their smart Egyptian clothes from their sophisticated background as his own sons, part of this shabby family.

Can you imagine the scene? These two teenage lads had to choose between Egypt and Israel, between the rich and cultured on the one hand, and the crude and despised on the other hand. I think for them it may have been a hard choice. But they chose to belong to their grandfather's family, and to turn their backs on the pride and pomp of Egypt. They took their place among the people of God.

I want to suggest that there is a very real sense in which the same choice faces every one of us today. The writer of the Letter to the Hebrews expresses it like this: The carcasses of the sacrificial animals 'are burned outside the camp. So Jesus also suffered outside the gate in order to sanctify the people through his own blood. Therefore let us go to him outside the camp and bear the reproach he endured. For here we have no lasting city, but we seek the city that is to come.'[7]

For those who would follow Christ, there is no other way. You and I still have to choose. On the one hand there is the world and its friendship with all that that implies. The world offers so much: parties, clothes, music and friends of a sort, together with thrills and spills and so much more. It seems sparkling and dazzlingly attractive and there is much that the very scent of it makes one's head go slightly fuzzy with an apparently lovely feeling.

Alongside all that excitement and fun, standing in the shadows is One who appears to be so out of date and old-fashioned that he is uninviting. His name is Jesus, and he endured the shame of the death of an outcast, despised and rejected. Today the choice is still between the disgrace of following a lowly Carpenter and this glittering tinsel world, with all it offers. But—and here is the vital point—we cannot have both. We must choose. For if we try to have both, we will be sucked down into the quicksands of alienation from our Lord and Maker; we will be drawn into the company of those who spat on Christ and delivered him to death. So all of us today must choose, as these two lads had to choose.[8]

Consider what this dying old man offered his two grandsons whom he claimed as his own sons. It is very beautiful poetry at that. There are three word-pictures tucked away in this ancient blessing on Ephraim and Manasseh.

---

[7] Hebrews 13:11-14.

[8] I am not suggesting that when a person first comes to know Christ, the initiative has been with him or her; it is always with God. Rather do I mean that as we live the Christian life we have to continue to 'strive to enter through the narrow door' for 'the gate is narrow and the way is hard that leads to life' (*Luke* 13:24; *Matt.* 7:13). The Greek verb 'strive' which Luke uses is *agonizo*, from which is derived our English word 'agonize'; it is a strong word suggesting that often Christ's followers will wrestle against the allurements of a godless society as they seek to be faithful to their Lord and Saviour.

May the God before whom my fathers Abraham and Isaac walked, the God who has been my shepherd all my life long to this day, the angel who has redeemed me from all evil, bless the boys; and in them let my name be carried on, and the name of my fathers Abraham and Isaac; and let them grow into a multitude in the midst of the earth.

May the God before whom my fathers Abraham and Isaac walked. The first picture is of 'God behind me'. Always as I walk *before* God, says Jacob, I am in front of him, and always he is there right behind me. Thus the Lord calls us to walk *before* him, as he walks behind us, so that he observes all we do, hears all we say, sees everywhere we go. In short, he calls us to holy living; we are to be pure, keeping our bodies clean and our words true; we are to be upright in all we do.

The Bible's teaching that God sees everything we do may seem to some to present the idea of a snooping deity who is spying on us and is always ready to pounce and catch us out when we make a slip. While it is true that God does know absolutely everything about us that there is to know, that is not the principal meaning of God always being behind us. Jacob was referring to a loving, caring God who protected him and provided for him all his days. For those who truly seek to obey the Lord, Hagar's words, 'You are a God of seeing . . . Truly here I have seen him who looks after me', were spoken on the occasion when God came to her in her distress and saved her life and that of her unborn child.[9] God's all-seeing gaze is always a source of immense comfort to his children, rather than a cause for dread. 'There is no fear in love, but perfect love casts out fear.'[10]

The God who has been my shepherd all my life long to this day. The second picture in this blessing is 'God before me'. In the east the

---

[9] Genesis 16:13.
[10] 1 John 4:18.

shepherd walks in front of his sheep, and they follow. He protects them, feeds them, and leads them. But he goes before them, showing the way. A party of tourists in Israel had just heard that middle-eastern shepherds always walk in front of their sheep, unlike shepherds in the west who walk behind with their dogs, when they saw two men driving a flock of sheep before them. The tourists at once asked their Israeli guide how what he had said could be true: 'Look!' they said, 'there are two men driving their sheep instead of leading them.' The Israeli guide was nonplussed. Then he went across to speak to the two men. He came back to tell his party that the two men were not shepherds at all, they were butchers taking the sheep to the abattoir to be slaughtered. The tourist guide was right when he said that in Israel the true shepherd always goes before his flock.

Our Lord calls on us to follow him. 'Follow me', he said to Simon and Andrew, James and John. Or again, speaking to the crowd milling about among his disciples, he said, 'If anyone would come after me, let him deny himself and take up his cross and follow me.'[11] Like the shepherd, Christ goes before us, leading the way. Of course his words 'follow me' take on an even fuller and richer meaning than those implied by Jacob when he called God 'my shepherd', for Jesus is our example, our teacher and our guide; as God incarnate he came to live among us and reveal to us exactly what God is like. 'He is the radiance of the glory of God and the exact imprint of his nature.'[12]

The third word-picture in Jacob's blessing is of *the Angel who has redeemed me from all evil*. This may be understood as 'God beside me'. He had been Jacob's travelling companion, a Comforter and Counsellor, a Defender and Deliverer. Looking back—and an old person's long-term memories can be very vivid and clear—Jacob

[11] Mark 1:17-20; 8:34.
[12] Hebrews 1:3.

could see how an unseen presence had preserved him, never leaving his side, but had been there to protect and deliver him when he least expected it. Today what the Angel had done for Jacob, God through his Holy Spirit does for his children, as Jesus promised.[13]

The blessing concludes with the boys being called upon to accept this triune God as their God, and to be part of his despised people rather than choosing 'the fleeting pleasures of sin'.[14] That is not to deny that there would be the compensation of the ongoing expansion of the Jacob family with all the material prosperity implied in that. Yet that material prosperity was bound up in a future promise based on faith in God's word.

So which bargain, do you think, was the better one: Egyptian society and all its luxury and wealth or being welcomed into the family of the Hebrew shepherds and cowherds with their faith in the one true God? Egypt and all its luxury offered only transitory, fleshly rewards; and when one died at the end, being mummified. To slow down the process of decay to dust and ashes, the dead person's stomach was opened up and all the organs except the heart were removed and stored in four 'canopic jars' to preserve them. The brain was smashed and drawn out of the skull through hooks inserted up the nose. The body was then wrapped in strips of white linen, with a final covering of canvas to protect it. Then (unless you were a Pharaoh with a pyramid for a tomb) your mummified remains were covered with heavy stones to preserve them from being eaten by hyenas!

In clear and sharp contrast to the offers of Egypt, the living Lord of the despised herdsmen and shepherds offered himself as a faithful God, a loving shepherd and a divine Angel. His invitation

---

[13] John 16:7; Acts 1:8; Ephesians 3:20, 6:10.

[14] The choice before them was exactly the same as that before Moses, some generations later (Hebrews 11:24-26).

to us today is no different to the one he gave thousands of years ago to the patriarchs, for he offers himself as Father, Son and Holy Spirit: a holy God, a loving Saviour and a faithful Counsellor. The challenge to men and women today is substantially the same as that delivered to Ephraim and Manasseh: Choose God for he has chosen you! Come and accept his blessing! Cross the line from the world's side and take your place among his people, not because a parent or relative or preacher urges upon you this choice, but because the initiative and call is from him. The promise is that you will have a God behind you, before whom you walk; a God before you, whom you follow; a God beside you, in whose company you travel. It adds up to the greatest gift in all the world, the gift of his own love.

A Striking Action

So why did the old man cross his hands over and, as these two young men knelt before him, put his right hand on the head of Ephraim and his left hand on the head of Manasseh? The right hand should have gone on the head of the elder, Manasseh, and the left hand on the head of Ephraim, the younger. Why did Jacob deliberately do it the other way round (verses 17-19)?

The principle embedded here is one of the lessons of this great book of Genesis: the blessings of God's sovereign grace do not follow the natural order.[15] The custom was for the oldest son to

---

[15] This point is forcibly made by the commentaries, not least by many of the early church Fathers: Ephrem the Syrian (A.D. 306-373), Ambrose (A.D. 333-397), Chrysostom (A.D. 344-407), *ACCS,* pp. 316, 318. Luther has an extraordinarily lengthy exordium, running to ten pages, as he expounds that Jacob's action, though 'like a monstrous act, according to all rights and laws, since by the right of nature and the nations, as well as by God's law, the primogeniture was assigned to the eldest son', yet he acted 'in faith and by the inspiration of the Holy Spirit'. Luther, pp. 178-88. Calvin is much briefer, but equally eloquent and clear: Jacob acting 'as a minister of divine grace . . . was but pronouncing on earth what God would ratify in heaven'. Calvin, pp. 430-32.

receive the blessing; he would inherit the birthright (that is, to be the temporal and spiritual head of the family). This natural order was reversed when Seth received the blessing instead of Cain; Shem instead of Japheth; Isaac instead of Ishmael; Jacob instead of Esau; and now Ephraim instead of Manasseh. It is a principle that underlies the entire Bible. It implies that not one of us becomes a child of God simply because our parents, or grandparents, are believers. The children of God are not like potatoes, growing from those under the ground. Faith is not inherited. It is all a matter of sovereign grace and that means that God himself must call us, we must hear his voice and we must answer his call. We must respond and we must answer. We may assume nothing!

Sometimes when someone is asked, 'Are you a Christian?' the answer is given, 'I think I am. I belong to a Christian family. I attend church. I was brought up in a Christian home, so I suppose I must be a Christian.' I cannot count the number of times I have heard that. Yet here in the very first book of the Bible we find it clearly taught that God's grace and his gifts are not hereditary. Sovereign grace does not work like that. The Lord must call us and we must hear and respond to him. Then we must walk before him, behind him and beside him. Has he called you? Have you heard his voice and invitation to come to his Son and yield to him? Then have you come?

However there was even more to Jacob's striking action than that. Because the old man, before he died, was transferring the birthright to the Joseph tribe in the person of his two sons, Ephraim and Manasseh, and making them head of the family. 'The sons of Reuben the firstborn of Israel (for he was the firstborn, but because he defiled his father's bed, his birthright was given to the sons of Joseph the son of Israel, so that he could not be enrolled as the oldest son; though Judah became strong among his brothers and a chief came from him, yet the birthright belonged to

Joseph).'[16] In this blessing Jacob was also giving to Joseph the land he had already won in Canaan: *Moreover, I have given to you rather than to your brothers one mountain slope that I took from the hand of the Amorites with my sword and with my bow* (verse 22). Thus Joseph and his two sons took on the leadership of the family.

Before he died, C. T. Studd (one time English cricketer, but later pioneer missionary to China, India and finally to Africa) gave his Bible to my mother who worked alongside him in the Congo; he wrote on the fly-leaf, 'May you so live and so die that men will call God by your name saying, "Blessed be the God of Lily Hard-castle."' In that comment Studd was alluding to the final words of Jacob's blessing on the two young men: *By you Israel will pronounce blessings, saying, 'God make you as Ephraim and as Manasseh'* (verse 20).

What do you want out of life: a successful career, lots of fun, a nice home, a lovely wife, or a kind and thoughtful husband? We may not assume any of these are ours by right; if we have some of them, it is because they are gracious gifts from God's hand. But to be known as someone on whom God's presence and blessing rest is surely the greatest blessing of life—that others should call God by our name! What higher privilege could ever be afforded to any man or woman?

Have you ever noticed that woven into this passage are faith, love and hope? There is a faith that looks up, a love that looks out and a hope that reaches forward. Only a few hours of Jacob's life were left. He knows he is soon to breathe his last. But in his final hours on earth he is granted remarkable spiritual insight and perception. To him it is crystal clear: God had spoken and he had heard; God had guided him and provided for him; God had changed his name from 'Supplanter' to the man who saw God—Israel. And now the future is brighter than ever before. There is an eternal light on the

[16] 1 Chronicles 5:1-2.

distant horizon, and it is growing brighter and drawing nearer. He is already hearing the call of his faithful friend, his fellow-traveller, his shepherd.

May we pray that we will face our final earthly hours as Jacob did, full of confidence, gratitude and faith. Because, for all that he had had a bent nature (and who has not?), God had straightened him out and transformed him into a saint. The Lord effects this 'metamorphosis' upon all who yield to him, the Almighty, and accept him as their Father.

Prayer

Loving God, the choice you set before us is no choice at all, for it is between life or death, pure gold or worthless trash, highest joy or deepest pain, noble fulfilment or shameful corruption. Yet we hesitate, our minds clouded, our vision misty, our wills wavering. Come to us by your Holy Spirit and take away the veil over our eyes that we may see clearly and choose life. Gather us in your strong arms, heavenly Father, that we may surrender to you as our God, our Shepherd, our guardian Angel. We ask all in the name of your beloved Son, Jesus Christ our Lord. Amen.

CHAPTER THIRTEEN

Reuben, Simeon, Levi, and Judah—Genesis 49:1-12

A few years ago, I heard an Australian doctor speak on the aborigines of her country. She told how these primitive people, many of whom still live far from civilization in the Outback and who are quite illiterate, never having seen books or writing, are able to recite for hours their tribe's history with its family trees. From their earliest years the children are taught their ancient people's traditions, and their family's ancestry. Apparently, it is something of a tourist attraction to visit their settlements, and pay them a fee to hear their children reciting off their carefully preserved oral tradition. Their history is gradually being added to with each new generation, but otherwise what they preserve remains unaltered, as far as scholars can tell, for hundreds of years.

It would seem that the dying words of Jacob were recorded, learned by heart and passed on from generation to generation until they became incorporated into the permanent record of Israel's history of which Genesis 49 is a crucial part. There is no doubt that this chapter contains a poem which is among the oldest surviving pieces of literature in the whole world. It is quite remarkable and we must handle it with reverence and care.

However, before we look at these verses, there is another point we should notice. I share the view of those who feel that today there is too great an emphasis in some ways on youth. I do not want to be misunderstood and perhaps I should re-phrase that and say rather that we are in danger of not giving to the elderly the respect which they are due, for 'age-ism' dominates our western culture. It was not so in biblical times. In the Scriptures we are urged to give due honour and respect to the elderly. I am not sure what Jacob's sons thought of their father at the time of his death. There are hints earlier in Genesis that at times they ignored him and even treated him with contempt, though, as we have seen, their attitude did gradually change. But if they thought of the old man as a dodderer, they were to receive the surprise of their lives, as in these final hours of his life Jacob pronounced the verdict of his assessment of each son.

Each of them stood to inherit the blessings of the covenant made with Abraham, renewed to Isaac and then to their father. But within that covenant there were rewards for obedience and chastisements for disobedience. Now we find Jacob enunciating a moral verdict on each of his sons. To what extent their future history was determined by Jacob's pronouncements on the one hand, and to what on the other hand it was the result of their fallen sinful characters with certain hereditary weaknesses, must remain a mystery. In some way that we cannot evaluate, heredity and destiny would seem to be intertwined. And so the prophecies made were appropriate to each son.

However, Jacob's words did not mean that each son's descendants were trapped by a predestined fate imposed on them, as we will see. Ezekiel states the case very clearly: 'Now suppose a man fathers a son who sees all the sins that his father has done; he sees, and does not do likewise . . . When the son has done what is just and right . . . he shall surely live. The soul who sins shall die. The son shall not suffer for the iniquity of the father, nor the father suffer for the iniquity of the son. The righteousness of the righteous shall be upon himself, and the wickedness of the wicked shall be upon himself.'[1] In this chapter we will consider the first three of Jacob's pronouncements.

Reuben

The firstborn son was naturally the head of the family. All the dignity and honour of the family was passed on to him. Therefore, Jacob begins his pronouncement on Reuben by saying that his potential had been enormous: *Reuben, you are my firstborn, my might, and the firstfruits of my strength, pre-eminent in dignity and pre-eminent in power* (verse 3). 'Might', 'strength', 'power'—these all lay at his feet as the heir of God's promises. None of his eleven brothers had greater advantages or better prospects than Reuben. The ball had been at his toe, as it were, the whole world at his feet.

But Reuben's mother had a maidservant, who would have been perhaps only ten years older than Reuben. By the custom of the day the maidservant, Bilhah, became the wife of Jacob and bore him children. Alas, Reuben cast his eyes on Bilhah, used his position of authority as the eldest son in a shameful way and seduced her. So he defiled his father's bed by his incest with Bilhah and brought shame upon his father's name.

The implication is that Reuben thought he had got away with his affair with Bilhah. There is no record of his father confronting him with his sin, though the record says that Jacob knew what his oldest son had done.[2] If we are right in assuming that Jacob had said nothing to Reuben, now the oldest son was in for a terrible shock. Because his father, in his dying hours, points to him and says, *he went up to my couch . . . and defiled it* (verse 4c). He concludes, not by saying 'you', Reuben, but 'he . . .', indicating that the assembled company is being addressed and that he is charging Reuben publicly with his wickedness. So for Reuben there is

[1] Ezekiel 18:14, 19-20.
[2] Genesis 35:22.

no blessing, only a judgment: *Unstable as water, you shall not have pre-eminence*... The word 'unstable' means 'turbulent', 'wild', 'lawless', 'without control'; the phrase can be translated as 'turbulent as rushing waters, you will no longer excel'.

In effect Jacob is saying, 'I take from you your headship of this family. You had pre-eminence, you had every opportunity, you had every advantage, but you have thrown it all away, and so from being the first and the greatest, you are made the last and the least. And that is the just reward for your sin.'

The films and DVDs make great play on the passion and excitement of getting into bed with someone, especially if the sexual partner is already married to someone else and the union is consequently blatantly immoral. But here we have the biblical perspective on such acts, so often depicted as passionate love; here is the divine perspective on immorality. We see a man brought down from honour to shame, from power to impotence, from strength to weakness. He once excelled. He now has nothing. Furthermore, it is significant to note that when the promised land was allocated, the Reuben tribe was given barren wastelands in trans-Jordan, where life would be a struggle for survival. And apart from an unholy challenge to the authority of Moses,[3] Reuben's family are hardly heard of again.

You see, the problem with sin—I mean all sin, not only immorality—is not simply that it is wrong. Of course it is wrong. We saw that vividly when we thought about Joseph's battle against the temptation presented to him by Potiphar's wife. This issue with sin is much more complex than that. It is that sin aims to destroy the life of God in our souls. Some years ago, before I left home for a month in the Far East, visiting missionaries there, I planted a row of summer cabbage seeds in my vegetable garden. But I made no

---

[3] Descendants of Reuben chose to associate themselves with Korah's rebellion against Moses (*Num.* 16).

arrangements for anyone to separate the seedlings and then plant them out; when I returned four and half weeks later, they were quite worthless, because they had been completely choked by a row of potatoes which had grown quickly and smothered them. Sin is like that. The tender plant of the life of God in our hearts grows in a very unkindly soil. If we allow evil acts to grow in that same soil, the tender plant of divine life is soon choked.[4]

And so we have here two devastating consequences of what at the time Reuben thought was an exciting love affair, a passion of the heart. First, God's life in his soul was all but stifled and choked; second, his own prospects and that of his family were ruined. We can hardly open our Bibles without coming across similar follies which carry solemn warnings. And we need them. Because every single one of us has the potential for the same ruination of our lives. There is a wild, weak, lawless strain in each of us. 'Turbulent as rushing waters', passion like a flood, pouring out through the breach in the dam wall, sweeping away everything in its path.

I once heard a chilling recording of a British pilot who was flying over the Netherlands just after the dykes had been bombed during the Second World War. He reported seeing the sea waters rushing in like a tsunami and, as darkness fell, he watched aghast from his plane as scores of cars, trying to speed away from the oncoming floods, were engulfed one by one, their headlights disappearing beneath the waters. So Reuben, turbulent as rushing waters, was engulfed by the consequences of his sin.

Simeon and Levi

Earlier in the story of Jacob there is recounted an incident which was the downfall of the two brothers, Simeon and Levi. We need to know a little about it as it forms the background to the next pronouncement. They had brought shame on their father's good

[4] Mark 4:7, 18-19.

name, as Reuben had done earlier, though the circumstances were very different.[5]

Jacob had a daughter, Dinah, who went to visit some of the Hivite women living nearby. While she was with them, Shechem, son of the Hivite clan chieftain, 'saw her, seized her and lay with her and humiliated her'. However, having treated her in this way, he fell in love with her and 'spoke tenderly to her'. At the young prince's request, his father called on Jacob and asked if his son could have Dinah's hand in marriage. Though Jacob agreed, his sons took a completely different view and 'answered Shechem and his father deceitfully, because he had defiled their sister Dinah'. They were indignant and angry because the young man 'had done an outrageous thing in Israel by lying with Jacob's daughter, for such a thing must not be done'.[6] Sexual relations outside of marriage were strictly forbidden, even in ancient Israel before the law was given by Moses.

Dinah's brothers allowed a nuptial agreement to be made, but when the men of the family were least expecting it, they fell on them and massacred them all. They seized everything the tribe possessed, including the women and children. Then they brought their sister home, leaving her betrothed prince and every male member of his entire tribe dead.

Their anger that Dinah's honour had been defiled by the prince sleeping with her before he was married to her was understandable. But the law later given by Moses simply decreed immediate marriage in such circumstances with financial compensation being paid to the young woman's parents for her loss of honour.[7]

Anticipating that Mosaic regulation, Jacob and his sons agreed to financial compensation. Having entered into a solemn covenant

---

[5] See Genesis 34.

[6] The quotations in the order in the text are from Genesis 34:2, 3, 13, 7.

[7] Deuteronomy 22:28-29.

with this family, they then savagely broke the covenant and embarked on a wholesale slaughter. The record clearly says that the originators and perpetrators of this dreadful deed were Simeon and Levi. As he rebuked them for their cruelty, their father said to them, 'You have brought trouble on me by making me stink to the inhabitants of the land.'[8]

We come then to Jacob's pronouncement on these two men and consider what their dying father says to them. First, he dissociates himself completely from what they did and says how abhorrent it was to him. In the Hebrew language there are two puns in verse 6: the verb *come into* also means 'desire', and the verb *joined* can also mean 'rejoice'. In effect Jacob says: 'Let me neither *desire* nor *enter into* their council, nor let me *be joined to*, or *rejoice in*, their council. I had nothing to do with it. They rejoiced that their evil plan to massacre a whole tribe succeeded. But I deplored it. I neither wanted it, nor approved of it.' The meaning is very clear and uncompromising.

Jacob also says that their cruelty is cursed: *their wrath . . . was cruel.* This is highly significant. Very often people bring the charge against the Bible that in the Old Testament human life was cheap, and murder could be ignored, even condoned. Yet here we have the strongest condemnation of such disregard for human life. Along with that condemnation, there is also a curse on the anger of these two brothers. We must not miss that.

Also notice that the judgment on Simeon and Levi for their treachery, murder and cruelty is that they will be divided in Jacob and scattered in Israel (verse 7c). Centuries later when the promised land was being allocated by Joshua, we find Simeon given land beside powerful Judah who soon swallowed up Simeon, while Levi was given no land at all, though for quite different reasons. So Jacob's pronouncement on the two brothers was fulfilled to the

---

[8] Genesis 34:12, 25, 30.

letter, though in the case of the tribe of Levi in another way to the tribe of Simeon.

At this point someone may object: 'This is all very fatalistic. Here are recounted certain sins, and later generations are apparently being discredited and punished for the atrocities their forefathers committed. Those later generations did not have a chance. Everything was already fixed and they couldn't do anything about it. Where is the justice in that?' Though that may be how it appears at first sight, the case of Simeon and Levi in fact proves the opposite: everything is not fixed in that way and indeed something can be done about it.

The later histories of these two tribes turn out very differently. It is recounted that Simeon was swallowed up and scattered, virtually losing its identity; but not Levi. Levi seized God's grace, and while this tribe was scattered, it was because Levi became the priestly tribe and the channel of the divine blessing. The Levites were entrusted with stewarding the things of God to the whole nation. So the judgment could have gone either way. In the event it went both ways. One tribe sank down under it, whereas the other was lifted above it. That is the marvel of God's severity, and it shows to us that his severity and his kindness can come together into harmonious gracious action.

Think of it like this. Here is someone who has always lived a decent life. Converted at a Christian camp in childhood and now a respectable member of the local church, this man attends worship each Sunday and lives a tidy, respectable life in a middle-class street. But he is doing little or nothing for the kingdom of God. As far as anyone can see, the only difference between this person and his neighbours is church attendance. There is nothing sacrificial, vibrant, or noticeable in his Christianity.

But here is someone else: over half her life has been wasted with abuse of alcohol, immorality and shame of all kinds. What deep dark stains have marked her past! Nevertheless, late in the day, well past the noon of her time on earth and well into the afternoon of life's short day, she finds living faith in Christ. Now how eager and hungry she is for the living word of God. Soon the green shoot of the first fruit of real godliness begins to appear, and with tears and trembling hands she weeds the poor soil of her heart to give that tender plant of the divine nature space and air to grow. And grow it does as the full ear begins to form. Maybe not a hundredfold, but certainly thirtyfold.

That is the contrast between Simeon and Levi in later generations. How important it is that we get the message of this awesome second pronouncement of Jacob!

Judah

Judah is the first son to receive a real blessing. While (as we saw in the previous chapter) the birthright passed to Joseph and his two sons, Judah is designated as the royal tribe, the one from which a sceptre and ruler will arise. And so in verse 8, Judah is told that his brothers will praise him, and will bow down before him. After the beautiful poetry of the next verse which depicts courage and daring, authority and wisdom, we come to one of the most remarkable statements of the whole Bible. Consider verse 10:

> The sceptre will not depart from Judah, nor the ruler's staff from between his feet, until tribute comes to him; and to him shall be the obedience of the peoples.

Notice a couple of points. There are liberal scholars who would give the book of Genesis a fairly late date. They would argue that Moses could not have written it, even parts of it. However, when it comes to this poem in chapter 49, there would be acceptance that (as we have already noted) it stands among the most ancient of all literature; its antiquity is beyond dispute.

A question then: How did old Jacob know that the kings of Israel would come from the tribe of Judah, especially when the first prince, Saul, was from the tribe of Benjamin? It was not until Saul had fallen on his sword on Mount Gilboa that David established the royal dynasty out of the tribe of Judah. How did this dying old man know that? You might say that he guessed; if so, it was a one in twelve chance that he would succeed in guessing correctly!

Here is a second question: Was Jacob not wrong when he stated that Judah would rule Israel until the promised One came, for verse 10 goes on to speak clearly of the Christ—*and to him shall be the obedience of the peoples*. Who is referred to as the one to whom the sceptre belongs and to whom is the obedience of the nations? That suggests a grander figure by far than a mere ruler or king of the despised nation of Israel. It is a king whose rule would know neither bounds nor limitations. It is an awesome picture.

The problem is that in 587 B.C., the nation of Israel was carried off into captivity and the monarchy was destroyed. Even after the return from the exile decades later, it was over five hundred years before the Lion of Judah, the kingly Jesus came. So had Jacob got it wrong? 'He must have made a mistake', someone says, 'for clearly Judah did not rule until this mighty promised Monarch came.'

But Jacob did not get it wrong, for when Israel returned after those long years of humiliation in Babylon, governors were appointed who belonged to the tribe of Judah.[9] And then when the governorships ceased, power passed to a kind of Jewish Parliament called the Sanhedrin, and the Sanhedrin was made up (predominantly) of the aristocracy of the tribe of Judah.[10] It was not until

---

[9] The first governor appointed by Cyrus was Sheshbazzar the prince of Judah (*Ezra* 1:8; 5:14-16); Zerubbabel was a son of Shealtiel and therefore a grandson of King Jehoiachin (*1 Chron.* 3:16-17; *Ezra* 3:2; *Hag.* 1:1; *Matt.*1:12).

[10] The great majority of those who had been taken into exile in 587 B.C. and who returned through the edict of Cyrus (536 B.C.) were from the southern kingdom (Judah). Commenting on the lists of returned exiles (*Ezra* 2:1-35), Keil-Delitzsch

Herod the Great severely restricted the power of the Sanhedrin that at last authority was removed from the descendants of Judah and the sceptre snatched from Judah's hand. But by then the Saviour had been born! King Jesus had come. Herod, you recall, tried to kill him. But the One to whom the ruler's staff belonged, and to whom would be the obedience of the nations, had arrived. So Herod could do his worst. The real Lion of Judah had taken the staff and sceptre as his own.

Verses 11 and 12 speak of a Golden Age. No one ever tethered his donkey to a vine. Vines were much too valuable for a man to use for tying up his donkey. Nor did you wash your clothes in wine. But he who changed the water into wine, the altogether lovely One—the expression, *His eyes are darker than wine, and his teeth whiter than milk*, speaks prophetically of the unsurpassed attractiveness of King Jesus—would usher in a golden age, when his kingdom would come and his Father's will would be done on earth as it is in heaven.

This blessing is quite remarkable. We are treading here on hallowed ground. 1,700 years before Christ, an old man on his deathbed sees the curtain of time parted for a fleeting moment, and he perceives that from his son Judah would come an authority and rule that would ultimately only end when the great King had come, a King before whom every knee would bow.

We can surely only draw one conclusion. It is that in those dim and distant years when this despised little family was living in Egypt, God already knew the end from the beginning. Mount Moriah where Abraham had gone to offer Isaac[II] would become

---

state: 'Most, if not all, of these races or houses must be regarded as former inhabitants of Jerusalem.' Keil-Delitzsch, *Ezra*, p. 36; therefore they would have been of the tribe of Judah. The conclusion is that members of Judah's elite controlled the Sanhedrin (along with a few Levites) and thus Judah ruled the Jews up to the time of Christ.

[II] Genesis 22:2, 9.

the Temple Mount, that selfsame spot where the Passover Lamb would be offered. There, the veil separating the Holy of Holies would be torn from top to bottom. There the Saviour would stand and cry, 'If anyone thirsts, let him come to me and drink.'[12] From there he would be led out to be crucified. And from a garden tomb nearby, he would be raised from the dead, the Lion of the tribe of Judah, the King of kings and Lord of lords. God knew and from eternity saw it all. That was how just a little of the secret was passed on to Jacob and was faithfully recorded by Joseph's secretary, learned by heart and preserved by the little family. Thus these words directed his people's prayers, and quickened their hopes for centuries to come, until the day came when Philip would at last declare to his friend Nathaniel, 'We have found him of whom Moses in the law and also the prophets wrote, Jesus of Nazareth, the son of Joseph.'[13]

Sometimes we may feel very small and very insignificant in this busy, bustling, teeming world. Sometimes we may wonder, 'Do I really matter? Does anyone care for me?'—I mean apart from your immediate loved ones and family. Read and think about these words we have been studying in this chapter. See the clear, unmistakable shadow of the hand of God. Feel the breath of his Spirit on your soul and the pulse beat of his heart, as you reach out to receive from him his reassurance and grace. So marvellous is the God who planned all this, whose severity and holiness are seen in this chapter so vividly, and whose majestic purpose is revealed so clearly. This God is our God. He is my God. Is he your God too?

In the final book of the Bible where the risen and glorified Jesus is called the Lion of the tribe of Judah, he is also called the Lamb that has been slain.[14] He is both King and Saviour! All who

[12] John 7:37.
[13] John 1:45.
[14] Revelation 5:5-6.

will come to him in faith and kiss his feet are welcomed by his embrace; such may be assured that this mighty One is their living Lord and Redeemer. And the quite amazing fact is that those who thus come are in very truth included and referred to in this dying patriarch's words, *and to him shall be the obedience of the peoples!*

CHAPTER FOURTEEN

Zebulun, Issachar, and Dan—Genesis 49:13-17

MY wife and I were recently in a restaurant where a young father with his five year old son had just received their main course. The peculiar thing was that the father appeared to show no embarrassment at the quite unacceptable behaviour of his boy. The youngster was walking around among the tables of diners, shouting at them. Meanwhile, bemused and apparently helpless, his father sat and watched him as the youngster ignored his feeble calls for him to come and sit down to eat the food that had just been served.

Too often believers ignore the commands of God through his word. We wrongly assume that because our God is loving and gracious that he is also perpetually indulgent. But so far in these blessings pronounced by Jacob upon his sons we have clearly seen that we reap what we sow and that God's ways are firm and strong. His love is not a soft, weak love like so much that passes for love today. Rather his divine love is a tough love.

More than that, God's blessing is conditional upon our obedience. I am not for one moment saying that salvation is conditional; our adoption into the family of God as his sons and daughters is entirely of his free, unmerited grace. However, thereafter the Lord's blessings are given to the obedient and withheld from the disobedient. Chapter 49 of Genesis abundantly illustrates this. It teaches that God will and does judge his people. Too often the church today forgets that judgment begins with the household of God.[1] It is easy to look out on a wicked world and even to tremble as we think of the coming final day when those who have spurned Jesus Christ shall be summoned to stand before the Almighty to give an account of their deeds. That will be the day when 'the kings of the earth and the great ones and the generals and the rich ones and the powerful will hide themselves . . . calling to the mountains and rocks, "Fall on us and hide us from the face of him who is seated on the throne and from the wrath of the Lamb."'[2] All that is very solemn, but let us never forget that the divine judgment begins with the Lord's own people. There is a sense in which Jacob's pronouncements on his deathbed anticipate that coming day of reckoning.

Having said that, we must not forget that the stern sentences against Reuben, Simeon and Levi were not irreversible. These three sons and their families were not necessarily written off as of no use to God. One of the three, Levi, came into the richest of God's blessings, winning her place as the priestly tribe in Israel. Levi produced Moses and Aaron, Samuel and Zechariah, and in the New Testament John the Baptist. The severest of the divine judgments can be withdrawn when with all our hearts we turn again and return to the Lord in sincerity and truth. Let us then consider the three blessings on Zebulun, Issachar and Dan.

Zebulun

> Zebulun shall dwell at the shore of the sea;
> he shall become a haven for ships,
> and his border shall be at Sidon.

[1] 1 Peter 4:17.
[2] Revelation 6:15-16.

Three simple statements are made here about the future of the tribe of Zebulun. First, this tribe would be given an appointed place—*the shore of the sea*. Second, this tribe would be awarded an appointed occupation—*he shall become a haven for ships*. Third, this tribe was to have appointed neighbours—*his border shall be at Sidon*.

Here we have a wonderful picture of how our lives are destined by God for our good and in order to serve his purposes. We can properly say that in God's plan there is a place for us to live, a job for us to do and even neighbours he plans for us to have. Do you realize and believe that God is as interested and concerned as that about the daily lives of his children? Yet it all makes such practical common sense.

Take a rather clumsy illustration of this from something very material in daily living. There are not many pipe organs being made nowadays as computerized instruments are cheaper and far easier to install. But when a new pipe organ is being designed for a church, the organ builders need to know precise details about the sanctuary, its height, length and width, the acoustic potential, the exact position where the new organ will be sited, as the complex system of pipes, connecting rods and reeds will have to be accessible to the tuners and maintainers of the instrument.

No one would dream of installing a huge organ designed for a vast cathedral into a tiny little chapel; the congregation would be deafened and the windows would rattle, perhaps even shatter, with the vibration of the decibels. Similarly, no one would take a small organ specially built for a drawing room and install it in a vast building such as Spurgeon's Metropolitan Tabernacle which was built to accommodate thousands of worshippers. People would say, 'That's ridiculous, we can't hear the organ once the singing starts—how stupid to put such a tiny little instrument into this huge church!' The two organs were designed for very different places and purposes.

Sometimes we hear it said, 'She's just the woman for that job', or, 'He's just the person for that post—he was the right choice.' Unfortunately, we also have heard it said, 'Oh dear, what a disaster! Whoever appointed him? He is completely the wrong person to serve there!' It is surely obvious that certain people fit into certain places like a hand into a glove, whereas others are like square pegs in round holes.

We are taught in the Christian Scriptures that God has created and fashioned us for a particular purpose. He knows us better than we know ourselves. He is not only fully aware of the gifts he has given to us, but also of the capabilities that he has not given to us. He knows our strengths, but he also knows our weaknesses. Therefore he knows all that is required for us to have a life of the most complete fulfilment. Coupled to that, he knows exactly how we can best serve his gracious purposes: where he would have us live, what he would have us do, the neighbours he would have living alongside us—just like the tribe of Zebulun.

Now that is all very well. We can nod our assent to such statements: 'Yes, the sovereign Lord knows best and his ways are perfect', we say. But there is a major problem in these words of Jacob addressed to Zebulun. For when we read on in the Old Testament we find that, as far as is known and recorded, this tribe never lived by the Mediterranean coast, nor ever had any harbours for shipping, nor had Sidon as a neighbour. Instead, we read, 'Zebulun did not drive out the inhabitants of Kitron, or the inhabitants of Nahalol, so the Canaanites lived among them, but became subject to forced labour.'[3]

It is in Judges chapter 1 that we read a summary account of the early years of Israel's entry into the land. All went well with the tribe of Judah (accompanied by Simeon). God's power was clearly present: 'the LORD gave the Canaanites and Perizzites into their

[3] Judges 1:30.

hands' (verse 4). Then Ephraim and Manasseh gained some initial successes and again we are told that 'the LORD was with them' (verse 22). But these two tribes, along with Zebulun, Asher and Naphtali, failed to press home those early successes, and so we read five times 'they did not drive out' (or 'dispossess') the people living in the land (verses 27-31). It is also stated that they subjugated the indigenous population and therefore were strong enough to subject them to forced labour (verse 28). That may well mean that instead of taxing them they demanded from them a certain amount of work in their fields each year. In other words, these five tribes (I am excluding Judah and Simeon) which Judges names became the dominant ruling powers in the northern part of Canaan.

Zebulun was an essential part of this compromise. God's instructions had been very clear: 'Do not let those people live in your country; if you do, they will make you sin against me. If you worship their gods, it will be a fatal trap for you.'[4] In other words, the picture we are given in the book of Judges is of a successful but disobedient people. 'Pragmatic success, and spiritual failure— a strange but possible combination. So Israel is dominant, if not obedient; she enjoys superiority even if she does not maintain fidelity.'[5] Success in life is not the same as pleasing God.

Sometimes when we speak about God having a purpose for our lives we run the risk of being fatalistic. We can slip into the error of hyper-Calvinism which suggests that everything is fixed, that God is sovereign and thus, come what may, his will shall be done. The false corollary to that is: Therefore we need not be too concerned about our neighbours' salvation or even about our obedience to the divine express commandments, for the Lord himself will make sure everything turns out as it should in the end.

---

[4] Exodus 23:33 (GNB).
[5] Dale Ralph Davis, *Such a Great Salvation* (Grand Rapids, MI: Baker, 1990), p. 25.

Such an attitude is very far from the teaching of the Bible. The Scriptures most certainly teach that God has a purpose and plan for every one of his children; further, that ultimately God's purposes will prevail, come what may. We must never doubt that. But alongside that, Scripture also makes it abundantly clear that you and I have a responsibility to obey God, for disobedience is not only possible, it is an ever-present hazard for every believer and will inevitably lead to loss and failure—as it did with Zebulun, and as Jacob, inspired by the Spirit, foresaw.

Every day of my life I look out from my living room window and I see a magnificent mansion house about three hundred metres away which is now standing deserted and derelict. In my childhood and youth, I lived in that house. My wedding reception was held there. Until comparatively recently, it was in good order. But latterly it was left standing empty and thieves stripped the lead off the roof, vandals broke the windows, others entered and took away the beautiful stained glass windows and marble fireplaces; in winter the water pipes froze and then burst in the thaw and for months the floors were flooded until they rotted and fell through. That mansion house is no longer fit for purpose. Yet it stands there, outwardly imposing, handsome, one of the finest examples of Scottish Victorian architecture; but anyone coming up close to it sees that in its present condition it is utterly useless.

What a tragic parable of many a believer's life. As far as we know, God's purposes for Zebulun were never fulfilled, though they could have been.[6] The Lord's appointed place and task and neighbours never became a reality. Scripture and experience teach us that although God's purposes cannot ever be thwarted, at times he may choose to work *in spite* of a believer rather than *through* a believer. How infinitely sad! Thus, though outwardly successful, the story of this tribe counted for nothing in terms of the divine

---

[6] See 1 Corinthians 3:10-17; 9:24-27.

plan. What a solemn warning Zebulun brings to us all in her failure to possess her promised possessions.

Issachar

> Issachar is a strong donkey;
> Crouching between the sheepfolds.[7]
> He saw that a resting-place was good,
> And that the land was pleasant,
> So he bowed his shoulder to bear,
> And became a servant at forced labour.

The first point to notice about Issachar is his potential strength: *Issachar is a strong donkey.* There may well be here a reference to the battle on Mount Tabor between Barak—though a woman, Deborah, was really the leader—and a Canaanite king, Jabin, and his commander, Sisera. Issachar receives honourable mention in Deborah's song of victory: 'The princes of Issachar came with Deborah, and Issachar faithful to Barak; into the valley they rushed at his heels.'[8] This was the occasion when Jael offered Sisera sanctuary in her tent, and then when he slept, drove a tent peg through his temples.[9] That apart, it was one of the great victories the Lord gave Israel over her oppressors, and Issachar was in the vanguard of the attack against Sisera's nine hundred iron chariots. If you feel sorry for Sisera being killed by a woman, remember that in careful biblical language we are told his speciality during those twenty years of his oppression of the Lord's people was raping young girls.[10] So I think he got exactly what he deserved, and I do not in the least mind if you disagree with me in that.

---

[7] Or, 'between its saddlebags' (ESV margin).
[8] Judges 5:15.
[9] Judges 4:17-22.
[10] Judges 5:30.

Further, it would appear from the summary statement of the entry into Canaan that Issachar was one of the tribes that did successfully occupy the territory allocated to it. Unlike Zebulun, Issachar won a good foothold in the land and thoroughly established himself there.[11] And aged Jacob saw in his son all this potential for success.

The second point that Jacob makes about this tribe is that they would fall heir to a rich inheritance: *He saw that a resting-place was good, and that the land was pleasant.* The area of Canaan allotted to Issachar was the region of lower Galilee, with its beautiful plain of Jezreel, fertile and prosperous. Some of you may have stood at the top of Mount Tabor (today it is called the Mount of Transfiguration) and gazed down at the Plain of Jezreel—the bread-basket of Israel. How very pleasant for this tribe. The land occupied, its inhabitants dispossessed and expelled, so that all remained was for the people of Issachar to enjoy the inheritance God had given to them.

Or was that all? Apparently Issachar thought so. They forgot their past strenuous efforts and battles and settled back to enjoy the good things of the land. Alas, in the process of enjoying life for its own sake, this tribe became indolent and idle, like a strong man who ceases to do any physical exercise and whose ligaments and tendons begin to atrophy so that his muscles are wasted and he is enfeebled.

You have probably guessed what gradually overtook this tribe when it was too late for them to do anything about it. Just as aged Jacob foretold, *so he bowed his shoulder to bear, and became a servant at forced labour.* A new generation of Canaanites saw what was happening to Issachar's former strength, they realized that this

---

[11] Issachar is not mentioned in Judges 1, but is included with Zebulun in Moses' blessing (*Deut.* 33:18-19); sixteen cities with their associated villages were within the bounds of this tribe's allotted territory (*Josh.* 19:17-23).

tribe was drained of the will and power to resist (as they had done rushing into the attack close on the heels of Barak). Now Issachar weakly made a treaty with his Canaanite neighbours from some adjacent territory and agreed to be subjected to forced labour in return for keeping his inheritance.

Consider carefully then, what we have here: potential greatness, immense strength, and a rich inheritance; but moral and spiritual decline which led to subjugation, if not to slavery. Though Issachar began so well, the tribe ended up a tragic failure, serving a pagan Canaanite tribe. In New Testament terms that reminds us of the Lord's warning that 'the one who endures to the end will be saved'.[12]

Many still begin well. It is clear to all who know them that their potential to serve God is considerable. They strike out bravely and at first they conquer for Christ. But after a few years of notable service for him, something goes slightly wrong. The enemy of souls comes to them in some new guise; there occur different and more subtle battles to be fought. Maybe there are temptations to doubt the full authority and inspiration of God's word, or else to slacken off in their devotional lives; or perhaps they bend before the desire to court popularity by compromising over fundamental tenets of faith and conduct. But whatever the cause, the enemy begins to make inroads, little by little, until their spiritual power has evaporated and their love for Jesus Christ has been replaced by love of other things. By then it is too late and the one who showed such promise awakens from spiritual lethargy to discover he has become a slave to his own arrogance and selfishness. Like Issachar, he has become a strong donkey, and in this context donkeys were never renowned for their intelligence or nobility. Forgive me for what is perhaps an unwarranted spiritualization of a couple of Old Testament donkey references: when Abraham climbed Mount Moriah with Isaac, the donkey stayed behind; and when Saul was chosen

[12] Matthew 10:22.

to be a prince in Israel he was searching for lost donkeys!

We must all be warned by Jacob's solemn words; had the tribe of Issachar kept them alive in their memory and soul, perhaps they would have remained watchful and alert. So we should never assume a victory for the Lord in our lives or that the activity of service is the be all and end all. Many believers and servants of Christ fall victim to the devil's snares later on in their lives. There have been some very notable and tragic examples of that in recent years—evangelists and preachers who have been at the forefront of the Christian world, but who have become enslaved to sin of one kind or another and so have ended up as castaways and have been disqualified from the Lord's service.[13]

> You shall eat and be full, and you shall bless the LORD your God for the good land he has given you. Take care lest you forget the LORD your God by not keeping his commandments and his rules and his statutes which I command you today, lest when you have eaten and are full, and have built good houses and live in them, and when your herds and flocks multiply and your silver and gold is multiplied and all that you have is multiplied, then your heart be lifted up and you forget the LORD your God, who brought you out of the land of Egypt, out of the house of slavery, who led you through the great and terrifying wilderness ... who brought you water out of the flinty rock, who fed you in the wilderness with manna ... that he might humble and test you to do you good in the end ... you shall remember the LORD your God.[14]

We used to sing a little chorus which I occasionally still hum to myself:

---

[13] This was the godly fear of the apostle in 1 Corinthians 9:27.
[14] Deuteronomy 8:10-18.

> Lest I forget Gethsemane,
> Lest I forget thine agony,
> Lest I forget thy love for me,
> Lead me to Calvary.

We come now to the tribe of Dan and Jacob's pronouncement on the progeny of this son.

Dan

> Dan shall judge his people
> as one of the tribes of Israel.
> Dan shall be a serpent in the way,
> a viper by the path,
> that bites the horse's heels
> so that his rider falls backwards.

Dan was to be the smallest tribe, not very great and not very strong, but by careful, well-timed strategy Dan would succeed. The metaphor which depicts this tribe as possessed with the wiliness of a serpent is not intended to be insulting or to insinuate that Dan would be deceitful. It simply means that Dan would rise above his natural weakness and disadvantages by cleverness and cunning, in the best sense. Against great odds, this tribe would win through by outwitting his opponents.

That was how future events transpired. Jacob's words were an accurate foretelling of Dan's subsequent history. This smallest of the twelve tribes became a formidable force by means of their skill. When they first entered Canaan, they found they were not strong enough to take possession of the territory allocated to them. At that time the Amorites were being squeezed out of their terri tory by the Philistines who were steadily migrating from Medi- terranean coastlands such as Egypt, the Aegean and islands such as Cyprus; they were settling along the seaboard area of Canaan known today as the Gaza strip.

The Danites knew they could never overcome the Amorites by force, and so they moved into the northern hill country of Canaan and carved out for themselves a homeland there near to the source of the river Jordan. That was accepted as their territory and there they lived and flourished. There is a common expression, 'from John o' Groats to Lands End', meaning from the furthest point in the north of Britain to the most southerly point. In Israel a similar phrase was used to denote from the far north to the far south: it was 'from Dan to Beersheba'. Samson was a Danite and his sad story encapsulates the description of his tribe's characteristic cunning prowess and illustrates how against huge odds significant victories could be won over their enemies.

We have seen how Issachar was given a rich inheritance which he failed to use to the full; therefore we might say that Issachar typifies those who are born with promising prospects, but whose lives end up seriously underachieving and failing to serve God as he would have had them serve him. By contrast, Dan typifies for us those who are not born with any great advantages at all, but whose start in life is right at the bottom of the socio-economic ladder. Some people have it hard all the way; unlike Issachar, they appear to have no great potential or innate strength, far less a home environment that resembles his allocated territory on that rich, fertile plain of Jezreel.

It may be that some are reading this who feel like insignificant little Dan—weak and disadvantaged. Out of the seven tribes that we have looked at so far, this may be the first one that strikes a chord with you. If that is so, then it could be that you are the very person for that special blessing of which Jesus spoke: 'Blessed are the poor in spirit, for theirs is the kingdom of heaven.'[15] Scripture

---

[15] Matthew 5:3. I am not forgetting that in its context this beatitude is the first

teaches us that God has a deep concern for the weak and feeble ones, those who appear not to have the best opportunities in life. God delights to help the despised ones. The reason is that disadvantaged people can sometimes be more teachable, more humble, more aware of their need of his grace and help than the high and mighty.[16] If you are like Dan in this, then you do not have to learn your own inadequacy and stupidity; you already are only too well aware of it. That is a good thing, for you may well be someone in whom God will do a singular work of his grace.

The great biblical principle that grows from the 'seed' of Dan's natural weakness and is unfolded little by little throughout the ongoing divine revelation is this: "'Not by might, nor by power, but by my Spirit", says the LORD of hosts.'[17] Zebulun with all his wealth of opportunities appears never to have learned to trust in the power of God. Issachar, who was endowed with affluence and enjoyed the richest of home comforts, forgot how to trust in the Lord's mighty power and became enslaved to his enemies. But weak, feeble Dan fought through and enjoyed his inheritance right up until the days of the captivity.

So which tribe represents your story? Zebulun who was given great opportunities, but failed to grasp them? Or Issachar who was strong and able, but was lulled into spiritual torpor by the things of this world and became a defeated people? God grant that you may rather be like Dan in this, that in spite of all the odds being against his people and his church, you battle through and win, even when faced by apparently insuperable obstacles. May we all accomplish

---

rung on the ladder that leads to biblical righteousness, that is, a right relationship with God, with others and with oneself, as exemplified in 'acts of righteousness' evidenced in the relationship with God, 'when you pray . . .'; relationships with others, 'when you give . . .'; and the relationship with oneself, 'when you fast . . .' (*Matt.* 6:1, 5, 3, 16). I take it that by synecdoche Christ is including in these three pericopes in Matthew 6 much more than the examples he gives.

[16] 1 Corinthians 1:26-29.

[17] Zechariah 4:6.

the impossible, surmount the insurmountable and, through faith that is no bigger than a speck of dust, cast those metaphorical mountains into the sea.[18]

> All things are possible to those
> Who can in Jesu's name believe;
> Lord, I no more your name blaspheme,
> Your truth I lovingly receive.
> I can, I do in you believe;
> All things are possible to me.
>
> Though earth and hell your truth gainsay,
> The Word of God shall never fail;
> The Lord can break sin's iron sway;
> 'Tis certain, though impossible.
> The thing impossible may be,
> Yet all is possible to me.[19]

[18] Matthew 17:20.
[19] Charles Wesley (1707-88).

CHAPTER FIFTEEN

Gad, Asher, and Naphtali—Genesis 49:18-21

I recently had a conversation over lunch with a man whom I knew only slightly; we had met to discuss at length a subject of some importance. We must have spent at least an hour and half talking about this topic that was of great concern to us both. When we parted we appeared to have reached firm agreement on certain salient points, so we arranged to meet again one week later to take the matter on to the next stage. However, when we again had lunch together, imagine my astonishment when I discovered that we had not understood each other at all. My understanding of the action we had agreed should be taken was completely different—not just slightly different—to the action the other person thought we had agreed should be taken.

That kind of misunderstanding sometimes happens. This is why councils and committees write minutes and at the beginning of each meeting the minutes of the previous meeting are read and approved. Once the minutes are approved, the members of the committee know where they are: agreement is set out in black and white.

Why begin with this? Because as we have been looking at the words dying Jacob spoke about each son gathered around his deathbed, we have been understanding the old man's words in a spiritual sense. We have been taking these prophecies about each tribe's future problems and struggles and giving them a meaning for Christians today. I wonder if you have thought to yourself: 'That's a bit much. Those men all standing round their father's death bed never dreamed that over 3,000 years later people would take his words and use them as if they had a timeless meaning. Aren't you stretching it a bit far!'

Is that a valid objection? Are we misunderstanding and twisting this chapter to suit an agenda of claiming divine inspiration and omniscience for events far into the future? This is actually a very good question and one that is worth considering and facing up to.

Sometimes when you are on a journey and you are travelling through a strange town, you become unsure whether you are on the right road. You carry on and on, getting more anxious as you wonder, 'Am I going in the right direction?' Then suddenly you see a signpost confirming your route, and you relax and drive on with an easy mind. In Genesis 49:18 we reach just such a signpost. The words of this verse assure us that we are understanding Jacob's words correctly. We are not wrenching them out of their context. We are on the right track in our interpretation of what he has said.

I wait for your salvation, O LORD. (I look for your deliverance, O Lord. [NIV])

Dying Jacob has his eyes fixed, not on his sons gathered round his bed, but on the distant future. He is peering through the mists of time and is seeing spiritual truths that point to the Messiah and to his great victory and gracious reign. He is seeing the One who is to come, to whom will belong the sceptre and the ruler's staff, and to whom will be the obedience of the nations. And so he pauses and says to the future expositor, wrestling with all these enigmatic words, 'I am looking and waiting for the Lord's salvation; that is my meaning.' Reverently we say, 'Thank-you, Jacob, for your sign-post, for assuring us we are not doing violence to your words.' And so we resume the task of seeking to understand these sayings as we turn to the next three pronouncements.

Gad

> Raiders shall raid Gad, but he shall raid at their heels.

For those who enjoy puns there are four in this blessing, because out of six words in the original Hebrew, four of those six words come from the same root. Gad means 'a band' or 'a troop' of raiders. So Jacob says: You, *Gad* (a band or troop of raiders) will be *raided by raiders,* but you will *raid at their heels!*

When the promised land was allocated by Joshua, Gad was given that stretch of mountainous, barren land east of Jordan. It was occupied at that time by two warlike tribes, the Ammonites and the Moabites. Gad quickly secured a foothold for himself, but down the generations was constantly harried and attacked. Gad's life was a dangerous one; so he had to be ever watchful, ever vigilant. And though molested and troubled, he always fought back and ultimately conquered and possessed his inheritance.

The Jewish Rabbis strongly spiritualized this blessing, for Elijah was from the tribe of Gad, and Elijah was the great exemplar of the people of God being attacked and molested by the enemies of the Lord, both from within the nation (King Ahab) and from without (Jezebel and her false prophets). But at last, fighting back, not by human means but entirely through divine intervention, Elijah saw the enemies of the true worship of God routed and scattered.

It is Calvin who comments on this verse, 'This prophecy may be applied to the whole church, which is assailed not for one day only, but is perpetually crushed by fresh attacks, until at length God shall exalt it to honour.'[1] What Calvin means is that we are called to fight against principalities, against powers, against the rulers of

---

[1] Calvin, p. 465.

the darkness of this world, against spiritual wickedness in high places.[2] We are to be soldiers of Christ, soldiers of the cross! We are called to fight, knowing full-well that we will sustain attack after attack upon us. But while we will be wounded, harassed and often beaten back, the victory will at the last be decisively won. We may lose many a battle, but we will ultimately win the campaign.

An illustration of what I mean might be that of the Duke of Wellington who was defeated many times by Napoleon during the Peninsular War in Spain, but after seven years of continuous conflict Wellington at last finally defeated his nemesis at the Battle of Waterloo.

So how is the spiritual battle going in your life? You might say that you have had no particular attacks recently. I suppose that is possible, for the Lord does at times cause us to lie down in green pastures and lead us beside still waters.[3] But even if sometimes a week or two slip by quietly, we will hardly get many weeks like that. However, it has sometimes happened that the soldier who is supposed to be on guard has fallen asleep, and the enemy is quietly plundering the army's ammunition stores while the sleeping soldier snores. Another possibility is that if you or I are facing in the same direction as the devil, then we will be unlikely to encounter him face to face for some time—though the head-on confrontation will ultimately come.

The truth is that all those who are following the Lord Jesus closely will undergo attacks on their spiritual lives. Our peace of mind may be attacked. Our purity may be attacked. Or our integrity may be attacked. Most certainly our fellowship with our Lord will be attacked. We will discover that at times we will often be hard-pressed and driven back.

[2] Ephesians 6:12 (AV).
[3] Psalm 23:2.

It is not only the individual Christian who will be attacked by 'bands of raiders'. Congregations also undergo attacks, for Satan is out to defeat the church of God as well as to defeat the children of God. He will use divisions, jealousies, misdirected and wasted efforts which divert the church from her real goals and which send her off on wild goose chases. Whole congregations can be persuaded to do battle with imaginary enemies the way Don Quixote attacked windmills. How often have churches been led by Satan down by-path meadow and consequently rendered ineffective because they have been aiming at the wrong goals!

Before we leave Gad, this soldier-tribe attacked and driven back but refusing to surrender, just a word of comfort. Like many an embattled, heroic battalion of infantrymen pinned down on all sides and facing impossible odds, our motto must always be, 'No surrender!' Some of us are hard pressed in our struggles against Satan and his wiles. At times we think all is lost and that we have been defeated once and for all. We are ready to give up, to resign, even to backslide. But, 'No Surrender!' Never ever forget that the battle is the Lord's, not ours.

Asher

Asher's food shall be rich, and he shall yield royal delicacies (delicacies fit for a king [NIV]).

Asher's name means 'happy' or 'blessed'. It is the word we know so well in our Bibles. We often meet it in the Psalms; indeed the Psalms open with this very word: 'Blessed (asher) is the man who walks not in the counsel of the wicked.'[4] So here Asher is truly blessed by Jacob who sees that this tribe will settle in the fertile land north of Mount Carmel, where olive trees will grow along with wheat and barley, lemons and grapes. Indeed we find in the

---

[4] Psalm 1:1; see also, e.g., Psalm 119:1, 2.

days of Solomon that this tribe of Asher is listed among those who brought provisions for the royal household. Perhaps most blessed of all was Anna the prophetess, who at the age of eighty-four years was constantly in the temple, fasting and praying day and night; when the baby Jesus was brought to the temple for Mary's purification, the Holy Spirit revealed to her that the Messiah had been born and she told the good news to all whom she met as she praised God for the privilege and revelation given to her and to Simeon. Anna was from the tribe of Asher. Happy and blessed was she, indeed![5]

Being a Christian brings such a varied life. Yes, there are battles; what is said about Gad holds true; not a word can we take away from it. But the battles, wounds and attacks of the devil are only one side of Christian living. There are other sides, other facets. So we thank God for Asher, because the blessings and happiness of being Christians are innumerable. As the old hymn says, 'Count your blessings, name them one by one, and it will surprise you what the Lord has done.' Asher's blessing calls us to forget for a moment the dust, heat and toil of Christian service and to remember that God's grace abounds and overflows towards us. 'You prepare a table before me in the presence of my enemies; you anoint my head with oil; my cup overflows.'[6]

It is not that we take 'time out' from the spiritual battle. Rather is it that right there, in the thick of the fight with the forces of unbelief and hatred of God all around us, the Christian sits down to a sumptuous meal of turkey and pumpkin pie. Only instead of the chief guest being the President of the United States visiting his troops in Afghanistan on Christmas Day, the chief Guest is our Lord himself, assuring his humble servant and soldier that he is always right beside him in the spiritual warfare.

[5] Luke 2:36-38.
[6] Psalm 23:5.

There is a project I have never undertaken but which I think I would rather like to engage in: it is to study all the sayings in the Psalms which begin with the word *asher*, 'blessed', 'divinely happy'. What a treasure chest is waiting there to be enjoyed— promise upon promise, like diamonds and costly gems dazzling one's eyes as the lid of the chest is prized open. Christians can have the wrong attitude towards these rich treasures. We are too often like the miser who carefully hides them away in the vaults of some bank to keep them secure. We have a kind of built-in canniness, a caution against overspending. So we hoard God's blessings as if they might run out if we use them too lavishly.

But that is not the way the Christian life is to be lived. Indeed, that is exactly the opposite of what we should be doing. We should be constantly plunging our hands into the divine treasure chest and taking, taking, taking. We should be feasting at his rich table and eating our fill every day because the food he provides for us never runs out. There is always a fresh supply. Christ's provision is grace and more grace—more and always more!

Before we leave Asher, one further comment. Satan invariably attempts to copy what God does. He always provides his evil alter- native. So he also produces a richly spread table and an overflow- ing cup. But his table makes a man sick with selfishness, deceit and lies; his cup confuses the young woman's brain as she over- indulges on drink and her brain cells are steadily but imperceptibly destroyed. Relationships are broken and families fall apart. Satan's imitation of Asher looks the part, like the cheap imitations the cowboy producers fob off on to the public all the time. The fake goods look genuine but they soon break, fall apart or pall. Beware of Satan's imitations of Asher's rich blessings. The real happiness endures and is an essential part of God's gracious work to trans- form us to being more like his Son. Whereas Satan's fake blessings ultimately rob us of our peace and finally destroy us.

'How can we distinguish between genuine, divine happiness and transient, worldly happiness?' someone asks. The difference is that God's blessings are always in King Jesus' character. As Jacob said, *they are delicacies, fit for a king.* Although the initial fulfilment of that prophecy referred to king Solomon, for you and me in the age of the new covenant in the blood of Christ, the King to whom Jacob referred is the King of kings: *I wait for your salvation, O LORD.* And if the joys and delights in which we are revelling are joys and delights we can share with our Lord and Saviour, and if our fellowship with him and his people is made sweeter and closer through them, then they truly come from Asher's table and are from the Father's hand. For all that the Father gives brings us into closer communion with his beloved Son.

Naphtali

Naphtali is a doe let loose that bears beautiful fawns

The name 'Naphtali' means 'my struggle' and originally referred to Rachel's bitter rivalry with her sister Leah.[7] There is something of a problem in these words which are obviously a play on the meaning of Naphtali as 'struggling' or 'wrestling', and I confess I have not found much help from the commentaries which I have consulted.[8] The word picture we have here is of a trapped deer struggling in the net of its captor; it is then set free and bounds off into the forests and hills which are its natural habitat, and there it finds a mate and is able to give birth to fawns. But who catches the doe and who then sets her free?

---

[7] Genesis 30:8.

[8] Martin Luther suggests that since Naphtali's territory was closest to the Syrians it was assailed rather often by their ambushes and as a result of these afflictions 'became accustomed to greater zeal and love for the word of God. Thus Isaiah says (28:19), "Vexation gives understanding"'; (see AV marginal reading). Luther, vol. p. 293.

Let me explain the problem in understanding this blessing. The hunter could be a goody or a baddy. If the hunter is a goody, the capture could be to protect the deer from predators by trapping it and then loosing it into some nature reserve where it can safely flourish. On the other hand, if the hunter is a baddy the capture could be to kill the deer, but either it breaks loose itself or is set free by some rescuer, and dashes off into the wild. The reason for the doe's captivity and struggling will have to remain a mystery. But nonetheless Jacob's meaning is clear that the beautiful creature begins its life afresh on being given its freedom, a freedom leading to fruitfulness. Moses' final words of blessing on this tribe reflect that promised fruitfulness: 'O Naphtali, sated with favour, and full of the blessing of the Lord, possess the west and the south.'[9] Naphtali held on firmly to the land allocated to him though, like some of his fellow tribes, he did not fully possess his inheritance. However, the conquered indigenous Canaanites became subject to Naphtali, rather than *vice versa*.[10]

We can trace the historical fulfilment of Jacob's prophecy in the fleet-footed warriors of Naphtali who, alongside Issachar and other tribes, played a crucial part in the defeat of King Jabin and his army commander Sisera.[11] We should not neglect the important part played by Hiram, the craftsman from Tyre, who masterminded much of the furnishings in Solomon's temple. Hiram's mother was from the tribe of Naphtali. Nor should we forget the princes of Naphtali in the procession of those entering the sanctuary to worship Israel's God.[12]

However I want to attempt to unlock the meaning of the blessing on Naphtali by focusing on that salvation for which dying

---

[9] Deuteronomy 33:23; I have taken the ESV margin's translation.
[10] Judges 1:33.
[11] Judges 4:10; 5:18; 7:23.
[12] 1 Kings 7:13-51; Psalm 68:27.

Jacob sighs: *I look for, I yearn for, I wait for your salvation, O LORD.*[13] We need to follow through the blessing of being *let loose* or 'set free'. For in the exquisite poetry of this blessing are encapsulated first the 'wrestling' or struggling of the captive soul and then the great gospel principle that it is our Lord Jesus Christ who brings liberty to the captives.

We read in John's Gospel of the slavery which binds us all in its invisible chains. 'Truly, truly, I say to you, everyone who commits sin is a slave to sin.'[14] We are slaves to so much.

Some of us are slaves to bad habits, perhaps even vicious habits, with the result that by the time we reach the age of forty, about ninety percent of our thoughts and actions flow from those habits which bind us. We have become set in a mould and we no longer have any—or at least many—new thoughts. That is a frightening prospect. I suppose it means that we become bores; others can predict what we are going to say and do, and how we are going to react. We lose our flexibility. The life we live runs along tram lines, and if we are derailed from those tram lines, we are at a loss.

There was a period when London trams were horse-drawn. Then motorized buses were introduced and the horses were sold off to milkmen who still needed them for daily deliveries in the city. But those animals were useless because for years they had been following tram-lines and their brains were irreversibly conditioned to those routes. No amount of flogging or coaxing or leading could persuade the poor horses to plod along any other route than between the tram-lines, so they had to be put out to grass until they died off.

Habits are all very well if they are good habits. But not all habits are good. Some habits cause our brains to fossilize; others cause

---

[13] Genesis 49:18; notice that Jesus made his earthly home in Naphtali's territory (*Matt.* 4:13, 15; quotation is from *Isa.* 9:1-3).

[14] John 8:34.

our health to deteriorate; yet other habits lose us our friends. But the paradox is that we protest we are exercising our rights as we twist the chains of our habits around our hearts and souls. 'Of course I am a free agent', we insist, 'I'm free to do as I please', and we plunge on into what we call our freedom, becoming more and more entangled in a web of behaviour which is uncontrollably conditioned.

Bad habits have another name, that nasty three letter word: they are nothing else but 'sin'. I remember having a discussion at a fireside with a man who insisted that sin consisted simply in wrong words spoken, or wrong actions done; he told me that Christianity had it wrong—people were naturally good and thoughtful, but just occasionally said the wrong thing or slipped up in what they were doing. I tried to point out to him that words and actions are sins (plural) and are the fruit of sin (singular), just as the apples on the tree are the fruit of the apple tree.

The real meaning of sin is not just a wrong thought or word or action. Sin refers to a root that goes right down into our innermost being. Its tentacles reach into every part of us, like an evil nerve-system. You cannot cut off any part of your body without the rest of your body feeling the pain, because you have a complex nerve-system which extends throughout your entire frame. And sin is like that; we all have it right through us. Here is another illustration of the way in which sin permeates our whole being. I understand that when a pinch of salt is dropped into a glass of water, even before the salt dissolves, instantly every single molecule of the water is affected by the salt in a lightning reaction. In the same way sin permeates our beings, our minds, our wills and our emotions.

Do you see what that means? Our freedom is actually an illusion. Our wills are not really free at all—not since the Fall, because our wills have these 'veins' of sin, little capillaries, affecting every single decision we make. Take just one example of sin's expression:

pornography. There are those who argue that people have to be free to buy and enjoy feeding their minds on pornography. The basic premise of their argument is that each individual has the right to choose what they want to enjoy. From there they demand to know who has the right to stop them. What right does anyone have to rob them of their freedom to do as they please in the privacy of their own homes? That is the illusion of freedom. But that kind of freedom is completely false. Sociological research is now concluding that pornography can lead on to child pornography and then to child abuse; then child abuse can sink into even lower depths of depravity in ritualistic foetal sacrifices. But those unthinkable foetal sacrifices, which surely all right thinking people abhor, could well have begun with the so-called freedom to 'enjoy' pornography.

Someone might object that I am using an extreme example of sin of which only a minority of people are guilty. But my argument is from the greater to the lesser. The principle firmly stands: our human freedom is an illusion, because the fallen mind, will and heart are warped and crooked from birth. That is the bad news that must always come before the good news: at birth we were born sinners and from our earliest days had no genuine freedom. Indeed, one of the first works of the Holy Spirit in our hearts is to show us that. The effect of discovering the truth of our real spiritual condition is called 'conviction of sin'.[15]

[15] This is not to deny that all humans are created in the image of God (*Gen.* 1:26-27) and that, although that image has been marred by sin, rich vestiges of it remain. We are all, therefore, capable of noble actions arising from compassion, kindness and love; furthermore, we have varying gifts of creativity as evidenced by great architecture, paintings, music, literature and engineering. When the apostle writes of 'the futility of [unregenerate] minds' which 'are darkened in their understanding, alienated from the life of God because of the ignorance that is in them' (*Eph.* 4:17-18), he is not denying human ability for greatness in countless spheres of living; rather, his underlying theme is the impossibility of men and women, by their own efforts, attaining righteousness before God because of the problem in every human being of innate sinfulness. For an exposition of Ephesians 4:17, see

So the lovely doe is captured, losing her freedom. But there is another hunter treading the hills. This other hunter is out to find the captured doe to set her free. However, in her captivity the terrified animal hears him coming and tries to bolt. She does her utmost to run from him. It needs all the hunter's skill and understanding to corner her. And when he does, she falls frightened and trembling into his control. But he has taken her to set her free, and so he takes her from the tiny enclosure where she was a prisoner, and lets her loose into the great forests and hills where she can bound away to roam and enjoy the God-given freedom for which she was created.

The parable implicit in this blessing becomes plain. I vividly recall talking with someone who had been cornered by the Divine Hunter; he had been well and truly captured. A slow, patient tracking process had gone on not merely for months, but for years. Now, by circumstances at work and home, he was hopelessly cornered. Finding himself alone in the house one evening, he went into the shower-room, knelt down on the bathmat, and there the Divine Hunter gathered in his arms that trembling, frightened soul. He found himself gently carried from the enclosure of his captivity to his sin and selfishness and delivered to run into the glorious woodlands and meadows of God's blessed earth.[16]

We need to see from this beautiful couplet that the salvation for which Jacob is sighing and longing is not merely freedom, but also fruitfulness. For the doe bounds away to find her mate and her subsequent history is collapsed down into just four words, *that bears beautiful fawns*. So we next see her grazing in the copse with her fawns. The message has become clear that Naphtali stands not

---

D. M. Lloyd-Jones, *Darkness and Light* (Edinburgh: Banner of Truth, 1982), pp. 33-6.

[16] Compare the well-known poem by Francis Thompson, 'Hound of Heaven', part of which is quoted at the end of this chapter.

only for the release from the chains of sin that Christ brings, but also for the fruitfulness in his service which must follow.

That brings us to the parable of the Sower and the thirty, sixty and one hundredfold which the seed in the good ground produces. We must conclude that the real freedom of Christ's deliverance will bear the spiritual fruit of bringing others to know him. No one is released by Christ from sin's captivity without beginning to influence others for him. It is a spiritual law as firm and fixed as the law of gravity. Drop a brick and it will fall and hit the ground, or hit your toe if you do not watch out. Live in Christ's freedom and there will be a reaction in others—your husband, wife, neighbour, work colleague. It will happen, because it must happen. If the branch is grafted into the vine, it will produce grapes. And if we are enjoying the freedom of Jesus Christ because we are joined to him, then we will and must bear his fruit.

Not that we are to be impatient if others do not respond immediately. We tell our neighbours, friends and family that we have been set free, and invite them to discover the joy of the Lord Jesus, but we find they are not interested. They give us the cold shoulder. Ah, we must be careful! Of course they are interested. But they are going to wait and watch and see. They want to witness for themselves how genuine this deliverance of Jesus Christ really is that we are telling them about. It may take months. Probably, it will take years. But if our lives are faithful and true to Christ, and his life of love, joy and peace along with the other fruit of the Spirit is growing in us, then the fruit will begin slowly to grow, ripen and be ready for picking.[17] Do not forget that fruit always takes time to mature and ripen. So do not be discouraged. Enjoy your Saviour! Keep very close to him! And at last there will be fruit in your family, at your work place, in your street, even though it takes a long, long time.

[17] Galatians 5:22-24.

Gad—attacked incessantly but, refusing to give up, at length driving back his enemies. Asher—there in the presence of his enemies, his table spread with a royal feast and his cup overflowing. And Naphtali—gloriously delivered and bearing fruit for God's glory.[18] Three lovely blessings, especially when we take all three together, for they are three complementary aspects of Christian living and serving. Take these short verses and make them your own. Though uttered nearly 4,000 years ago, they are the word of God about his salvation which has now come to us in our Lord Jesus Christ, whose final consummation and eternal victory we too wait and long for!

---

[18] Francis Thompson's, 'Hound of Heaven' (see note 16 above), contains the following lines:

I fled Him, down the nights and down the days;
I fled Him, down the arches of the years;
I fled Him, down the labyrinthine ways
 Of my own mind; and in the mist of tears
I hid from Him, and under running laughter . . .
From those strong Feet that followed, followed after.
. . . But with unhurrying chase,
 And unperturbèd pace,
 Deliberate speed, majestic instancy,
They beat . . .
Halts by me that footfall:
Is my gloom, after all,
Shade of His hand, outstretched caressingly?
'Ah, fondest, blindest, weakest,
 I am He Whom thou seekest!
Thou dravest love from thee, who dravest Me.'

CHAPTER SIXTEEN

Benjamin and Joseph—Genesis 49:22-28

ABOUT fifty years ago a woman called Chrissie Wilson, who lived in an east coast town in Scotland, received an unexpected call from her GP. During the course of the conversation (which was a little bit strained as the doctor had not been asked to call), he suddenly asked Mrs Wilson a question about her daughter, 'Is it true that Lorna is going out with that dreadful young man?' And he named him. 'You should tell her to keep as far away from him as possible. He's an absolute scoundrel!' Mrs Wilson was quite taken aback. 'Doctor', she said, 'My daughter is not going out with John. It's his twin brother, David, whom she is going out with. He is completely different from his brother!'

My twin brother was forty-seven years old when he was soundly converted. He had been a professional gambler and, in his own words, a heartless wretch and waster until that time. If ever there was a 'trophy of grace' it is my brother John. My point is that brothers who have the same parents can nonetheless be very different to each other. Think of Jacob and Esau—how completely different in character they were. Or Moses and Aaron. Did not Aaron make the golden calf while Moses was on Mount Horeb receiving the Ten Commandments from God? As we come now to two blood brothers, Joseph and Benjamin, we will find that they too were very different, and their blessings clearly reflect that. We will take Benjamin first, and then Joseph.

Benjamin

> Benjamin is a ravenous wolf, in the morning devouring the prey
> and at evening dividing the spoil.

As the youngest son of Jacob, Benjamin was what we might call
'the baby of the family'. His mother, Jacob's beloved Rachel, died
in childbirth, giving him the name Benoni, which means 'child
of sorrow', but his father changed his name to Benjamin, which
means 'child of my right hand'. He was his father's favourite. A
late child, born in his father's old age, he was perhaps spoiled, not
only because of his mother's death, but especially because when
Joseph was sold into slavery, Jacob lost Rachel's only other son. We
always find him being looked after by others, or being jealously
guarded by his doting father. Therefore we would expect a very
special blessing promising dainties, luxuries and prosperity for the
tribe of Benjamin. Instead, we find a very different kind of blessing. This tribe was to be warlike, living by plundering; it would be
a tribe of soldiers, fierce and formidable.

Using a concordance I read through some of the biblical references to Benjamin. The members of this tribe are almost always to
be found in the forefront of the battle. Indeed they are singled out
for mention as expert with the sling, able to aim at a hair and never
miss. They had a battalion of seven hundred men who could aim
with unerring skill using their left as well as their right hands; pre-
sumably the left hand is mentioned as in their right hand would
be their swords. David was supported by a crack company from
Benjamin who were deadly archers. The youngest son of Jacob produced a people who were fiery and martial.[1]

Not only was this tribe marked out for military prowess, but
she produced great generals as well. Ehud in Judges, and Saul,
first anointed prince of Israel, were both from Benjamin; so was

---

[1] Judges 5:14; 20:16-48; 1 Chronicles 12:2; 2 Chronicles 14:8,17:17, 25:5.

Mordecai and therefore Queen Esther, his relative. Perhaps the most fascinating example of a leader from this tribe is that of the Apostle Paul.[2] There is little doubt that Benjamin's fiery nature was also in Paul. Before he was a Christian, Paul was like a plundering wolf, ravaging and destroying the church.[3] But once he was converted to Christ, God took up his campaigning, fiery nature, and turned it round to wage war against sin and wickedness. So that in the evening of Paul's life, we find him rejoicing over a new kind of spoil—the lives of people from all over the Roman world who had been captured for Christ.

This brings us to the meaning and value of this blessing for us today. The Old Testament is set in a world of wars and fighting; to survive, a man had to be armed along with his sons and servants. But the Lord Jesus introduces us to another kind of society, in which the battle-front has changed very radically from conflict with flesh and blood to spiritual warfare between principalities and powers. For although King Jesus is the Prince of Peace, he still rides out conquering and to conquer. And so, like Benjamin, you and I are called to fight. And no Christian can live in any other way. Christ is our Captain and we enter the fight following him, with the helmet of salvation on our heads, the breastplate of righteousness covering our hearts, truth round our waists, and the gospel of peace upon our feet; on our arms must be the shield of faith, and in our hands, the sword of the Spirit, which is the word of God.[4] Ranged against us is an enemy full of wiles and cunning stratagems.

---

[2] Judges 3:15; 1 Samuel 9:1-2; Esther 2:5; Philippians 3:5.

[3] Acts 9:1, 26:11; Galatians 1:13; 1 Timothy 1:13. 'This a brief blessing, one that is understood very beautifully as referring to the Apostle Paul ... the sense is almost literal, for Paul devoured Stephen like a wolf. Afterwards he divided the spoils throughout the world by spreading the doctrine of the gospel abroad as he carried on his apostolic office in the church.' Luther, vol. 8, p. 306.

[4] Ephesians 6:10-18.

I would suggest that we have a war on three fronts. The *first battleground* is within our own hearts and lives. In Galatians 5:17-21 Paul writes:

> But I say, walk by the Spirit, and you will not gratify the desires of the flesh. For the desires of the flesh are against the Spirit, and the desires of the Spirit are against the flesh, for these are opposed to each other, to keep you from doing the things you want to do . . . Now the works of the flesh are evident: . . . enmity, strife, jealousy, fits of anger, rivalries, dissensions, divisions, envy . . . and things like these. I warn you, as I warned you before, that those who do such things will not inherit the kingdom of God.

There is no getting away from that battle-ground. We have seen that again and again as we have studied each of these blessings pronounced by Jacob on his sons. But I want to make a rather different point arising from this blessing on Benjamin.

There are two extremes we have to avoid in the inner battle between our sinful desires and the Holy Spirit of God. The first extreme is found in Christians who are truculent and even impertinent. They flaunt their valour against what is wrong. They make a great display of their fight against uncleanness and greed and selfishness. Brother Andrew, in his book *God's Smuggler*,[5] tells how when as a young man he was fighting in Indonesia with the Dutch army, he deliberately exposed himself to the enemy. He wore a ridiculous yellow straw hat which made him an obvious and easy target for sniper fire; and when his platoon was creeping through the undergrowth, knowing they were in hostile territory, he swaggered along openly, deliberately courting death. It was only by the grace of God that he emerged from that war still alive.

Some Christians behave as foolishly as that. And the ethos of much evangelical teaching in the past actually trained and

[5] Brother Andrew, with John & Elizabeth Sherrill, *God's Smuggler* (1967); reprint (Grand Rapids, Chosen Books, Baker, 2001).

encouraged young Christians to be blatant and even insolent in their style of Christian living and witnessing. That is the first extreme I believe we must avoid. In words of Jesus himself, 'Behold, I am sending you out as sheep in the midst of wolves, so be wise as serpents and innocent as doves.'[6]

The other extreme is for the Christian to go almost completely underground. Obviously, that is a reaction against the first cavalier attitude, as the pendulum swings from one side to the other. Sensing there is something wrong with the truculent, brazen impertinence of some Christian witnessing, others have responded by living their Christian lives as if they were spiritual woodlice hiding under a fallen tree-trunk. They are never seen, never heard, and certainly never engage the enemy. In fact they are so quiet and still that they are not even sure if there is a real enemy out there.

But there is a deadly enemy alright. And all who follow the Lord must be willing to face that enemy in their lives. There is no other way if we are to be faithful to our Lord. I suspect that few, if any, will fall into the trap of the first extreme of trying to draw Satan's attention directly on to themselves. But I guess quite a few slide into the other extreme of going into hiding: being so tactful, so careful, so gentle, so obliging, that they resemble kiddies in a nursery school rather than soldiers in an army. This, then, is the first front on which we must engage in warfare—the fight in our own lives, that battle within our hearts and minds.

There is a *second front:* the warfare flares up during the faithful preaching of God's word. Whenever the word of God is preached, the enemy sets up spiritual road-blocks and barricades. And those who have never really come to know the Lord grab their tin helmets and duck down behind these barriers in the hope that they will be able to stay out of the line of fire of the living word of God. Hearts become hard, ears are stopped, eyes are blinkered. Time

---

[6] Matthew 10:16.

and time again, people have said to me after a service, 'That was just the word for someone I know who was in church today.' And I have always been tempted to ask, 'Didn't God have anything to say to you today?' Because God's word is not aimed at the person behind me, or the person in front of me, or someone sitting upstairs in the balcony. God's word is always aimed directly at my will, my life, my mind, my heart. And when the word is preached, the war is on. Always. Without exception.

There is a *third front* where the battle rages: it is in the place of prayer. Now I know only a very little about personal, private prayer. And I know just a little about corporate prayer. All that we learn about both private and corporate prayer is to be found in our text book on warfare—the Bible. In the battle-zone no army commander would allow a tank commander to go off on his own to do battle unaided against the enemy's opposing forces. When the hour comes for the attack, the tanks will move forward together, keeping in constant communication.

The war films depicting the lonely hero who thwarts single-handed the entire opposing force are sheer fiction. A single courageous soldier might succeed in knocking out one enemy gun emplacement, but not the entire battalion. It just does not happen.[7] In the 1962 classic film, *Lawrence of Arabia,* at one point in his desert campaign Lawrence's hoard of Arab warriors on camels and horses come across a village which has been destroyed by the retreating Turkish forces; men, women and children have all been massacred; not a living soul remains. One of Lawrence's men had belonged to that village and, crazed with fury and grief, he breaks ranks and with heart-rending screams charges alone after the Turkish force. It is a heroic moment. But as he approaches them at full gallop, waving his scimitar, he and his horse are mown

---

[7] This is not to deny individual acts of outstanding valour which are recognized by awards such as the Victoria Cross or the Military Cross; but though such actions may save several lives, by and of themselves they do not win wars.

down by machine-gun fire. A few moments later, Lawrence gives the order to charge and in a disciplined pincer movement the Arab forces totally overwhelm the Turkish line. Offensives against an enemy line require to be controlled by a corporate, organized, co-operative strategy.

To move from the horror of human warfare with swords and guns to the reality of spiritual warfare through prayer, this is why we read of the early believers in Acts 2, that when the Holy Spirit was poured out upon them, 'they were all with one accord, in one place'.[8]

Further, there is a cost involved in corporate prayer. The television news bulletins show clips of tearful army wives embracing their husbands and saying their goodbyes to them as they leave for the front line in some far-off land. War always demands sacrifice. There are our soldiers far from home, training, working, sweating it out and thinking of their loved ones back at home: how hard for them when it is Christmas, or the time of their sons' or daughters' birthdays! They fight for Queen and country, always living on the edge of mortal danger.

There is a close parallel between that kind of warfare, and the spiritual warfare of prayer. For in prevailing prayer sacrifice is demanded. It can be hard, even painful. On a winter's night we would often far rather be at home beside the fire, rather than braving icy pavements and biting winds to reach the congregational prayer gathering. On a lovely summer's evening perhaps we would rather be enjoying a walk in the park. But prayer is warfare, costly, near to the danger-zone, confronting the enemy head-on.

I suppose that is why gatherings for prayer are the least attractive of all our various activities. Why else, when we have a choice, do we choose not to pray but to opt for some other less demanding alternative? Remember how Gideon sent home to their firesides

---

[8] Acts 2:1 (AV).

first 22,000 men and then, out of the 10,000 who remained, another 9,700. Only the handful who stayed shared in the victory.[9]

> Must I be carried to the skies
>   On flowery beds of ease,
> While others fight to win the prize
>   And sail through bloody seas?
>
> Are there no foes for me to face?
>   Must I not stem the flood?
> Is this vile world a friend to grace,
>   To help me unto God?
>
> Since I must fight if I would reign,
>   Increase my courage, Lord!
> I'll bear the toil, endure the pain,
>   Supported by Thy Word.[10]

Joseph

Jacob's blessing on Joseph is a most beautiful poem, gathering together the salient points about his son's life and work. It seems to fall into three main parts: there is a short introduction summarizing Joseph's life and work; there is a short epilogue which places a crown on his brow; there is the main part of the blessing which forms the body of the poem. We will consider each part in turn.

First, the introduction which summarizes Joseph's life and work:

Joseph is a fruitful bough, a fruitful bough near a spring; his branches climb over the wall.[11]

---

[9] Judges 7.

[10] Isaac Watts (1674-1748).

[11] The NIV uses the word 'vine' instead of 'bough'; ESV follows AV, NKJ, RSV. Leupold, p. 1193, is very critical of the translation which GNB adopts: 'Joseph is like a wild donkey by a spring, a wild colt on the hillside', calling it an 'unwarranted alteration' and commenting that 'the text [as in AV] makes sense and the sense is good.' Although ESV offers the GNB's version in a marginal note, most other commentators concur with the reading that the majority of English translations

As in several others of the blessings, Jacob introduces a pun. Twice we have the word 'fruitful', and that is the name of Joseph's second son 'Ephraim', whom Jacob made head over his older brother.

Often when you are walking in the hills and you cross a barren, wind-swept mountainside where only the heather and heath grow and there is no tree in sight, you will come across a deep gully in which you will find some trees growing, rowan or birch or gean.[12] You wonder how these lonely trees have managed to survive on such a bleak hillside, constantly swept by high winds and storms. Then you discover why: in the gully is a burn, and the rowan or birch or gean trees are growing along the banks of that wee burn as it tumbles its babbling way through the gully between the rocks and over the stones.

Jacob says that Joseph was like those unlikely trees, fruitful in such a hostile environment. There in the wilderness years of his lonely life, his roots had found a deep gully with an ever-flowing spring from which his soul could daily draw fresh supplies of inner strength. And so while others had withered and died, Joseph's inner life had stayed fresh and green, as each day he drew his succour from God. I cannot prove it, but I like to think that the psalmist drew his metaphor from these words when he introduced the book of Psalms:

---

adopt, though admitting the Hebrew of this verse is obscure. LXX translates as: 'Joseph is a grown son, my enviable grown son; my youngest son, turn to me' (In response to my enquiry regarding this translation, Prof. Howard Marshall wrote: 'Lust's Lexicon of LXX suggests that the imperative verb *anastrepson* translates the Heb. verb *shub*, instead of the noun *shor* = 'wall' used in the MT. The literal Heb. use of 'son' lies behind this.') In that regard Luther (vol. 8, p. 295) relates these words to Psalm 80:14-15, 'Look down from heaven, and see; have regard for this vine, the stock that your right hand planted, and for the son whom you made strong for yourself.'

[12] 'Gean' is an old Scots word for a wild cherry tree (*prunus avium*), often found growing in the Scottish glens and hills.

> He is like a tree planted by streams of water
> that yields its fruit in its season,
> and its leaf does not wither.
> In all that he does, he prospers.[13]

A vine is a climber. It needs support. Therefore Joseph is pictured as growing beside a wall, supporting his branches and the heavy bunches of ripe grapes by clinging to its great stones, until he reached the top of the wall and his boughs overran it, and so hung, laden with fruit, over both sides. It is an exquisitely beautiful summary of this great man's life, his secret strength and fulsome fruitfulness. That had been Joseph through his years of slavery, imprisonment and finally, during his brilliant service as lord of Egypt.

Second, consider the main part of Jacob's blessing in verses 23 to 26a:

> The archers bitterly attacked him, shot at him,
> and harassed him severely,
> yet his bow remained unmoved;
> his arms were made agile
> by the hands of the Mighty One of Jacob
> (from there is the Shepherd, the Stone of Israel),
> by the God of your father who will help you,
> by the Almighty who will bless you
> with blessings of heaven above,
> blessings of the deep that crouches beneath,
> blessings of the breasts and of the womb.
> The blessings of your father
> are mighty beyond the blessings of my parents,
> up to the bounties of the everlasting hills.

---

[13] Psalm 1:3.

Dying Jacob has no intention of passing over the appalling injustices Joseph's ten brothers inflicted on him. Now he knows of those years as a slave and a prisoner and of his son's suffering and loneliness. And so he incorporates that too into his poem: *The archers bitterly attacked him, shot at him, and harassed him severely.*

The picture is of a lone warrior, hard-pressed by attackers: outnumbered, facing impossible odds because he is alone and without any help or a single friend. In studying this account of his privations in earlier chapters, we have seen vividly the dark, dark days of Joseph's life. And now his father, deeply moved, expresses those years of suffering in these immortal words of poetry.

However, in Jacob's dramatic poem, to the astonishment of the silent onlookers, this lonely archer does not fall as his enemies rain down their arrows upon him. Contrary to all expectations, he stands firm. With deadly accuracy and untiring strength, he looses shaft after shaft against his attackers and thus holds them back: his bow remained steady, his strong arms remained supple. Then Jacob expresses more fully the secret strength and power of Joseph that he has already hinted at in the picture of the roots reaching down to the moisture of the spring of water. Only now, the picture is changed as he opens our eyes to see something quite wonderful: this lonely archer under such heavy attack is, in fact, not alone at all. There is beside him, behind him, and all around him, a shining shadow, a towering figure, quite unseen by his enemies. And his invisible companion has his hands over Joseph's hands, his arms over Joseph's arms.

While Joseph appears to be standing firm, on a closer look, we find him weary, exhausted, ready to collapse; but he is upheld by the One surrounding him; and he is leaning hard on him, supported by him, else he would be overwhelmed, and those arrows loosed against his attackers with such ferocity and accuracy, are empowered and directed by the strength and aim of his Companion who is holding his hands. Lest any of us should think that Joseph was a bonny fighter, able to take on anyone, Jacob names this mysterious Champion beside, behind and around Joseph: he is none other than the Mighty One of Jacob, the Shepherd, the Rock of Israel, his father's God, the Almighty, (El) Shaddai.

Imagine a father teaching his son to use a bow and arrow. The father stands behind the boy, who holds the bow in his small hand. But father puts his strong left hand over his laddie's tiny left hand. Then as the arrow is slotted into the string and the boy's right hand begins to draw it back just a little, the father's right hand closes over his son's right hand, and steadily and surely, he draws the string back, still holding the bow firm in his left hand as it takes the strain. And the father's eye guides the aim until together father and son release the shaft and it speeds with deadly accuracy towards its target. That is the picture.

And then the blessings:

> ... by the Almighty who will bless you
> with blessings of heaven above,
> blessings of the deep that crouches beneath,
> blessings of the breasts and of the womb ...

Blessings of heaven above, the deep that lies below, blessings of children and family, blessings of a sun-kissed hillside, tilled, sown and watered, and now golden with fields that are ready to be harvested (*the bounties of the everlasting hills*). The bounties, riches and dominion of which Jacob speaks could not be greater, as he gathers up all the promises of the past made to himself, to his father Isaac and to his grandfather Abraham. So that instead of being obstacles to be surmounted or barriers barring the way, the mountains have become rich and abundant with overflowing blessings.

Today Jacob's words stand as an accurate and authentic description of Christian living. He is right about the discouragements and at times the loneliness, hostility and often, too, the bitterness. He is also on target regarding the secret of endurance, blessing and ulti-mate victory. What is here in the text can be a reality in the lives of those who would follow and serve Jesus Christ in their daily living. We may have to endure far more than we ever could on our own. The odds against us are still impossible. The sooner we realize that alone we do not stand a chance, the better.

During my years of pastoral ministry I have seen young people sitting through the services Sunday by Sunday, attending various congregational organizations, all taken up with the fellowship and the fun, their friends' parties and their nights out together. And I have seen them excitedly saying goodbye as they leave home to go off to college or university. But many of them we have never seen again, unless it has been when they have been home at Christmas and we have caught a glimpse of them drunk, staggering along the road home. Or I have bumped into them in town, and they have said with a laugh, 'I'll not be back . . . I don't need God . . . I have found a better way to live than the bigotry of churches and the hypocrisy of your supposed Christians.' Sadly, that is what I have heard and seen.

What went wrong in their lives? There were no roots going down deep into the secret spring. There was no constant Com-panion beside, and behind, and all around them. And so, when the attacks came, sooner or later they caved in, mostly sooner. Therefore the challenge comes to us all, are we learning from God's word? Have we understood the meaning and relevance of this account of Joseph's life? Have we discovered the code to unlock the door of our understanding? Or do we think that this is just an ancient legend, romantic and lovely, but with little or no reference to life in the twenty-first century? The key to the blessing on Joseph is that it is about finding the Son of God as our Lord and Redeemer.

The code that unlocks the meaning of Joseph's story is that this man combines in himself two 'types' or 'role models'. He foreshad-ows both the obedient, faithful Christian and at the same time he typifies the faithful, loving Saviour of the world. That is the meaning of the third part of the blessing:

> May they be on the head of Joseph,
> and on the brow of him who was set apart from his brothers.

For Christ is the golden shadow beside, behind and all around Joseph in his darkest hours. Christ is the one who was the Rock, the Shepherd, the Mighty One, Shaddai. It is his dear hand that brings the blessings and the bounties that begin to grow on those mountain slopes that once stood as impenetrable barriers barring our way. He rides on the thunder and unleashes the storms, yet all the while retaining complete control over them. And it is his head that is crowned, his brow that is princely, for he who was once separated[14] from his brothers and sisters is now crowned with glory and honour and power.

As Martin Luther once said, the word of God is the manger in which we find the Christ lying. Not only is he lying there as a new-born baby, but he rises up from these inspired pages, walking, talking, teaching and acting. Rejected by his brothers and crucified by foreigners, we find him being raised by the glory of the Father, victoriously exalted as his erstwhile enemies draw near in trembling to bow before him and confess he is Lord. And now he is at his Father's right hand as he reigns in majesty and power in the heavenly places.[15] But most wonderful of all, he mysteriously steps out of the cradle of the Bible's pages and falls into step with all those humble enough to accept as their travelling Companion the Carpenter of Nazareth—King Jesus, our Redeemer, Lord and Friend!

---

[14] Cf. Hebrews 7:26; 2 Corinthians 6:17.

[15] John 1:11; Romans 6:4; Hebrews 2:11; Ephesians 1:20-23; Philippians 2:9-11; Revelation 5:12.

CHAPTER SEVENTEEN

Guilt—Genesis 50:15-21

OVER the past few decades a great deal has been written and spoken about guilt. There is a point of view which says that much guilt is unnecessary and even harmful, and is brought on by the moralistic Christian teaching. Sigmund Freud took that line. He spoke about our 'Id', our 'Ego' and our 'Superego'. Our id is the dark, inaccessible part of our personalities, which can only be traced through our dreams; it is that part of us from which our 'primitive passions' arise. The ego, said Freud, represents what may be called reason and common sense, in contrast to the id, which contains the passions . . . In its relation to the id the ego is like a man on horseback who has to hold in check the superior strength of the horse; with this difference, that the rider tries to do so with his own strength and skill, while the ego uses borrowed forces from outside of himself. In other words, according to Freud, our ego tries to organize our thinking and our acting, and keep the id in check in accordance with the people and events happening around us.

The 'superego' can be thought of as a type of conscience that punishes misbehaviour with feelings of guilt—for example, over having an extra-marital affair. The superego retains the character of the father, while the more powerful the Oedipus complex was in childhood and the more rapidly it succumbed to repression (under

the influence of authority, religious teaching, schooling and reading), the stricter will be the domination of the superego over the
ego later on—in the form of conscience or perhaps of an uncon-
scious sense of guilt.

There it is—that word 'guilt'! Largely as a result of Freud's teaching, many people now believe that guilt is repression. As such, it is
argued, it is a bad thing; it has been superimposed on our personalities—our ego—by strong moralistic teaching in our early years.

But is that really so? If we go right back to the beginning of our
Bibles, to Genesis chapter 3, we find that the man and woman in
the garden both had a powerful feeling of guilt because they knew
they had disobeyed God's clear commandment. They were afraid,
they hid and they tried to cover up themselves. Therefore right at
the beginning of the Scriptures we find a plain description of guilt
as a deep emotion in those who realize they have done wrong and
are responsible for what they have done. So for Adam and Eve
there was no id or ego or superego, just an awareness of disobedience against a loving Father who had lavished only kindness and
bounty upon them.

Freud spoke and wrote about repression. There is certainly
one sense in which we can all repress our guilt. We can push it
to the back of our minds and try to lock it in some subconscious
basement deep within ourselves. The passage we are looking at in
Genesis 50 is an example of this. We have reached the encounter
between Joseph and his ten brothers after the return to Egypt from
Jacob's elaborate funeral in Canaan. Now that the old man is dead
and buried, the brothers who had originally sold Joseph into slavery have become afraid that Joseph would now look for revenge,
and throw them all into some dark foul dungeon in order to let
them experience what he had been through on their account. Or
else perhaps he would set them to work under slave drivers to give
them a taste of what they had intended to subject him to.

So they devised a scheme. They sent a messenger to Joseph who claimed that before he died their father Jacob made a special plea that Joseph should not exact any revenge on his ten brothers. Through the messenger they made a moving plea for forgiveness. Of course Jacob had not left any such message at all and Joseph knew that perfectly well. He was grieved that his brothers were afraid of him and thought him capable of attempting to avenge himself. But there was more to their scheme. The ten brothers then appeared in person, fell down before Joseph, pled with him for mercy, and swore to be his slaves if only he would spare them. Joseph was both embarrassed and upset: he *wept when they spoke to him*. He reassured them and spoke words of comfort to them: *do not fear; I will provide for you and your little ones*. And he heaped kindnesses on them.

We see, therefore, that this passage is about forgiveness. However, there is an important theme that comes earlier than that, one that also occurs in all our personal stories. I am referring to guilt: deep guilt feelings, which must have been repressed for years, suddenly floating up and materializing like ghostly apparitions to haunt these ten guilty men. That was exactly what they were—guilty men.

The Fact of Guilt

You and I can have guilt on a fairly trivial level. You have a friend who has left home to work some hundreds of miles away. You promised to keep in touch with this friend and you have never written so much as an email, far less a letter; so you feel guilty about it. But that is no big deal, just a niggling feeling that you have not done what you promised to do.

Take another example of a young person in her teens. She has been out in the evenings too much recently and her family is complaining: 'You're never at home with us, always off with your friends.

And that newest friend, we just don't like her, she's a bad influence on you; you're always with her and never with us.' That leads to an argument. She defends her new friend and says she is fine, there is nothing wrong with her, apart from her rather embarrassing laugh that gets on people's nerves. And then she feels guilty, and when she sneaks out the next evening, she wonders if she should not be staying in for a change instead of gadding about with her friends. Consequently she has twinges of guilt that she is out at all.

Or here is another example of guilt: failing an exam and knowing you have not worked sufficiently hard for it. Maybe some readers will not know anything about this because they have never failed an exam in their lives. But to fail an examination can be the most devastating experience. I remember after I sat my Scottish Higher physics exam I was so sure I had failed that I shut myself in my room for about two hours and cried and cried. (After all that, I actually did very well in that exam and easily passed.) However, failing can be really painful. You believe you have let everyone down, especially your loved ones. And you feel guilty about it. I know that some guilt can be induced by others making unreasonable demands on us, and there are parents who have a lot to answer for because they put unreasonable pressure on their children. But in my own case and my intense feelings of guilt over what I wrongly thought was a failed exam, there was absolutely no pressure; I had set myself certain standards and had worked hard to achieve them.

However, put aside guilt we bring on ourselves and the guilt arising from others who have put too much pressure on us. There can be no doubt at all that the fact of guilt is a reality. It is not a mere fantasy. Nor is it necessarily induced in us on by parents or teachers or a boss at work being too demanding. I have just referred to Adam and Eve. Their guilt was real. God had said there was something they must not do. As soon as they disobeyed, they felt guilt. They knew perfectly well that they had disobeyed God. And, with that knowledge, came an overwhelming feeling of guilt. Never before had they experienced such an emotion. Now it filled their minds and deeply troubled them.

That was how it was with Joseph's ten brothers. We have seen throughout their story how God had dealt with them through Joseph, as he tested them to find out if they held a grudge against their youngest brother, Benjamin, the way they had detested himself. He had also been concerned to find out if they still had a complete disregard for their father's feelings in the way they had tortured him with their lies about his favourite son being torn to pieces by a wild beast.

But we have also seen how Joseph had forgiven those ten men, sons of his father, but not of his mother. 'And now do not be distressed or angry with yourselves because you sold me here, for God sent me before you to preserve life . . . So it was not you who sent me here, but God.'[1] There can be no doubt that Joseph really had forgiven them, and for him there could be no going back on that.

Nevertheless, his brothers still felt their guilt: although for seventeen years they had lived in Egypt, all this time they had suppressed their feelings of guilt. They evidently had felt a kind of security while their old father was still living. They believed that Joseph would never do anything drastic while Jacob was still with them. So their guilty feelings were pushed back into their subconscious and forgotten about. Yet the guilt was still there. It was there because these ten men had done something unspeakably wicked; their sin against their brother was truly atrocious. They knew that. Although their guilt was concealed beneath the surface, it had never been dealt with; there had been no genuine spiritual healing.

Indeed, I quite believe that the brothers were hardly aware of any guilt for those seventeen years that Jacob lived with them in

[1] Genesis 45:5, 8.

Egypt. Perhaps at first they had been a bit sensitive about it. But, as the first months passed, they began to forget and to think everything would be alright. Joseph would not take his revenge after all. And so I suspect they themselves thought they had got away with their past wickedness. But no, the memory of what they had done to Joseph was still there deep in their subconscious minds.

The human brain is quite remarkable. Our brains have a vast capacity to store memories in some ten billion cells, each of which is thought to be able to store a mini-DVD of some event, whether a meeting, or an experience, or even some fantasy of our minds. It is fascinating that it appears you and I not only store in our brains memories of such past events, but we also store the emotions we felt at the time. If we were happy about some event we experienced, then those feelings of pleasure are recorded in our brains along with that particular memory. If the event recorded in our brains was accompanied by sadness, then that emotion of sadness is recorded too along with that particular memory. No wonder, then, that feelings of guilt are also recorded when we engage in some action or relationship that is plainly wrong.

If you or I deliberately break the law of God and fly in the face of his word, if we seize the reins and go our own way, then, as sure as night follows day we will store up guilt within our minds—even though we may attempt to suppress that guilt or try to explain away to ourselves what we have done. The guilt will become part of us. Every day, doctors write out thousands of prescriptions to try and help men and women with deep emotional problems. But what is really needed is some way of wiping the slate clean, and removing the awful pain of guilt that has come back to haunt them, often many years after the event. This is the plain fact of guilt.

Fear from Guilt

We must notice carefully that these ten brothers of Joseph were afraid. Their fear was quite understandable. My guess is that it was the return journey from Canaan where they had been to bury their father that had brought it all back. Perhaps they remembered their own fears as seventeen years earlier they had travelled back along the same route from Canaan to meet the mighty governor of Egypt, having found the money for their corn in their sacks and having been accused of being spies. But however it happened, their false sense of security was now shattered, and they found themselves haunted by ghosts they believed had long since disappeared, but which unexpectedly reappeared from apparently nowhere. And so this scheme they devised and their throwing themselves down and offering to be Joseph's slaves for the rest of their lives.

Psychiatrists tell us there are various ways in which guilt can affect us. Sometimes, for example, guilt can make us depressed. You might find yourself being very moody and preoccupied with feelings that you have no worth and that there is nothing to hope for. It is possible that your depression has been caused by suppressed guilt. Something may be hidden in your heart that has never been dealt with, and the secret guilt is making you depressed. I am certainly not suggesting that all depression comes from guilt, only that there are occasions when guilt can cause depression.

Or take feelings of aggression. You may find yourself reacting very negatively towards people close to you; you snap at them and attack them without any real reason. That might happen especially when you notice in them exactly the same failings you know you yourself have. Are you behaving like that because you are feeling guilty? Once more, I am not saying that all aggression in us is caused by guilt. But at times it can be. If you bite your husband's or wife's head off, so to speak, or are negative towards someone else close to you, perhaps deep down there is a guilt complex that goes back many, many years. Like these ten men, you and I can act in the most bizarre ways on account of events that occurred in our lives years before.

I have known some people to have spells of being ridiculously fastidious. They become perfectionists. They do their best to create an ideal world. No dust in the house. Not a thing out of place. The casual observer would think that everything in their lives must be just perfect. But that has been exactly their problem. Deep down inside everything is anything but perfect. Instead there has been an unholy mess and now there lurk the memories of horrid hidden things, deeds and sins that would make your hair stand on end. The truth about them was that they have been trying to get rid of all that suppressed guilt by creating a perfect world, an ideal home. But the reality was that they have known perfectly well that their home was extremely unhappy and full of foul memories. I have seen such families. I can assure you that the deep, suppressed guilt has been very real.

I will mention one further way in which suppressed guilt can force us into unexpected and false behaviour. (Of course, there are many others, but one more example will be enough to make the point.) Call it 'self-depreciation'. This person constantly says to himself what a hopeless person he is. He keeps on being negative about himself and is always running himself down. But what he is really trying to do is to get others to compliment him. He actually wants them to contradict him and say that he is not such a bad person at all. He is subconsciously trying to take the pressure off himself, and relieve his guilt by persuading others to commend him.

But, and this is my contention, all these are psychological tricks we play on ourselves to try and escape from the secret apprehension that our guilt induces deep within ourselves. Whether it is depression, or aggression, or perfectionism, or self-depreciation, or apathy, or anger—whatever pose we put on—we are on the run, trying to escape from the fear of knowing we have done wrong. The voice of our conscience is being ignored as we attempt to rid ourselves of the fear arising from our suppressed guilt.

(Very briefly, in just a couple of sentences, I want to add that there is a guilt which is quite false. As we have already observed above, others can set standards for us and make demands on us which are unreasonable. At times parents can be very unwise and put their children under too much pressure. As a result we can find ourselves needlessly overtaken by guilt. But that ought not to happen if we live by a balanced understanding of the word of God and his grace and love.)

Freedom from Guilt

We are to be deeply grateful for this penultimate paragraph of the book of Genesis. Here we have the divine prescription for dealing with real guilt.

First, we must recognize what we have done wrong. Listen to the ten brothers: *It may be that Joseph will hate us and pay us back for all the evil that we did to him.* These men have taken the first step: they have admitted their sin. Now you might argue they had already done that, and no one could deny it. We thought about that when Joseph made himself known to them.[2] But that remains only the first step, and it is not an easy step to take.

Our problem often is that we are very ingenious at making excuses for ourselves. We admit our wrong, but with other names which make it sound not quite so bad. And we give very clever (and sometimes, not so clever) explanations of all the extenuating circumstances: we did it because of this and that and the other; we were provoked; we were under pressure; we were taken in ... and so we rhyme off the excuses. What in fact we are doing is refusing—or at least failing—to face the hard, red-hot facts and say, 'We have

[2] See above on Genesis 42:21-22

sinned against God.' David, after his sin with Bathsheba, began his prayer of repentance with these words, 'Against you [God], you only, have I sinned and done what is evil in your sight.'[3] We have to face up to the truth. Rather, we have to face up to God and admit we have flung his holy laws to the winds, and deliberately disobeyed him. There can be no avoiding step one.

The second step is to believe and embrace the glorious truth that for Jesus' sake God does forgive those who truly turn to him. However, it is important to notice that Joseph's ten brothers in their plea to him, and Joseph in his reply, bring God into the picture. Hear them speaking: *And now, please forgive the transgressions of the servants of the God of your father.* For his part, Joseph answers: *Do not fear, for am I in the place of God?* He is acknowledging that God alone can forgive sins.

Have you ever come into your home after doing some really dirty job, maybe in your garden or garage? You have got yourself quite filthy. The grit and grime is in your hair, eyes and ears; it is all over you. So you stand under a shower and wash and wash until you are clean and you can throw your dirty clothes into the washing machine (occasionally, straight into your wheelie-bin if they are too filthy to clean) and put on clean things. In the spiritual realm, only God can do that for us, and he does it only at one place—the foot of Calvary. Sometimes each particular sin needs to be named, not necessarily to anyone else, but to God alone: confession, genuine heart-felt confession, even with tears.

In my years of pastoral ministry I have been with people of all ages who needed that treatment very urgently. (Indeed, I have too often been in the same situation myself.) But there were some who were unwilling to admit their wrongdoing. They refused to name each sin before God and ask for his great cleansing stream to wash them and make them clean. Nevertheless, this is step two,

---

[3] Psalm 51:4.

to believe that God does forgive us for Jesus' sake and to ask for his gracious pardon.

It is hard to think of many things more blessed than hearing someone weeping before the Lord as they confess their guilt. Those sacred moments, when it is has been my privilege to lead someone in that, are preserved forever in my memory. One can never forget such occasions of divine grace as a person rises from his knees, washed, sanctified and justified.[4] The joy and release as the burden rolls away and as the blood of Christ cleanses from all sin—to witness that is to come very near to actually hearing the angelic rejoicing as one sinner repents.[5]

There is a third step which is equally important as the first two. However, it is at this point that many stop short, for the third step is to receive God's forgiveness. That was precisely what these ten men had never yet done. Joseph had forgiven them. So, I believe, had God; the whole movement forward of the story tells us so. Yet they themselves had never come to terms with God's grace nor had they ever actually received God's gift of forgiveness and cleansing. Consequently their guilt was still there, tormenting and haunting them. They still had no peace, no inner tranquillity or joy. Not believing in Joseph's forgiveness, they were afraid.

Repeatedly throughout this book of Genesis it has been made abundantly clear that we have to receive the living and abiding word of God. We must believe God. The whole ground of our relationship with him is founded upon receiving and resting upon his word. That principle applies equally to accepting his forgiveness. We must hold out to the Lord our empty hands of faith and close them tight over his grace as he freely gives it to us. If we have confessed our sins, let go of them and turned our backs on them, and if we have asked God to forgive us, then we have his word for it that he has forgiven us. His word says, 'If we confess our sins, he

[4] 1 Corinthians 6:11.
[5] Luke 15:7, 10.

is faithful and just to forgive us our sins and to cleanse us from all unrighteousness.'[6] He is *faithful* and *just!* His word is *faithful* for he cannot deny himself; his forgiveness is *just* because his Son has paid our debt in full.

Some readers may be haunted by their past sins, and are still afraid because of their guilt. Is your problem that you cannot really believe that God is faithful and will always keep his word? Do you realize the enormity of your error in refusing to believe that God is faithful? Not only is he faithful, he is also just. John uses this word 'just' because Christ has fulfilled the law's just demands by carrying in himself our sins. Now God's inscrutable justice enables him freely to forgive those who turn wholly to him, for our debts have been fully paid. Those who refuse to accept God's mighty forgiveness are denying both his faithfulness and his justice.

Joseph reassured his brothers, he treated them kindly and tenderly. He pointed out to them that God had worked marvellously to use his presence in Egypt *for good, to bring it about that many people should be kept alive, as they are today* (verse 20).[7] Our living, loving God does just that. He puts his arms around us and draws us to himself with bonds of deepest, truest love, and calls us his own dear children. Our response to such grace needs only to be one word, 'Father!'

Finally, I must add one more point about guilt. There is someone who has a vested interest in our refusing to accept that God has truly forgiven us and that our sins have been completely and

---

[6] 1 John 1:9.

[7] 'Somewhere Augustine says: "God is so good that he does not permit evil to be done unless he can draw great good from it." But what irreligious men infer from this does not follow. Their inference is refuted by Paul in Romans 3:7-8: "If through my falsehood God's truth abounds to his glory, why am I still being condemned as a sinner? And why not do evil that good may come?" as some people slanderously charge us with saying. For Paul adds: "Their condemnation is just." It is godless reasoning to say: "If our sin praises the mercy of God, then let us sin." For God does not want or permit this . . . He does not do good for the sake of sin . . . [rather, he] gives help and assistance on account of sin.' Luther, vol. 8, p. 328-29.

forever washed away. We have an adversary. His name, Satan, means 'Accuser', and we are told in Revelation that he accuses the people of God night and day before God himself.[8] But the devil is a liar[9] and a slanderer, and he will come at times and try to persuade us that Christ has not forgiven us. He will argue that we are not loved by God. He will point to sins still in our lives and use them to cast doubt on God's forgiveness. And his foul, deceitful aim is to take away our peace of mind and heart, and to torment us by implanting false guilt in us.

There is only one way to deal with such pernicious, mocking taunts of the devil. It is to resist him and at the same time to remind ourselves that God is both faithful and just. That is the final word: Christ has died; God has forgiven us; we have accepted his forgiveness, and all because he is eternally faithful, and supremely just.

I believe that the unwritten conclusion to this story of Joseph and his ten brothers was that they lived happily ever after. For that is what the Lord wants for all his children. God desires our good, our happiness, our contentment. And when we are aggressive, or depressive or foolishly perfectionist or self-denigrating or indifferent or whatever, we are being robbed of the peace which the Prince of peace came to bring us. God is the God of peace. His great gift to all his children is first and foremost peace: the peace of God from the God of peace. And that peace is like a great fortress, the massive inner keep of an impregnable castle, to guard our hearts and minds through Christ Jesus our Lord.

His name shall be called . . . Prince of peace.

And the peace of God, which surpasses all understanding, will guard your hearts and your minds in Christ Jesus.[10]

---

[8] Revelation 12:10; see also Job 1:10-11, 2:4-5.
[9] John 8:44.
[10] Isaiah 9:6; Philippians 4:7.

CHAPTER EIGHTEEN

Funerals—Genesis 49:28–50:14, 22–26

BEFORE we come to the topic of funerals, we should notice in passing the words of 49:28: 'All these are the twelve tribes of Israel. *This is what their father said to them as he blessed them, blessing each with the blessing suitable to him.*'

We might be tempted to say, 'How on earth can you call those stern pronouncements about Reuben, Simeon and Levi "blessings"? Surely they were the opposite of blessings; they were, in effect, severe chastisements.' But no, they were blessings alright, for this reason: those pronouncements implicitly declared that these deeply flawed characters were nonetheless still within the covenant of grace given to Abraham and renewed to both their grandfather Isaac and their father Jacob. Yes, painful discipline was visited on these brothers during their lifetime. But by his words Jacob nevertheless acknowledged his sons' place and part within the chosen people of God. Therefore they are rightly termed 'blessings'.

Thus we are reminded again of the paradoxical balance that is always there between the severity of the holy God who will never overlook the sin of his people, and the mercy of the gracious Father who is faithful to his promises in Christ. You and I must never assume we can disobey God and get away with it. I think it is the most difficult task of every preacher to walk along the straight and narrow path of biblical truth; on the one hand, to avoid leaning over so far to one side that he becomes antinomian—that is, talking as if the Ten Commandments no longer matter because God is such a loving God;[1] and on the other hand, leaning so far over to the other side that he becomes a legalist, talking as if there is no fountain of grace and mercy flowing freely from Calvary. Our Lord never erred in this way; he never deviated from the balance of holiness and love. John says he was 'full of grace and truth'.[2] He poured out from his life, lips and actions the *grace* of God; but he also spoke the *truth*, however unpalatable it might have been.

We turn now to the death of Jacob and his burial in Canaan. The embalming of the remains took forty days[3] and the official period of national mourning seventy days. (Probably these days ran concurrently.) Because they will have entered Canaan south of the Dead Sea and travelled up its east coast, the journey to the burial place must have taken several weeks, to which we have to add the seven days of mourning after the burial. I reckon the whole event from Jacob's death to Joseph's return to Egypt could not have taken much less than three to four months. It must have been quite a funeral! So what is there here for us living as Christian people in the twenty-first century?

Conviction

We have to go back to Genesis 23. When Sarah died, Abraham had approached a local tribe of Hittites with the request that they sell him a field with a cave so he could bury his wife. The account of the negotiations between Ephron and Abraham is rather droll. Ephron at first pretends Abraham can have the field as a gift, but when Abraham insists he must buy it, Ephron ends up demanding

---

[1] To be 'antinomian' is 'to deny the fixed meaning of moral law'.

[2] John 1:14.

[3] For a full description of Egyptian embalming (though we do not know if it was practised in this way on Jacob's remains) see article 'The Ritual of Embalming' on website, http://iw-chameleon.bravepages.com/5emba.htm.

a whacking price for it—four hundred silver shekels. It is almost impossible to guess how much that would be in today's currency, but bear in mind that centuries later David paid only fifty shekels for the threshing floor of Araunah together with his agricultural equipment and at least two yokes of oxen; also Jeremiah bought a field for a mere seventeen shekels, but that was during a siege of Jerusalem when no doubt prices were at an all time low.[4]

We must ask why Abraham insisted on the purchase of the field and cave and why without any bargaining he handed over four hundred silver shekels. Remember he was an alien in Canaan, a nomad who owned no property or land, even though he was wealthy in terms of livestock and servants. However, he was quite resolved to secure for himself and his successors a stake in his adopted land for two reasons. First, it would assure the generations after him that this was where they belonged. The purchase, witnessed by the elders of the Hittites who were gathered in the city gate, the equivalent of today's town hall, would have been regarded as legally binding. And so Abraham at last had gained for himself a permanent claim to belong to the land which God had promised to his descendants.

Second, it is important to bear in mind the occasion of this land purchase. It was for a burial place for Sarah. We have already noticed that belief in an afterlife was common in Abraham's day. But the implication of the desire for a tomb in the promised land was that his faith, like that of Moses, was not in a god of the dead but in the God of the living, as the Lord himself pointed out to the sceptical Sadducees. Calvin makes this comment:

---

[4] 2 Samuel 24:24; Jeremiah 32:9. A shekel weighed about two fifths of an ounce, therefore 50 shekels would weigh 20 ounces; at £40 an ounce (average 2012 value), 50 shekels would be about £800; Abraham's 400 shekels would be worth about £8,000. It is, however, obviously impossible to estimate the relative value of shekels in biblical times, especially in Abraham's day.

[Abraham] wished to have his own family tomb in that land, which had been promised him for an inheritance, for the purpose of bearing testimony . . . that the promise of God was not extinguished, either by his own death or by that of his family, but that rather then it began to flourish; and that they who were deprived of the light of the sun, and of the vital air, yet always remained joint-partakers of the promised inheritance. For while they themselves were now silent [in death], the sepulchre cried aloud that death formed no obstacle to their entering on the possession of it . . . he saw the half of himself taken away; but because he was certain that his wife was not exiled from the kingdom of God, he hides her dead body in the tomb, until he and she should be gathered together.[5]

This then was the conviction that caused Abraham to be willing to spend a huge amount of money on the purchase of a field with a cave which was to be the family tomb. That same conviction is why Jacob in the very hour in which he passed away referred back to his grandfather's faith in the purchase of that field, and insisted that he himself should be buried there.

I am to be gathered to my people; bury me with my fathers in the cave that is in the field of Ephron the Hittite, in the cave that is in the field at Machpelah, to the east of Mamre, in the land of Canaan, which Abraham bought with the field from Ephron the Hittite to possess as a burying place. There they buried Abraham and Sarah his wife. There they buried Isaac and Rebekah his wife, and there I buried Leah . . . (verses 29-31)

We must conclude that Jacob shared the same faith as his grandfather, and though he only dimly saw the fulfilment of the promises—'I wait for your salvation, O LORD'[6]—nonetheless, his

[5] Calvin, pp. 579, 583.
[6] 49:18.

faith was firmly holding to the covenantal promises of his God. He is there today among that cloud of witnesses who encourage us in the gruelling race of this mortal life to look 'to Jesus, the founder and perfecter of our faith, who for the joy that was set before him endured the cross, despising the shame, and is seated at the right hand of the throne of God'.[7]

The account of Jacob's death is very simple and unadorned. *He drew his feet into the bed and breathed his last and was gathered to his people.* I think we can safely say that his passing was serene and peaceful. We can almost write into the narrative the Lord's own words, 'Father, into your hands I commit my spirit.'[8] He had pronounced those covenantal blessings on his sons with their words of rebuke, judgment and encouragement. He had given instructions concerning his funeral. He had proved God's faithfulness to him down the long years of his life and had seen his beloved Joseph, specially chosen by God, exalted to the highest station in mighty Egypt. And Joseph now stood beside him to close his eyes in death and then to carry his remains from Egypt to the covenantal resting-place in the land of promise. We may say without fear of contradiction that he died in full conviction of faith.

Convention

I wonder what you think about Joseph's elaborate arrangements for his father's funeral? He commanded the physicians to embalm his father's body. That process took forty days.[9] The whole population of Egypt was commanded to mourn for seventy days, thereby giving highest honour to their ruler's departed father. He himself could not enter the king's presence as he would have been ceremonially unclean, having been in recent contact with a corpse,

---

[7] Hebrews 12:2.
[8] Luke 23:46.
[9] See note 3 above.

therefore he then sent word to Pharaoh by messengers, asking for permission to leave Egypt in order to bury his father's remains in the family tomb in Canaan. Thus a large company on horseback and in chariots made the long journey to the family sepulchre, with great lamentation and mourning there for a further seven days. We can imagine the wailing and weeping in which they would have engaged, witnessed by the local Canaanites and incorporated into their folklore. Indeed, the place became known as 'Abel-mizraim' which means 'mourning of Egypt'.

What are we to make of all this? I remember as a boy seeing a dog barking at the moon; it struck me as being quite ridiculous. I am about to bark at the moon, so to speak, because I am going to disagree with some of John Calvin's comments on Jacob's funeral. Calvin is severe in his criticism of Joseph and all that he did on this occasion: the pagan embalming, the seventy days of mourning, the great company of his household servants in their chariots and on horseback, the seven days of grieving when they reached the family tomb. Calvin sees Joseph as compromising his faith. He ridicules the crocodile tears of the servants and officials whom Joseph took with him. He says the 'tumultuous clamour' by this company of Egyptians who accompanied Joseph and his eleven brothers 'cannot be excused'.

Basically, Calvin is accusing Joseph of weakness in not standing firm and saying to Pharaoh that his Hebrew family had been promised the land of Canaan as their eternal inheritance and therefore his father must be laid to rest there; he implies that Joseph was hypocritical in blaming his father's instructions for the journey back to Canaan, instead of having the courage to nail his colours to the mast. Calvin therefore urges true children of God to stand by a simple and upright confession of their faith and not do as Joseph did in 'stooping to the perverted customs of the Egyptians'.[10]

[10] Calvin, pp. 479-80. I have yet to find any other commentator who agrees with

I remain to be convinced that following the conventions of Egyptian burials was of any consequence or significance. Different cultures have different customs when it comes to funerals. I remember as a boy of fifteen years old hearing a missionary speaking about her many years of fruitless work in (then Portuguese) Guinea in West Africa. For years she and her husband had toiled among primitive people, but they had seen absolutely no response to the gospel. However, gradually it occurred to her that they were not sufficiently identifying with the people in the village where they lived. She decided she would try and find ways to sit with them where they sat and to share in their joys and sorrows. So when one of the village women lost her baby, she joined the other women in watching with her all night over the tiny corpse as together they mourned the child's death. She then joined them the next day in the funeral rites. From then on whenever there was a death she sat all night with the village women, weeping and grieving with them. It was that identification which brought the breakthrough for the gospel and on account of a change of attitude on her part the women began to listen and to be converted. Slowly some of the men followed and a new, if tiny, congregation of believers was born.

The way funerals are conducted in the Outer Hebrides is different to the burial conventions followed in the north-east of Scotland.

Calvin's criticism of Joseph over Jacob's burial. On the contrary, the few who do offer an opinion express the same views as Chrysostom (A.D. 344-407): 'For your part, however, dearly beloved, don't simply pass this by on hearing it; instead, consider the time when it happened and absolve Joseph of all blame. I mean, the gates of the underworld were still not broken or the bonds of death loosed. Nor was death yet called sleep. Hence, because they feared death, they acted in this way; today, on the contrary, thanks to the grace of God, since death has been turned into slumber and life's end into repose and since there is a great certitude of resurrection, we rejoice and exult at death like people moving from one life to another . . . from a worse to a better, from a temporary to an eternal, from an earthly to a heavenly.' *ACCS*, p. 350.

Similarly, funerals in central Scotland are very different to Indian funerals of believers, which in turn are different to Japanese funerals. So I am giving a few short barks at the moon as I take issue with Calvin on this. However, having stated that the seven days of lamentation in Canaan should never have taken place, Calvin then proceeds to give some credit to Joseph by stating,

> Nevertheless, it was not without reason that the Lord caused this funeral to be thus honourably celebrated: for it was of great consequence that a divine trophy should be raised, which might transmit to posterity the memory of Jacob's faith.

He goes on to say that had it been a quiet funeral the memory of Jacob would quickly have been extinguished. But with such a noble burial a lasting memorial was set up to remind Jacob's sons of the deliverance that would one day be visited on the chosen people of God. He even goes as far as to say that, without realizing what they were doing, by their excessive seven days of phony lamentations the Egyptians carried a torch before the sons of Israel to teach them to remain steadfast in their divine calling. That of course is typical of Calvin's thinking: he is always quick to perceive where God can and does use the actions of the ungodly to accomplish his own inscrutable purposes. I doubt whether any thinking Christian could ever dispute that.

I now cease my barking at the moon! It is sufficient to conclude that whatever the convention we follow in the burial of our loved ones our faith in Christ and our blessed hope of the resurrection must be there. You and I stand on the near side of Calvary, the empty tomb and our Lord's resurrection and exaltation to his Father's right hand; Joseph stood on the far side of the cross. Compared to the glorious sunshine of grace that streams from the face of the exalted Redeemer, the pale light that dimly lit the rich promises in which Joseph and his father trusted only provided them with shadows and symbols to engender and direct their faith.

Yet those shadows of Old Testament theology were revealed by the very word of God. It is only because the radiant light from Jesus which has shone on you and me has illuminated the pages of Genesis that we can clearly understand the covenantal promises which to the patriarchs were dimly lighted hopes, held on to because they came from the word of God.

Consolation

Our funeral conventions, then, do not greatly matter provided they give full place to the blessed hope we have in Christ. In whatever way we arrange our family burials—or make preparations for our own burials for that matter—let us not be ashamed that there is bound to be genuine grief wherever there has been genuine love. Indeed, the intensity of our grief is always in direct proportion to the depth of our love. Nevertheless, let us always remember that those who are Christians cannot ever grieve in the same way as those grieve who have no hope.[11]

Our sorrowing is bound to be different. I am sure that Calvin is absolutely right when he suggests that the Egyptians' mourning over the passing of Joseph's father was expressing a grief without any true hope or understanding of the promises of Israel's God. It could be conjectured that Joseph had brought some of his household to genuine faith in the one true God; but that is an argument from silence. To find out if there is any substance in such a conjecture we shall have to wait until we no longer 'know in part' but when 'face to face . . . we shall know fully'.[12]

Let us think, then, about the consolation of the gospel which must radically affect our grief in the face of death. We turn to the final verses of the book of Genesis.

[11] 1 Thessalonians 4:13.
[12] 1 Corinthians 13:9, 12.

So Joseph remained in Egypt, he and his father's house. Joseph lived 110 years. And Joseph saw Ephraim's children of the third generation. The children also of Machir the son of Manasseh were counted as Joseph's own. And Joseph said to his brothers, 'I am about to die, but God will visit you and bring you up out of this land to the land that he swore to Abraham, to Isaac, and to Jacob.' Then Joseph made the sons of Israel swear, saying, 'God will surely visit you, and you shall carry up my bones from here.' So Joseph died, being 110 years old. They embalmed him, and he was put in a coffin in Egypt (50:22-26).

The book of Genesis gives us precise details about Joseph's age. He was thirty years old when he began to serve Pharaoh. At the time of the first year of famine he would have been thirty-seven years old. We are then told that when Jacob and his family migrated to Egypt there were still five years of famine to come, therefore Joseph must have been thirty-nine years old when he was reunited with his father. Next we learn that Jacob lived in Egypt for seventeen years and since he died at the age of one hundred and forty-seven, he will have been a hundred and thirty when he left Canaan, and at his father's death Joseph will have been fifty-six years old. He lived a further fifty-four years and saw not only his grandchildren but also his great grandchildren—*Ephraim's children to the third generation*.[13]

These details are not unimportant. After Jacob's death, for fifty-four years Joseph continued to ensure that his entire family were

[13] '"So Joseph died, being 110 years old." Why does it indicate to us his age? For us to learn how long he had been entrusted with control of Egypt . . . for eighty years. Do you see how the rewards were greater than the hardships and the recompense manifold? For thirteen years he struggled with temptations, suffering servitude, that illicit accusation, ill treatment in prison. Since he nobly bore everything with thankfulness, he accordingly gained generous rewards even in the present life . . . it was by faith that he did all this (Hebrews 11:22).' Chrysostom (A.D. 344-407), *ACCS*, p. 352.

provided for. However, this deathbed scene makes it very clear that in his old age Joseph identified himself fully with his family. He continued to be unashamed to call them his brothers.[14] We can only guess how he reconciled that with his personal wealth, but I believe we can correctly surmise that he also ensured his own sons and their families fully identified with their peasant uncles, aunts and cousins; they too must have been taught not to be ashamed to call them brothers.[15] Calvin goes as far as to suggest that, during those fifty-four years that he lived after his father's death, Joseph 'employed all his efforts to bring himself and his children into submission, lest his earthly greatness should alienate them from the Lord's little flock'. I am sure that Calvin has good grounds from these final verses for saying that.

Deathbed scenes are rarely dramatic. My own mother passed away while softly singing the verses of a little hymn she had taught her own children. My father died in his sleep. Neither of them made any final significant statements of faith on their deathbeds; instructions regarding their funerals had been made several years earlier. However, Joseph's passing was extremely significant. Knowing that he only had hours or possibly a few days left to live, Joseph summoned the heads of his brothers' families. Remember he had been given the birthright which Reuben had forfeited, and so he himself was rightly the head of all Israel. He was resolved to give a clear lead and to impress upon them the promises of the covenant. His wealth and worldly possessions were of no account. His hope of a true inheritance that he now shared with his family was in the word of God alone.

---

[14] The allusion is to Christ who 'is not ashamed to call them brothers' (that is, 'those who are sanctified') Hebrews 2:11; see also 11:16 where we read, 'God is not ashamed to be called their God.'

[15] Calvin writes, '[Joseph] now counts it necessary to . . . descend to an ignoble condition, and wean his own sons from the hope of succeeding to his worldly rank.' Calvin, p. 490, from where the next quotation is also taken.

We must not lightly gloss over Joseph's final words. When he tells his brothers that he is about to die and therefore leave behind his worldly wealth, authority and dignity, they know he cannot bequeath any of that to them, even though through his influence they themselves were settled in a fertile area and had become exceedingly prosperous. In effect, he is informing them they may not rely any longer on his power as lord of Egypt, for they are about to lose their earthly provider and protector. It does not take much imagination to guess that for many of them the prospect of Joseph's death would give them cause for concern. What would happen to them when he was no longer there? They were only too well aware they were immigrants, a peasant people, despised by their Egyptian neighbours. So on his deathbed what hope was Joseph able to offer them? What consolation?

We have in the sacred record the account of direct revelations God gave to the three great patriarchs. Several times God spoke to Abraham in visions assuring him that he was chosen and that a covenant of grace had been made with him along with firm promises regarding his posterity's future in the promised land. That covenant with its promises was renewed to his son Isaac and to his grandson Jacob. All three men were privileged to experience direct encounters with God.[16]

There is no such account of any personal revelation made to Joseph, in spite of the fact that he was filled with the Spirit of God and through the Spirit's inspiration could interpret dreams. However, what Joseph did have was full knowledge of God's word to his father, grandfather and great-grandfather. There are certain key statements in Scripture where the weakness and frailty of humanity is startlingly contrasted with the power and grace of God. For example, there are Paul's words in Ephesians 2:3-5, where he says to believers, '[you] were by nature children of wrath, like the rest of

---

[16] Genesis 12:2-3; 13:14-17; 17:1-8; 22:15-18; 26:1-5, 24; 31:3, 42; 32:29; 35:9-12; 46:3-4.

mankind. **But God,** being rich in mercy, because of the great love with which he loved us, even when we were dead in our trespasses, made us alive together with Christ . . .' We have a similar vivid contrast in Joseph's dying words: *I am about to die, **but God will** visit you and bring you up out of this land to the land that he swore to Abraham, to Isaac, and to Jacob.*

'But God'—this is pure gospel, Old Testament gospel it is true, but nonetheless evangelical gospel. 'All your worldly security is being stripped away', says Joseph, 'and the human power in which you have been trusting is about to be taken from you forever. But God is faithful. I have his word. I received it from my father and his father. To you now I commit that word. It is on God alone you must rely; his promises must be your hope and expectation for the future. *I am about to die; but God . . . .*

He himself was not yet to be buried in the promised land as his father had been, though no doubt he could have arranged that without any difficulty. Rather, in a final solemn act, Joseph summoned the heads of the twelve tribes of Israel and had them swear that they would wait upon God's time, and when at length that hour came, they would then take his remains with them back to Canaan and bury them beside the remains of Jacob and Leah, Isaac and Rebekah, Abraham and Sarah.[17] And so we find that when ultimately God's hour did arrive, and those Hebrew slaves were safely brought out of Egypt and across the Red Sea, as the pillar of cloud and fire went before them, Joseph's remains were also taken with them according to the oath sworn on his deathbed.[18]

Just think of the years of slavery that were to come. Reflect on the taskmasters' lashes that would fall on Israelite backs. Remember too the baby boys who would be thrown into the Nile. Consider the slaves' suffering throughout those awful years. What sustained

[17] Hebrews 11:22.
[18] Exodus 13:19-21.

them? During the first few years of his life when Moses' mother was entrusted by Pharaoh's daughter with the task of nursing and feeding him, what teaching did she give her young son? Whatever it was, it most certainly included the promise transmitted through Joseph that God would visit his people, for we read that Moses when he grew to manhood refused to be called the son of Pharaoh's daughter, but chose 'rather to be mistreated with the people of God than to enjoy the fleeting pleasures of sin'.[19]

Can you see, then, how relevant these final verses of Genesis are for you and me today in the hour of bereavement? With the death of a loved one life will never be the same again. Part of our very existence is torn from us. The wound may heal, but the scar will always remain. Whoever it may be who has died, whether a relative or a dear friend, our loss cannot but be great, for death after all is 'the last enemy'.[20] But our sorrow can never be greater than the living hope that God will one day visit us and transport us to the promised land. Our inheritance is not a house or a bank balance or some bonny china or valuable silver handed down from granny. Nor is it even a field and cave in Canaan. Rather is our inheritance an eternal tenancy in rooms already prepared for us by the Saviour in his Father's house.

'I go to prepare a place for you. And if I go and prepare a place for you, I will come again and will take you to myself, that where I am you may be also. And you know the way to where I am going.' Thomas said to him, 'Lord, we do not know where you are going. How can we know the way?' Jesus said to him, 'I am the way, and the truth, and the life. No one comes to the Father except through me.'[21]

[19] Hebrews 11:24-25.
[20] 1 Corinthians 15:26.
[21] John 14:2-6.

And again:

For this we declare to you by a word from the Lord, that we who are alive, who are left until the coming of the Lord, will not precede those who have fallen asleep. For the Lord himself will descend from heaven with a cry of command, with the voice of an archangel, and with the sound of the trumpet of God. And the dead in Christ will rise first. Then we who are alive, who are left, will be caught up together with them in the clouds to meet the Lord in the air, and so we will always be with the Lord. Therefore encourage one another with these words.[22]

---

[22] 1 Thessalonians 4:15-18.

SELECT BIBLIOGRAPHY

(The works below are cited in the book simply by the author's name or by the abbreviation listed below)

Ancient Christian Commentary of Scripture (ACCS) (Downers Grove: IVP, 2002).

Baldwin, Joyce G., *The Message of Genesis 12 to 50* (Leicester: IVP, 1986).

Barocas, Claudio, *Monuments of Civilization, Egypt* (London: Reader's Digest, 1974).

Calvin, John, *Genesis* (London: Banner of Truth, 1965).

Douglas, J. D., *The Illustrated Bible Dictionary, (IBD)* Org. Ed. (Leicester: IVP, 1980).

Hastings, James, Ed. *Dictionary of the Bible* (Edinburgh: T & T Clark, 1931) 11th Imp.

Keil-Delitzsch, *The Pentateuch* (Grand Rapids: Eerdmans).

Kidner, Derek, *Genesis* (London: Tyndale, 1967).

Leupold, H. C., *Exposition of Genesis* (London: Evangelical Press, 12th Printing, 1972).

Luther, Martin, *Lectures on Genesis vols 7 & 8* (St Louis: Concordia, 1965, 1966).

Meyer, F. B., *Joseph, Beloved Hated Exalted* (London: Marshall, Morgan & Scott, 1955).

Palau, Luis, *The Schemer and the Dreamer* (London: Marshall, Morgan & Scott, 1976).

Ryle, Herbert E., *Genesis* (Cambridge: CUP, 1914).

Wallace, Ronald S., *The Story of Joseph and the Family of Jacob* (Grand Rapids: Eerdmans, 2001).

Skinner, John, *ICC on Genesis* (Edinburgh, T & T Clark, 2nd Edition, 1956).

Still, William, *Genesis & Romans* (Edinburgh: Christian Focus/ Rutherford House, 2000).

Thomas, W. H. Griffith, *Genesis, A Devotional Commentary* (Grand Rapids: Eerdmans, 1960).